To Sara Clair,
my Spodee girl, with all my heart

Special thanks are in order to Charles Horan, M.D., for the detailed information which I hope I summarized accurately; to Jane Berkey and Don Cleary for their tireless support; to Stephanie Laidman for her global efforts; to Maureen Egen for insight and enthusiasm; to Shellie Collins and especially to Mary B. Hackler for the time and peace of mind to write it, and to my husband, Art Bourgeau, for being my trusted critic, my unwavering corner man.

Prologue

October

Crystal Showack used a manual can opener so that the whine of the electric opener would not awaken her grandparents. The fishy odor of cat food filled the tiny kitchen of the bungalow. Crystal pulled on her jacket, put a handful of cookies in her pocket for later, packed her schoolbooks in her knapsack, and checked the ceramic clock shaped like an apple pie that hung above the stove. Forty minutes until she had to catch the bus. Carefully balancing the can of cat food and a plastic fork in one hand, she opened the back door and slipped outside.

The sky was just beginning to lighten and there had been an early frost during the night that left the trees and scrubby bushes a dusty silver. Crystal looked back at the bungalow as she hurried off down the road. It was a typical New England–style beach cottage, with dark cedar shingles and white trim that had begun to peel from the constant exposure to salt air. Her grandfather used to keep that trim perfectly painted, but lately, although he kept mentioning that he needed to paint it, he seemed to have lost the will to get out there on the ladder.

Crystal had always loved coming to visit in the summer, especially after her grandparents permanently retired to their little summer home in the seaside town of Bayland, Massachusetts. She and her mother, Faith, had lived in a dingy studio apartment in New York City, and a visit to Bayland was a slice of paradise in an otherwise dreary existence. Crystal loved her narrow bed with the old quilt on the enclosed sleeping porch and the sound of the ocean crashing just a few streets away and beyond the dunes. But then, last summer, when Crystal was a few weeks shy of her ninth birthday, her mother, Faith, had died, and Crystal came to live with her grandparents for good. People tried to tell her that Faith died of pneumonia, but Crystal had lived around drugs all her life and she understood about overdoses. She just pretended to believe them. No use arguing about it.

The beach road was deserted at this hour. Crystal crossed the sandy tarmac and arrived at the entrance to the nature preserve that separated the street from the dunes. There were three trails inside, marked by different-colored arrows. Each one was a cedar plank walkway with railings on either side. One led to the beach. The other two wound through the preserve marked by widenings at various points where you could sit at a bench and little signs told you what birds and shore vegetation you were likely to see there. Crystal knew just where the cats would be. She followed the markers for the blue trail.

"Goddamn summer people," her grandfather had grumbled when she told him about the cats she had spotted living in the bird sanctuary a few weeks back. She had been hoping that he might suggest they try to catch them and bring them home. But right away she knew he wouldn't go for that idea. "These people want a pet for the summer and then they go and abandon them when they leave. And we get stuck with them," he said darkly. The way he said it gave Crystal a kind of funny, bad feeling in the pit of her stomach. She thought of joking with him that he used to be a summer person himself until he retired, but she could tell he wasn't in a joking mood. The other night she had heard him telling her grandmother, "This isn't how I planned on spending my golden years—raising another kid." She heard her grandmother murmuring to him to keep his voice down.

"Here, kitty, kitty," she crooned. Crystal's sneakers squeaked and thudded along the cedar walkway. On either side of the trail, brown sea grasses rooted in the marsh and, twice her size, rustled constantly. Bare trees, bent by the winds with gnarled, gray, intertwining branches, formed a brittle barricade around her. It always reminded her of the story of Sleeping Beauty when she was in the sanctuary, the way the briars grew up and surrounded her as she slept. "Come out, come out, wherever you are," she called out, a little quaver in her voice.

There were three cats that seemed to live together at

one particular spot along the blue trail. When Crystal first spotted them they had startled her, staring out at her from their lair in the marsh. And then they had darted away. She had come back the next day with food, leaned over the side of the walkway, and emptied it out on a dry spot. The cats had stared at her from deep within that twisted vegetation, staying well back from the trail. But each time she came back the food was gone. Crystal didn't blame them for being wary. Dumped off like that, left alone. Who wouldn't distrust people? But, lately, one of the cats had gotten bold. It was the littlest one, a calico. As soon as she would dump out the food, the calico would sidle up and quickly eat its fill, casting frequent dire glances in her direction, while the others hung back fearfully. After her last visit, Crystal made up her mind. She couldn't let that one little cat eat everything while the others went hungry. And she hated the thought of them killing the birds in the sanctuary for food. She knew it was not allowed to leave the walkway because it was a preserve and also because it was very marshy. You couldn't really tell by looking which ground was solid and which would sink away beneath you, sloping into those wine-dark pools of salt water with their deceiving grids of broken shafts and branches undulating so close to the surface. But this was an emergency. Winter was coming. The cats could starve without her help. Crystal had studied the spots where the cats lurked. She thought she could safely make her way through on the solid patches. It would probably be okay. As long as one of the park rangers didn't catch her going in. That was why she came early. She had the whole preserve to herself.

Putting her book bag down on the walkway, Crystal peered through the rushes. In a few moments the cats assembled there, looking back at her. The little one began to inch forward as usual.

"Oh, no, you don't," said Crystal, "not today."

After glancing back to be sure there was no one near, she climbed over the railing and dropped the short distance to the ground below. As she hit the ground with a thud the cats scattered as if a gunshot had been fired in their midst. "Don't be afraid," she murmured. "I'm your friend."

The calico was the first to come back, of course. Crystal had already figured this part out. She shoveled out a little mound of food with the plastic fork and left it on a bare patch near the walkway. Then, stepping carefully to avoid the spongy, swampy areas, she started back through the dense sanctuary, pushing aside the crackling grasses as she went. She looked back, and sure enough, the little one had crept up to the food and was sniffing it. Crystal smiled to herself. Good, she thought. That will keep him busy. She came to the area where they always seemed to appear, marveling at how they were able to move so quickly and not end up in one or another of the shifting tidepools. Cats were so careful that way.

Crystal squatted down and overturned the rest of the contents of the can onto the ground, using her plastic fork to get every last fishy bit out for them. She could not see them, but she could sense that they were nearby. Near enough so that when she returned to the trail they could pounce on the food and finally have their share.

There, she thought, straightening up, feeling proud of her idea. If this worked, she might have to do it this way for a while. Until they learned to trust her. Until they realized she was only there to help them.

About five feet away from her, the black cat appeared, watching her balefully. Still holding the empty can and plastic fork, Crystal backed away, hoping it would come nearer. Intent on the cat, she did not pay attention to where she was going. She did not notice the spongy ground until her foot sank down and brown water seeped into her shoe. "Oh, no," she cried, muffling her voice at the last minute. She jumped back and looked down at her feet ruefully. One of her shoelaces was soaked, and she could feel her socks wet inside her shoes. Crystal sighed.

The sanctuary was alive now with the twitter of birds, and the sky was turning a yellow-gray color. Crystal stared into the swampy pool, trying to think what to do. If she went back to the house to change her socks and shoes, she would miss the bus. But if she wore these wet socks all day, she would surely catch a cold and have to stay home, and then who would come out and feed the cats?

So intent was she on solving this dilemma that it took her a few moments of staring into the murky water to realize that the dark shape below the pattern of sodden rushes was not a rock covered with seaweed. The undulating tendrils on the pale surface was hair. The dun-colored rock had eyeholes. The long stick was not a branch, but a bone. Crystal flailed out and jumped back, her heart pounding a tattoo. She was too frightened to scream. For a moment she thought the thing would rear up out of the water and come toward her. The skeleton remained where it was, trapped, facedown in the pool, ensnared by the fallen branches, the stiff grasses. Crystal began to cry. "Mommy," she whimpered to the rustling reeds, to the wind. "Mommy." She shivered uncontrollably in her wet socks.

Dale Matthews, chief of the Bayland Police Department, made a smooth, right-hand turn into the unpaved parking lot nearest to the nature preserve and parked his blue Lincoln between two black-and-white police cars, their radios squawking. He'd been here on the scene most of the morning but had had to leave to give a scheduled speech to the local Rotary Club luncheon. While he was gone, the search of the preserve had continued under the direction of his senior detective, Walter Ference. The chief had checked on his radio after leaving the luncheon and learned that despite the intensive search, joined by police from several surrounding towns, no other bodies had turned up— only the skeletal remains that had been found by the schoolgirl out feeding kittens.

As Chief Matthews slid from behind the wheel of his car he was accosted by a frizzy-haired woman wearing a "Recycling or Else" button and leading a group of four women wearing similar buttons. Dale waved a placating hand at her. The woman ignored the greeting.

"How much longer," she demanded in a shrill voice, "are you people going to keep this up? This is a fragile ecosystem. There are men clomping in and out of these marshes in boots, raking through the grasses, totally disturbing the environment. We have some very rare species of birds nesting in these marshes. You have got to put a stop to this."

Dale's smooth, unlined face wore a patient expression. "Just as soon as we can, madam, we'll be out of here," he said politely.

"You people are ravaging this sanctuary," she cried, her small but indignant band of fellow protesters nodding in agreement. "We insist that you call off these pillaging hordes right now."

"Madame," said Dale in a soothing tone, "these 'pillagers' are simply policemen doing their job. We are looking for bodies. We have to put human beings before the birds in this case."

"That's what's wrong with this world," the woman snorted. "If we put the birds first, we'd be a lot better off."

Dale smiled graciously. "Perhaps you're right," he said. "Will you excuse me now?" He was relieved to look up and see his man in charge, Lieutenant Ference, and George Jansen, a local retired GP who was serving as medical examiner, coming out of the preserve and heading in his direction. Chief Matthews walked toward them waving a kid glove in greeting. He stepped gingerly, trying not to kick up too much sand that would grind the shine right off his good black oxfords.

Dale knew perfectly well that a lot of people in Bayland thought he was too young to be chief of police, and that an experienced local cop should have gotten the job over an outsider. But, he reflected, in addition to having the education and the credentials, he had something that a lot of these older guys lacked—tact, diplomacy, and a way with words. Like his speech at lunch. Or the way he'd handled the environmental nuts just then. You had to be someone at ease in any circle.

Doc Jansen and Walter Ference had their shoulders hunched against the chilly October day as they approached him. Walter was dressed in a substantial wool jacket, but he had the graying, anemic look of a man who would really feel the cold, no matter what he wore. Even his steel-rimmed glasses looked as if they were frosted over. The only part of his face that was not that same bloodless gray was the wedge-shaped scar that formed a dent over his left eyebrow. It had turned a vaguely purplish hue. The doctor, on the other hand, in addition to being a good fifty pounds overweight, had the shiny pink complexion of a man who chased the chill with abundant food and drink.

"No news?" asked the chief as they reached one another.

Walter shook his head. "Looks like just the one."

"How many men have we still got in there?" he asked.

Walter squinted back in the direction they had come.

"About a dozen, I'd say."

Dale pulled up his gloves and stuffed his hands into the pockets of his gray flannel overcoat. "We'll keep looking until sundown," he said. "Did they take out the remains yet?"

Walter and the doctor nodded.

Dale looked at Doc Jansen. "Homicide, I presume."

Doctor Jansen shrugged. "We'll have to see what we

turn up in the autopsy. If we find a bullet, all well and good, but as it stands we'll be lucky to ever even ID this one. There's nothing left to her."

The chief shook his head, but he could not help thinking that he did not need an insoluble case in his lap in these early days of his tenure. "So, all we know is what you told me this morning?"

The doctor nodded. "White, female, teenaged. That's it. What's left of the clothing you'll need a fiber expert to describe. Of course there's always dental records."

"Any idea how long she's been in there?" asked the chief.

"The lab's going to have to pin that one down for you, too. A few years at least, I'd say."

The chief grimaced.

"What's that all about?" Walter asked, pointing toward the knot of protesters who had waylaid the chief and were now talking animatedly to a female reporter and photographer from the local paper who had been on the scene most of the day.

The chief sighed. "Bird lovers. They want us to call off the search because we're disturbing the birds' habitat."

"Good God," said Dr. Jansen angrily. "What's wrong with people? They're unbelievable, aren't they? There are parents of missing children out there wondering if their little one might be dead in that marsh. Don't they ever stop to think what it must be like for those people? The suffering it is to lose a child. And all these wackos can think about is ruffling a few feathers."

Chief Matthews nodded uneasily and stole a look at Walter, who stood by stoically, his face unreadable.

Both of Walter's children were killed years ago in a freak car accident. Walter's wife was driving and she lost control of the car on a rain-slicked causeway. The car plunged into the bay. Both children died, but she survived. Walter never mentioned it, but it was one of the first stories that had been whispered to Dale when he arrived in Bayland. He had never asked Walter about it because, well, it simply was not the sort of thing you asked a person about. But Dale often thought of it as he watched Walter go quietly, efficiently, about his job.

In a way, Dale had to admit, that long-ago accident was part of the reason why he was chief and Walter Ference wasn't. Walter had seniority on the force, and he came from a well-respected family in Bayland. He was a good officer, highly regarded, the kind of candidate who might have slipped easily into the chief's job. But it all came back to that business of diplomacy. A chief's wife had to be able to hold up her end of the social duties. And there was no way that Emily Ference could do it. It was common knowledge that she'd become a closet drinker after the accident, and who could blame her? I'd drink too, Dale thought, shuddering at the idea of the mental anguish she must have suffered. He thought gratefully of his wife, Denise, and their daughter, Sue. The perfect family. And Denise was a whiz at entertaining.

"By the way," he asked. "How's the little girl that found her?"

Walter's distant gaze became focused once again. "I called the hospital a little while ago. She's doing better. They just wanted to watch her for a bit, make sure she's over the shock of it. They're going to let her grandparents take her home tonight."

"Poor little kid," said the chief.

"Special-interest groups," Dr. Jansen raved on. "That's what's ruining this town. Hell, it's what's ruining the country. Nobody cares about the other guy anymore. They just want to lobby for their own little piece of the action. It just galls me."

A green Ford pulled into the parking lot and a man and woman emerged from the car. "Who's this now?" Dale wondered aloud.

Walter peered at the couple. "Some of the people you've been talking about, Doc."

Doc Jansen looked at Walter inquiringly. "What's their beef?"

"I didn't mean that," said Walter. "I mean they had a child disappear on them."

"Oh, God," said the doctor woefully.

"Their name is Emery. They had a teenaged daughter who up and vanished some years back."

"Oh," said Dale solemnly. "They must have heard on the news about the body."

The aging couple walked toward the cluster of officials. The woman wore glasses, a pale, mauve-colored raincoat, and running shoes. She came toward them with grim determination. The man, who wore a snap brim hat and a lightweight baseball-style jacket, hung back, fiddling with the keys on his key ring. They jingled like bells in the damp air. The wife was clearly in charge of this visit, and he was a reluctant participant.

"How many years back?" Dale whispered as an afterthought.

Walter stopped to think. "Must be . . . thirteen or fourteen years now. They come around the station periodically to ask . . . I know them. They go to my church. My wife's church, that is."

"This one hasn't been in the water any fourteen years," said the doctor abruptly.

"Excuse me," said Alice Emery. "Oh, Detective Ference."

"Hello, Mrs. Emery," he said. "Mr. Emery."

Jack Emery mumbled a greeting but did not look up. He was a wan, frail-looking man with rheumy eyes. His fingers continued to work the keys on their ring as if they were rosary beads.

"We heard you found a girl," said Alice. There was a quaver in her voice, but her tone was matter-of-fact.

"Detective Ference tells me you have a daughter missing," said Dale solicitously.

"Yes, our Linda. Of course it's been quite a while," she admitted.

"This isn't Linda," Walter said bluntly.

"How can you be sure?" Alice pleaded. "What was she wearing?"

Walter grimaced. "It's hard to tell anymore. But, the doc here says this girl hasn't been in the water that long."

"It's not her, Alice," said Jack Emery gruffly. "Let's go."

"Do we have all the information about your daughter on file at the station?" Dale interjected.

"Yes, we do," said Walter automatically.

"Let's go, Alice," Jack repeated.

"We'll be sure and let you know if there is any indication that it might be your daughter," the chief said soothingly.

Alice struggled to regain her dignity. "It's just that it's been very hard on us. All these years. Especially on my husband."

Dale placed a comforting hand on her shoulder. "We understand," he said.

"Thank you," Alice whispered, and turned away, now the reluctant follower as her husband headed toward the car. The female reporter and her photographer pounced on the Emerys as they reached their Ford.

Dale shook his head in disgust. "That Hodges girl is a pest, isn't she?"

Walter smiled and nodded. "Would you believe her dad used to be on the force? I remember her growing up. She was always one of those irritating kids that none of the other kids wanted to play with. She'll probably win the Pulitzer Prize someday."

Dale nodded. He did not like ambitious women. There was something unnatural about them, although he did his best to disguise that feeling. You had to, these days.

Dr. Jansen watched the Emerys extricate themselves from Phyllis Hodges and her cohort and lock themselves in their car. He shuddered. "Nothing more terrible than not knowing if your child is dead or alive. It's easier just to deal with their death than to live in limbo like those people."

Dale felt suddenly irritated at the old doctor. It had been a long time, but surely he knew about Walter's loss. He'd been in this town his whole life. The chief glanced furtively at Walter. As usual his expression was impassive, but Dale suspected that a loss like that did not get much easier to bear with time. There was no need to rub it in.

A redheaded officer in waders emerged from one of the nature trails into the parking lot, and the chief welcomed the opportunity to change the subject.

"Larry," he called out to the young cop, who was availing himself of the makeshift coffee wagon that had been set out for the searchers. "Anything?"

"Nothing, Chief," the young officer called back.

Chief Matthews looked at his watch. He had a meeting at City Hall with the town councilmen in twenty minutes. "I'd better get going. Walter, stay on top of this until dark?"

Walter nodded. "Sure will."

"We really aren't going to be able to do much about finding the killer until we know who the victim is," said the chief. Homicide was definitely not an ordinary occurrence in a town like Bayland. The truth was that he didn't have much hands-on experience with a murder investigation, and it was daunting to start out with so little in the way of information. But the people in this town were going to be panicked by the thought of a murderer in their midst. Someone who had killed a young girl and dumped her off in this desolate place. Dale sincerely hoped it was a family member. Even the most inexperienced cop knew that that was usually the case. All they had to do was put a name to these bones and they'd be halfway home. "We'll get him," he said, as much to convince himself as anyone else. "Just find out who she was, Doc."

Doctor Jansen sighed. "Easier said than done," he said.

Walter gazed thoughtfully back in the direction of the dunes and relentless rushing tides beyond. "The sea doesn't leave you a lot to go on," he said.

Chapter One

May

Which tie do you think?"

Karen Newhall, huddled in her bathrobe on the edge of the tub, turned to look at her husband, Greg, who had opened the door and was holding a red club tie in one hand and a green-striped tie in the other. He was dressed in a blue blazer, chino slacks, and a crisp, white shirt. "You look nice," she said.

"Hey," he said gently. "You better have your shower. Our reservation is for one o'clock."

Karen nodded absently and smoothed out the lap of her robe.

"Honey, do you feel all right? Why are you sitting there?"

"I'm fine," she said quickly. "I was just resting a minute." The grave look in his eyes made her feel guilty. "I'm perfectly all right," she said. "I like the green tie."

"Are you sure?" he asked.

"Well," she said lightly, "the red is nice, too. . . ."

"You know what I mean."

"Go put your tie on. I'll be ready in no time."

"Okay." Greg went back down the hall to their bedroom, and Karen closed the door and slowly untied the sash on her robe and hung the robe on a hook beside the shower.

Every Mother's Day for the last six years or so, Greg always took Karen and Jenny, their daughter, to the Bayland Inn for lunch. In this family they joked that anything you did more than twice was a tradition, and the Bayland Inn on Mother's Day definitely qualified.

Karen looked ruefully at herself in the full-length mirror behind the door. At thirty-eight, her body was lean and trim, thanks to years of teaching dance to young children. Of course when she was in her early twenties, trying desperately to conceive a child, the doctors had blamed that lean, disciplined dancer's body for her failure to ovulate, her inability to become pregnant. Karen had given up dancing for two years, gained twenty pounds, tried every suggested treatment, but nothing worked. Finally, she and Greg had begun the process that led to the adoption of their only child, Jenny.

And then, less than a year ago, a routine brain scan for persistent headaches had revealed a tiny, benign tumor on Karen's pituitary gland. The drug she took to eradicate the tumor had another, most unforeseen effect. Within a few months Karen was pregnant. The doctor had explained to the astonished parents-to-be that Karen must have had the tumor for years, and that it had probably been the cause of her suppressed ovulation. But in the years when Karen was trying to conceive, they did not have the technology to detect it. Karen and Greg had left the doctor's office in a happy daze, stunned but elated by this unexpected gift. They had rushed home to gently break the news to Jenny that she was going to have a baby brother or sister.

Karen stepped into the shower and let the hot water rush over her, stinging her. Under its steady beat, the tears that formed in her eyes mingled and fell with the water, dripping off her face. She had quit work immediately, rested each day, taken the prescribed hormones, and eaten every vegetable in sight. And then, just two weeks ago, when it had finally felt almost safe to look at baby clothes, to think of names, she awoke one morning with wrenching cramps and a feeling of terror resting like a boulder on her chest. By nightfall it was over. The wondering, the dreaming, the hope against hope. Life returned to normal.

She stepped out of the shower, dried herself off, and rubbed a window in the steamy mirror to check her eyes. She did not want Greg to see that she had been crying again. She knew that it was a kind of torture for him, not to be able to fix it for her, a painful reminder of those early years of their marriage when they first learned of Karen's infertility. And then, when Karen had adjusted to that reality, they began three years of frustration and anguish as would-be adoptive parents. Those years were a nightmarish blur in her mind of frustrating bureaucratic procedures and emotional upheaval as, with one baby after another, their hopes rose and then were dashed. Each disappointment left her more depressed, and time and again Greg bucked her up, prodded her to go on, never dwelling on his own pain. Karen could remember as vividly as if it were yesterday the day when they finally got their baby and brought her home. Karen had cradled her Jenny in her arms, and the sleeping infant's tiny hand had curled around Karen's pinky and held on tight. Although Karen and Greg had always dreamed of having a couple of kids, she vowed on that day that she would not try to adopt any more children. She would never forget the anxious, haunted eyes of the other couples who clogged the waiting rooms of the lawyers' offices and adoption agencies where they had been on their odyssey. It would be greedy to seek another child when so many people were waiting.

That's what you're being now, she told herself sternly. Greedy. Greedy and self-indulgent. Stop sorrowing for what you lost, and be thankful for all that you have, she told the wistful woman in the mirror. With Jenny's adoption, they put the sorrow and the tension behind them. Happiness reentered their lives. It was not fair to put Greg through it again. You are blessed, she reminded herself. Think how lucky you are.

She padded down the hall to their bedroom. Greg had finished with his tie and looked to her, as always, for her approval.

"Very handsome," she said, smiling. She rarely saw him dressed up this way. He was a contractor by trade, and his normal work clothes were sturdy shirts and rugged boots.

"I've got to look good for my girls," he said cheerily.

For the millionth time the unbidden thought flitted through Karen's mind. Would it have been a girl or a boy? Greg recognized the look on her face.

"Honey," he said, "if you don't feel up to this, we don't have to go."

Karen narrowed her eyes. "Are you trying to do me out of my lunch date? I've been looking forward to this all week." She took his favorite dress out of the closet and slipped it over her head. "Help me with this zipper, honey."

Greg drew up the zipper and kissed her neck.

"I'm sorry I've been such a drag," she said.

"You haven't," he said.

Karen brushed her hair and glanced at the silver frame on the dresser, the gap-toothed smiling child in the picture. "Besides, Jenny would be disappointed."

Greg looked at his watch. "We'd better get a move on. I told her to meet us there at one o'clock sharp."

"Does she need a ride from Peggy's house?" Their thirteen-year-old daughter had spent the night with Peggy Gilbert, a new friend from school. Greg had driven her over there the night before.

"No. Peggy only lives about two blocks from the inn," he said.

Karen dabbed on a little blusher to brighten her complexion. Her skin seemed drab to her now that the glow of pregnancy had vanished.

"You look beautiful," Greg said sincerely.

Karen smiled at him. They had met when she was

fifteen years old. Sometimes she thought they were like people suspended in time. It was as if they never noticed the passing of the years. When she looked at her husband she still saw the broad-shouldered boy with sandy-blond hair and liquid brown eyes, so like her own, who had dazzled her eye and made her heart race back in high school. Someday, she thought, when I'm completely gray and wrinkled and the mirror cries out "old lady," I will still be able to look in his eyes and see myself as a young girl.

"I'm ready," she said.

"It feels weird driving your car," Greg said as he pulled into the parking lot beside the old brick building. Usually he went everywhere in his van.

"I thought it might be nice to show up for lunch without sawdust all over me," she teased him.

"Well, excuse me, Mrs. Vanderbilt," he said, coming around to her side to open the door and bowing as he offered her his hand.

Karen giggled as she climbed out of the car and looked up at the inn. During Revolutionary War times, the Bayland had actually been an inn, housing the guests who had made the arduous fifty-mile trek from Boston. These days the Bayland was just a restaurant, and superhighways made the town of Bayland a long but possible commute from the city. Still, the seaside town retained much of its historic charm, was crowded only in the summer, and the Bayland Inn remained virtually the only place in town to go for a dress-up occasion.

Greg took her arm as they went inside and spoke to

the hostess. "We're meeting our daughter here," he said. "Her name is Jenny. Dark brown hair, blue eyes, about this tall."

"She's not here yet," the hostess said brightly. "I'll keep an eye out for her." She led them to their table. It was by the window, overlooking a little waterfall and a stream. Karen sat down and gazed out at the trees fuzzy with new growth, the pastel blue of the sky, and the daffodils and tulips blooming in disorganized profusion on the stream bank.

"What a beautiful day," she said.

"We do what we can," he said.

She made a face at him, picked up her menu and glanced at it, and then put it down again. She looked around the room. It was definitely a family day. Every table boasted a mom in her best, some with corsages pinned to their dresses, husbands and children encircling them.

A stout, henna-haired waitress came up to their table, but Greg indicated the empty place. "I'll come back," she said.

Greg followed Karen's gaze. "I should have brought you flowers," he said.

"Don't be silly," said Karen, returning to the menu.

"I did get you something, though," he said, producing a small, flat, gaily wrapped box from inside his jacket.

"Oh, Greg."

"Open it," he said.

"Should we wait for Jenny?" she asked uncertainly.

"It's all right. We'll show her when she gets here. Go ahead."

Karen couldn't help but smile. He was always impatient when he got her a gift. Like a kid itching to open a package, it was all he could do not to unwrap it himself.

"I saw this and I felt like you needed it," he said.

Karen opened the box and lifted the lid. An antique silver locket engraved with a pattern of leaves and vines rested on the black velvet in the box. "Oh, honey, this is beautiful."

"Open it up," he said.

Karen fumbled with the tiny button and pressed it. The locket snapped open. Inside were two pictures, carefully clipped from family snapshots, one on each side. Greg and Karen on the left, Jenny on the right. "You see," he said. "There's no room for anyone else. It's a full heart as it is."

Karen felt tears rush to her eyes, and she nodded. She knew what he meant to say—that he was happy as they were, just the three of them. He always said so. "It's true, darling," she murmured. "We're very lucky. I was just thinking that earlier today. How lucky I am. Thank you," She smiled at him, knowing there were tears standing in her eyes, but he seemed satisfied as he squeezed her hand. She did not say what she knew, deep down inside—that in a mother's heart there would always be room for one more.

"Well," he said, clearing his throat, pleased with the reception of his gift, "do you know what you're going to have?"

"I haven't decided," she said, turning to look at the door. "Have you?"

"I'm thinking about the baby lamb chops," he said,

glancing at his watch. Then he spoke Karen's thoughts aloud. "Where is that kid? It's quarter after."

"Oh, teenagers," said Karen, forcing herself not to look at the door again. "They lose track of time."

"I told her one o'clock sharp," he said irritably.

The waitress returned. "Do you want a drink?" Greg asked Karen. Karen shook her head.

"Just a few more minutes," Greg said to the waitress.

"Are you sure it was only two blocks?" Karen asked.

"Honey, I took her there last night."

Karen nodded. She had spoken briefly to Mrs. Gilbert on the phone, just to make sure it was all right for Jenny to spend the night. Jenny, who lately bristled at any questioning of her independence, was angry about the call. "I hate it when you check up on me," she complained.

"I'm sure Peggy's mother would have done the same," Karen had replied calmly. She was not about to mention to Jenny that in fact Mrs. Gilbert had sounded impatient, as if she could not see the need for the call, either.

"You treat me like I'm in the first grade," Jenny griped.

Karen sighed, recalling the exchange. All their conversations seem to go that way lately. Every decision Karen made met resistance, every suggestion was construed as interfering or dismissed as boring.

"What's the matter?" asked Greg.

"Oh, you know me and Jenny lately."

"It's just a phase."

"You always say that."

"No, this one is documented—insufferable adolescence, commonly known as the terrible teens."

Karen laughed, but then her expression lapsed into a frown. "I don't know," she said, trying to sound casual. "Maybe she decided not to come. Maybe she's mad at me."

"Mad at what?" Greg exclaimed, and then waved the possibility away. "Anyway, she wouldn't do that." But he looked grimly at his watch again. It was nearly one-thirty. "Do you want to go ahead and order?"

Karen shook her head. "You don't think something could have happened to her," she said.

"No," he said, too quickly, too definitely.

No, Karen thought. It's one-thirty in the afternoon. Don't even think it. The sun is shining. She had only two blocks to walk. But no amount of reason could dispel the memory of Amber. It had been seven months since the skeleton was found at the Bayland Nature preserve. In all that time, despite an artist's reconstruction of her face, a description of the fibers of her tattered clothes, the combing of the missing persons files, the Bayland police had not been able to identify the remains. In a big city those pitiful skeletal remains would probably have become a statistic in a week or two, but Bayland was a small town. One of the local reporters, Phyllis Hodges, dubbed the dead girl "Amber" in an article she wrote, because it seemed to fit the time of year, the autumn, when she was found. The name stuck. And when it became evident that no one was going to claim her, the town took up a collection to have a proper burial for her in the local cemetery. Although little new information surfaced about Amber, the townspeople had not forgotten her. This was a town where people knew one another's children, and people did not forget that someone had killed a teenage girl and left her in the marshes. That someone could still be here, in this town, a danger to anyone's daughter.

Greg frowned at his wife. "I know what you're thinking," he said. "You're being paranoid. I'm telling you, the Gilberts live two blocks away. You could probably see the house from here if you craned your neck."

"I'm sorry," said Karen.

"Don't borrow trouble."

"I can't help it," said Karen. "Maybe we should just call Peggy's."

Greg pushed back his chair. "Well, I'm tired of waiting for her, and you're about to wring that napkin of yours into accordion pleats, so I'll call."

Karen managed a shaky smile. "She'll be livid with you. At least it's not me for once."

Greg stood up and jingled some change in his pocket. "I'll be right back," he said.

Karen gazed out the window, her fingers clenched tightly in her napkin as she waited for him to return. Their waitress cruised by the table again, and Karen grimaced at her apologetically. Karen half expected the woman to glare at her for taking up precious time and table space on this busiest of Sundays, but the woman looked at her with a genuine kindly concern that only made Karen feel worse. She turned back to the window. The brightness of the spring day suddenly seemed garish to her. No matter how bad relations were between them, it was not like Jenny to just not show up. She had always been a tender-hearted child, and if that tender heart was less evident in adolescence, Karen knew it was still there. Still, that little face that used to light up at the sight of Karen was now most often a stormy mask. The guidance counselor at Jenny's school had told them it was an identity crisis, common to all adolescents, especially difficult for adopted children, who had doubts and unanswered questions about their origins that plagued them. After the conference, Karen had tried to bring the subject up with Jenny, asking her if it bothered her, "You mean does it bother me that my real mother gave me up to complete strangers?" Jenny had replied in that familiar, caustic tone that made Karen's heart shrivel up inside. "No. It's something I feel great about."

When Karen had tried to reassure her that she and Greg loved her more than anything, more than they could have loved their own child, Jenny had referred to this, in a bored voice, as "the party line. I've heard it before." Karen shook her head, recalling the defiant look on that small, white, freckled face, the ill-disguised hurt in those blue eyes as she pushed her dark hair back off her forehead in a familiar, unconscious gesture. There was no getting through to Jenny these days. It's a hard age, Karen reminded herself. It's harder on her than it is on you. But secretly Karen missed the old Jenny—the winsome, affectionate child she used to be.

Greg appeared in the dining room door, a grim look on his face. Karen's heart swooped down in her chest. She watched him fearfully as he crossed the room.

Greg resumed his seat and Karen could see at once

that he was not worried, but angry. "What happened?" she said. "Was she there?"

Greg shook out his napkin and picked up his menu. He did not meet her gaze. His voice was harsh. "I spoke to Peggy's father. It seems that Jenny and Peggy went to an afternoon movie."

At first, all she could feel was relief. And then her cheeks began to burn. Jenny had shunned her celebration on Mother's Day. There was no avoiding the blow.

Greg lowered his menu. "Wait until I get a hold of her," he said. His face was stony with anger, but Karen could see hurt and confusion in his eyes.

"Maybe there's some reason," said Karen, her voice trailing off.

"Don't defend her," he said. "There's no excuse for this."

"At least she's safe," said Karen.

"Goddammit," said Greg. "I can't believe she went trotting off to a movie."

"Don't," Karen whispered as the people at the next table turned to look at them. "It's bad enough."

"I'm sorry," said Greg, leaning back in his seat. "I'm sorry. . . ."

"It's not your fault," Karen said.

"Maybe she did forget," he said lamely.

"We both know she didn't forget," Karen replied.

Greg stared out the window for a minute. Then he turned back to his wife. "Well," he said briskly. "Let's order our lunch."

"I can't," said Karen. "I'm not hungry anymore."

Greg leaned across the table. "Sweetheart," he said.

"Don't let her ruin it for you. Just because she's not here. It'll be like a date. Just the two of us. . . ."

Karen looked at him helplessly. "It's Mother's Day," she said.

Greg sighed, defeated. "I know."

"Let's go home," she said.

"All right."

Karen groped for her purse and stood up as Greg scanned the room for the red hair of their waitress, caught her eye, and summoned her. Karen felt as if everyone in the restaurant were staring at them as Greg gave the waitress a tip and a hurried excuse. Karen trained her gaze on the floor as they left the inn.

Neither one of them spoke as Greg opened the door for her, then went around to the driver's side and got behind the wheel. "Put your seat belt on," he said gently as the motor idled. Karen did as she was told.

Just as Greg started to back out of the parking space, their waitress appeared at the doorway to the inn and waved to them. For a moment Karen's heart lifted as the woman trundled toward their car.

Jenny had called. It was all a mistake. She was on her way. Karen rolled down the window as the woman reached the car, her coppery hair agleam in the afternoon sun.

"You left this at your place," said the woman breathlessly.

Karen looked down at the box holding the locket that the woman extended to her.

Karen took the box and put it in her lap. "Thank you," she said numbly. She stared down at her gift.

"Hope you feel better," said the waitress kindly. She waved as they pulled away.

Greg turned down their street and up the long driveway to their house. Back when they were first married, Greg and Karen had bought their home, a run-down old Colonial on one of the prettiest pieces of land in town. In the ensuing years the surrounding property had been subdivided and dotted with new houses, but their house was still relatively secluded, with many shady trees and no near neighbors. Greg had renovated the house with loving care over the years. Occasionally they talked about moving, but they doubted they could ever find a like piece of land or a house with the character of the one they had.

Greg helped Karen out of the car as if she were ill, guided her up the path with a hand on her elbow, and opened the front door.

"I might go lie down," Karen said. She felt chilled despite the pleasant warmth of the day.

"All right," Greg said sadly. "Why don't you. Can I bring you a sandwich or something?"

"I'll get something later."

"I'm sorry," he said again.

"Don't you be sorry. You were just trying to give me a nice day." Slowly Karen climbed the stairs to their room and changed into some comfortable Sunday clothes—jeans and an old sweatshirt. She placed the locket in a drawer in her bureau. The photo of Jenny smiled up at her, bright and eager. Karen winced as if jabbed. Don't take it to heart, she kept telling herself. It seemed to take all of her energy to

lie down on the bed. Once she had pulled the comforter up over her shoulders, she dropped off into a
dreamless sleep.

Sometime later she was awakened by the sound of
the front door slamming and then of loud voices from
downstairs. For a minute she hid under the covers, the
painful rejection washing over her again. Finally she
dragged herself up and went downstairs, her slippered
feet quiet on the steps.

"I told you how important this was," Greg was saying, his voice clipped with rage. "I think I made it very
clear. Your mother has been through a lot lately. All I
asked of you was one happy, pleasant day to make her
feel better. But no, you couldn't manage that."

Jenny's small face was white, her freckles livid
against the skin, and her blue eyes were glittering with
anger. "I can't believe this. You start screaming the
minute I come in the door, like I'm some kind of criminal."

"What do you expect? You behave like a selfish little
. . . I don't know what. You don't think of anybody but
yourself."

"Nobody around here even gives me a chance to
speak!"

"Stop yelling," said Karen, standing in the doorway
to the living room.

Jenny turned and looked at her mother. For a minute
a guilty look flitted across her features. Then she stuck
out her chin belligerently. "He started it," she said.

Greg shook his head in disbelief. "Nothing is ever
your fault, is it? You're the poor, put-upon one. Did

you ever give a thought to how your mother might feel?"

"Of course I did," said Jenny defensively. "But Peggy wanted to go to the movies, and she wanted me to go with her."

"Oh, I see," Greg said sarcastically, "Peggy wanted to go. Well, what choice did you have?"

"Forget it," said Jenny.

"Did you stop to think we'd be worried about you?" Karen cried. "Why didn't you at least call and tell us where you were going?"

"I knew you'd say no," said Jenny.

"That does it," said Greg.

"Does what?" Jenny demanded.

"Have I got this right?" asked Greg incredulously. "You want to do something and if you think we'll say no, you just do it anyway and don't tell us?"

"No," said Jenny with a sigh. "I didn't mean that."

"You damn well better not mean that," Greg exclaimed.

"I knew you would be like this," said Jenny wearily.

"Jenny, for God sakes, how do you expect us to react?" Karen demanded in a shrill voice. "What are we supposed to think when we don't know where you are or what happened to you?"

"Don't say it," said Jenny, mimicking a querulous, high voice. "We can't forget what happened to Amber. Gosh, I'm so sick of Amber. Nothing happened to me. Why does it have to be such a big deal?"

"Don't you tell me it's no big deal," Karen said, her voice shaking, "I'm the one sitting here worrying about you. If you can't be trusted to let us know where you are, then you won't be allowed to stay with your friends. That's all there is to it."

"That's not fair," Jenny cried. "It was one time."

"You heard your mother," said Greg.

"You don't even listen to me. You just push me around."

"I've listened to you all I'm going to," said Greg. "You get up to your room and when you are ready to apologize to your mother and act like a decent human being you can come down."

Muttering under her breath, Jenny stamped out of the room and started up the stairs, her feet banging on each step.

Suddenly the doorbell rang. "Who's that now?" Greg said with a scowl. "What timing."

"I'll get it," said Karen. She walked out into the center hallway and opened the door. A stranger stood on the doorstep. She was around thirty, slim and nicely dressed, with dark, shoulder-length hair. She was holding a bouquet of flowers and a shining, ornate wooden box. Her face was pale and heart-shaped, with a dusting of brownish freckles across her nose. She looked at Karen with anxious blue eyes and swept her bangs off to the side with a nervous gesture that gave Karen's heart a queer little twist.

"Mrs. Newhall?" she asked.

Karen nodded.

"I know I should have called first, but I was afraid I'd lose my courage."

Karen's heart thudded in her chest. "That's all right," she said automatically, but a voice in her head was clamoring, No, no, it's not. This was a face she had never seen, a voice she had never heard, a name unknown to her. But instantly, instinctively, Karen knew her.

"May I come in?"

Karen stood back, and the woman stepped into the hallway. Jenny, who had halted at the top step when the doorbell rang, came halfway down and hung curiously over the bannister.

The woman looked up and saw Jenny there. Her eyes widened. "Are you Jenny?" she asked.

Jenny nodded and came down another step.

The woman looked apologetically at Karen. "I hope you don't think this is too terribly rude or strange, but I had to come."

"Who is it?" asked Greg, coming into the foyer.

Karen felt as if she were frozen where she stood, her gaze riveted to the woman's face, unable to reply.

The woman was staring at Jenny. "I've tried to picture you a million times," she said almost to herself.

Jenny looked questioningly from the stranger to Karen and then back. "Am I supposed to know you? What do you want?"

It was obvious to Karen that Jenny did not see it. To a thirteen-year-old girl, her own appearance was nothing more than a collection of insoluble problems, a source of constant anxiety. A mouth too wide, hair too greasy, a pimple no makeup could disguise. A thirteen-year-old girl could not be expected to see her reflection in a middle-aged face. But Karen could see it. And more than that, she could feel it, like a threat in the air. "Wait a minute," Karen blurted out.

But it was too late to stop her. The woman smiled tremulously.

"My name is Linda Emery," the woman said to the bewildered girl. "I'm your mother, Jenny. Your real mother."

Chapter Two

A paralyzing numbness seeped through Karen's body as she heard the words and watched their meaning register on Jenny's face. The girl froze on the stairway, holding the bannister in a white-knuckled grip, her stunned gaze fastened on the stranger. "You're my mother?" she said.

Tears formed in Linda Emery's eyes and rolled down her freckled cheeks. She nodded and then glanced at Karen apologetically. "I'm sorry," she said. "I shouldn't have blurted it out like that." She looked tenderly back at Jenny. "But seeing you here after all these years . . ."

Jenny looked first at Karen, then at Greg, who was rigid in the doorway to the living room, his face drained of all color. Karen could see the bewilderment in Jenny's eyes. She was looking to them for some answer, some explanation, as a child would do. Say something, she thought. Get it together. But all she could do was stare helplessly at the intruder.

"I have proof. Your birth certificate. It's in my purse," Linda said. She tried to reach for her purse, but she was encumbered by the bouquet of flowers and the shiny box. She held them up, offering them to Jenny. "These are for you," she said. Jenny did not budge from her spot halfway up the staircase.

Awkwardly, Linda placed the flowers and the box on the floor beside her. Then she stood up and began to fumble in her purse. "I put it in an envelope. One of these pockets . . . I don't know . . . here . . ." She held up the slip of paper in Jenny's direction, but Jenny just shook her head. Linda turned and offered it to Karen. Karen reached for it mechanically and stared down at it. Greg walked up and pried it gently from her icy fingers.

"Let me see that," he said. He frowned at the document as Linda lifted her gaze back to Jenny and drank in the sight of her. "You don't know," she said. "You don't know how I have dreamed of seeing you."

Greg's voice cut her off harshly. "What do you want?" he demanded. "Why are you here?"

Linda tore her gaze from Jenny's face and looked at Karen and Greg. "I'm sorry, Mr. Newhall, Mrs. Newhall. I know I shouldn't have just turned up on your doorstep like this. I had to see her. Please, if we could just talk. . . ."

Slowly, as if waking from a trance, Jenny came down the stairs, walked over toward Linda, bent down, and picked up the flowers and the box.

"It's a music box," Linda said eagerly. "It plays 'Beautiful Dreamer.' "

"Thanks," said Jenny, standing near Linda but not looking at her.

Karen finally recovered herself enough to speak. "Why don't you come in?" she said in a leaden voice. She gestured to the living room, throwing a warning glance at Greg, and preceded Linda into the room.

"Oh, this is lovely," Linda exclaimed. "So comfortable. You have a beautiful home."

Karen was about to thank her when Linda added, "I'm so glad." The implication hit Karen like a slap in the face. Linda hadn't said "for my daughter," but she might as well have. Karen turned and looked at Jenny. She was standing in the doorway holding her gifts, looking like a child who had lost her way home. Karen could see that she needed a chance to think, to collect herself. Karen walked back to her and gently took the music box from her. "Those flowers need water," she said. "Why don't you go put them in a vase."

Jenny nodded. "Okay," she said, and fled from the room, clutching the bouquet.

Linda had perched on the edge of the sofa. Karen seated herself in the rocker, the chair where she had rocked Jenny to sleep a thousand times, and placed the music box on the coffee table between them. Greg declined to sit.

"I'm sure you're wondering . . ." Linda began.

"How did you . . ." Karen said at the same time.

"Go ahead," said Linda nervously.

"What I want to know," said Karen, "is how you

found us. This was a blind adoption. Those records were sealed."

"I hired a private investigator," said Linda apologetically. "He was able to get the information from the lawyer's office."

Karen glanced at Greg, who was leaning against the mantel. She could tell he was as angry about this as she was. Arnold Richardson was careless, negligent, if he let this kind of information get out of his office. It was his job to protect them from something like this.

"I know it was . . . wrong for me to do that. Please, try to understand. I'm from Bayland originally, although I've been living in Chicago for many years. Recently I found out that my father had died, and I decided to make a trip back. I knew my baby had been adopted by a local couple, and when I knew I was coming back here, I just had to try to see her."

"We knew the mother was a local girl," said Karen in a dull voice. Her mind traveled back to that long-ago day when Arnold Richardson had called them to his office and told them about their baby. She could still recall the rapid beating of her heart, the clamminess of her hands, intertwined with Greg's, as they received the news. "The mother is a local girl," Arnold Richardson had said, and in her own heart Karen had said, God bless you, whoever you are. Thank you for this wonderful gift. I hope you have a rich and happy life. Karen looked at the woman on her sofa and tried to rekindle that blissful rush of joy and gratitude. But all she could feel now was something cold in her chest.

Linda continued to talk, trying nervously to fill the silence. "I was only seventeen when she was born. And all these years I've wondered about her. I'm sure you could understand that. . . ."

"I suppose so," said Karen stiffly. "You could have at least phoned us."

"I was afraid," Linda pleaded. "I was afraid you would turn me down." She took out a tissue and wiped her eyes.

Karen glanced up again at Greg, who had moved to the front window and was staring out. His jaw was clenched and his eyes were steely, but she could see that he was holding himself back from saying anything. He was trusting it to her.

"It's just such a shock, for Jenny. You can see how it has upset her."

"Well, I knew it would be a shock, but I thought she'd be happy, too. I mean, to finally find out about her . . . her natural mother."

Karen was almost ashamed of her own bitter feelings. Of course Jenny would want to meet her. How many times had she heard her wonder aloud who her real mother might be. But something inside of her could not give this interloper the satisfaction of admitting it. "This is not the sort of thing you just spring on a child. You have to prepare them for something like this. Besides, you made a legal agreement years ago. It's irresponsible to think you can just turn around whenever it suits you . . ."

Linda shook her head abjectly. "You're right, you're right. Everything you say is true. I'm just appealing to you, as a mother. Please forgive my impulsiveness. Please try to understand . . ."

In her mind, even in some part of her heart, Karen

did understand. To have a child and never know . . . It was unimaginable, a lifelong heartache. And she could sense the woman's sincerity. But she did not *want* to be sympathetic. She felt threatened. This intruder was laying claim to her child. She felt a primitive instinct, like some kind of bear with a cub. No matter how she tried to understand, there was an irrational side that just wanted to protect what was hers.

"Well, it doesn't really matter whether I understand or not, does it," Karen said, more bitterly than she had intended. "It's done now, no matter what I think."

Karen had not noticed Jenny returning to the room until she heard a small voice say, in a reproving tone, "Mom." Jenny carried the vase of flowers to the mantel and placed them there. Then she went and sat down on the couch, in the opposite corner from Linda, folding her coltish legs beneath her.

"No," said Linda, "your mom is right. Technically, I shouldn't have done this."

Greg finally broke his silence. "The word you want is legally," he said darkly to their visitor.

"Yes," said Linda. She did not look at him. "Yes, that's right."

"Well, I'm glad you came," said Jenny.

Karen felt stung. Of course it was true. Jenny was only being honest. She wished it did not hurt her to hear it.

"There are a lot of things I want to know," said Jenny.

"And I want to know about you," said Linda eagerly, turning to her.

"The main thing is," Jenny continued, her voice quavering slightly, "how come you didn't want me?"

The painful question made Karen want to reach out for her child, but Jenny was looking expectantly, almost defiantly, at Linda.

"Oh, Jenny," said Linda sadly. She pressed her lips together and shook her head. "I know it seems that way to you . . ."

"That's how it is. You gave me away," said Jenny.

Linda nodded. "There's so much about that time . . . if I could tell you . . ."

"I want to know why," said Jenny stubbornly.

Linda paused, a pained and distant expression in her eyes. "I started to tell your parents, when you went out with the flowers. I'm a local girl. I grew up here in Bayland. I was only seventeen when I got pregnant— just a few years older than you are now. And marriage wasn't . . . it wasn't an option."

"My father didn't want me either," said Jenny flatly. "I was a mistake."

"Oh, don't say that," Linda interrupted her. "Look at you. You've turned out so beautifully. Sometimes I wonder why I was ever born. But sitting here, looking at you, I see that I did one good thing in my life. Two good things. I gave birth to you, and I entrusted you to these good people . . ."

Karen could not help being touched by the woman's answer. For a moment she felt that old kinship with Jenny's unknown birth mother, this stranger sitting on her couch.

"But you could have kept me," Jenny persisted. "There are lots of single mothers . . ."

Linda shook her head. "Things were a little different thirteen years ago, Jenny. People didn't accept that quite the way they do now. Besides, I was a high school girl. And my parents would never . . . never have been able to live with it. They were strict Catholics. I was afraid to even face them."

"So, what did you do?" Jenny asked curiously.

"Well," said Linda briskly, "I made arrangements with a lawyer for you to be adopted, and then I went to a home for unwed mothers out in Chicago. The lawyer came and got you there when you were born. And I stayed in Chicago. I've been there ever since. I finished school at night, and got a job."

"What did you tell your parents?"

"I didn't tell them anything. I just left," said Linda.

Jenny mulled this over. "Did you end up getting married and stuff?" she asked.

"Nope," said Linda, an edge in her voice. "It's just me and my cat."

"I love cats," Jenny said cautiously.

"Do you have one?" Linda asked, looking around.

"No. Mom's allergic."

Karen bristled at the implied rebuke but bit back a protest.

"That's enough about me," said Linda. "I want to hear about you."

"I have a lot more questions," said Jenny. "Can you stay to dinner?"

Linda looked up at the startled expression on the faces of Karen and Greg and said, "I'm not sure that's a good idea."

Jenny turned to Karen and instantly perceived the

reason for Linda's reluctance. "Mom," she challenged Karen, "she's invited, isn't she?"

"I hadn't planned much. Just a cold supper," said Karen, flustered, "but I guess . . ."

"Jenny," said Greg, "don't put your mother on the spot."

"No," said Linda. "I've intruded enough."

"I want you to stay," Jenny cried.

"Actually, I'm going to see my own mother. It is Mother's Day."

This mollified Jenny somewhat. "How long since you've seen her?"

Linda looked at her gravely. "Not since I left home, I'm afraid."

"Wow," said Jenny.

"So, you see, I couldn't really stay anyway."

Jenny looked at Karen and saw the relief in her face. Jenny's expression hardened. "Well, I wish you could," she said stubbornly.

"I do, too. But, I'll tell you what. Let's . . . if it's okay with your parents, of course. Let's you and I get together tomorrow. Maybe we could have some lunch together. And get acquainted."

"It's a school day," said Karen before she could stop herself.

"This is more important," Jenny cried.

Linda stood up hurriedly. "Maybe after school. Why don't I call you and we'll make a time." She looked at Karen. "Would that be all right?"

"Well, I guess so," said Karen uneasily.

"We'll talk it over," said Greg.

"Why not? Am I a prisoner or something?" Jenny demanded.

"You have a short memory," said Greg. "You were sent to your room this afternoon."

Linda zipped up her purse and began to edge toward the foyer. The Newhalls followed her. "I'll call tomorrow morning," she said. "Thank you for letting me see Jenny. You don't know what it means to me."

"Wait a minute," Jenny exclaimed. "Don't leave yet. I'll be right back." She bolted up the stairs, leaving the adults in an uncomfortable silence.

"This is a nice old house," Linda said in an aimless manner.

"My husband's done a lot of work on it over the years," said Karen.

"Are you handy, Mr. Newhall?" Linda asked.

"I'm a contractor," he said shortly. "That's my business."

Linda nodded and fiddled with her purse.

"I hope you have a good visit with your mother," said Karen as kindly as she could.

"This will be a shock for her, too," Linda admitted with a nervous laugh. "She doesn't know I'm coming."

"You didn't let her know you were coming?" Karen asked incredulously.

Linda shrugged. "I guess I like surprises." But there was no cheerfulness in her tone. "I think some things are better done face to face."

Just then Jenny clattered down the stairs, a wrapped gift box in her hands. With a serious expression on her face she handed the box to Linda. "Happy Mother's Day," she said.

Linda took the box, a confused look in her eyes. "Why, Jenny . . ." she said.

"Open it," Jenny urged.

Linda fumbled with the wrapping while Karen stared at the box, immediately realizing that there was no way Jenny could have known that Linda would be here. There was only one possible explanation for how Jenny had this gift at the ready.

Linda lifted the top off the box and looked inside. It was a dove gray leather wallet that Karen had admired one day at the mall when she and Jenny were shopping. Karen stifled a groan.

"I hope you can use it."

"Oh, I really can," said Linda. "Mine's falling apart."

Jenny beamed.

"Well, I'm overwhelmed. Thank you." Suddenly it seemed to dawn on Linda that she was not the intended recipient of the gift. "I mean, it was very sweet of you, but . . . I mean, you probably, well, I feel a little guilty taking it."

"No," Jenny insisted. "It's Mother's Day. And you are my mother, after all."

Karen turned and walked out of the foyer, back to the living room.

"I'll call you tomorrow," Linda said hurriedly, clutching the gift box. Jenny followed her to the door and leaned out, waving shyly as Linda got into her car. When she turned back, both her parents were gone. She went to the door of the living room. Karen was seated in the rocker again. Greg was pacing behind her chair.

"Mom, I was going to give you that wallet."

"I know," said Karen in a dead voice.

"I'll get you another present. Something better. She

brought me those presents, and I just wanted to give her something."

Karen did not reply. She blinked back angry tears.

"I didn't mean to hurt your feelings," Jenny protested.

"Well, if you could have hurt your mother's feelings any more than you did today, I'd like to know how," said Greg furiously.

"I didn't know she was coming today. I was just trying to be nice," Jenny cried.

"And the hell with us," Greg shouted.

"Someone had to be nice to her," Jenny shot back. "You were both horrible to her."

"That woman had no business coming here," said Greg.

"No, she's only my real mother. Well, I don't care what you say. I'm glad she came. All my life I've prayed that she would come someday." Jenny's voice cracked on the words and she ran from the room.

"Dammit," said Greg, slamming his fist into the door frame. Then he turned and stared helplessly at his wife, who sat immobile in the rocker. He walked over and knelt beside her, rubbing her hand which was cold and limp on the padded arm of the chair. "Honey," he asked. "Are you all right?"

Karen turned her head to look at him, and there was a puzzled look in her eyes. "I'm her mother," she whispered. But it came out like a question.

"Of course you are," he said fiercely.

Karen leaned over and opened the music box on the coffee table. The melody of "Beautiful Dreamer" tinkled forth. She listened for a minute, then closed the lid on the box. She began to rock with purpose, as if she were trying to soothe a frightened child with its motion.

Chapter Three

Alice Emery took her best pair of silver candlesticks from the built-in corner china cabinet and placed them on the dining room table, stuffing each one with a pale pink taper. Then she stepped back to admire her table. It was set for five, and that seemed strange. It was the first family dinner since her husband, Jack, died. She had debated about it and finally decided to put Bill in his father's chair at the head. It wasn't meant to be disrespectful to Jack's memory. It was just a fact. Bill was the head of the family now.

Alice leaned over and adjusted the napkin beside her daughter-in-law Glenda's plate. She made sure the booster seat was tightly fastened to her three-year-old grandson's chair, and that both children had their own special "silver" that Grandma and Grandpa had bought for them to use when they came over.

Tears filled Alice's eyes at the memory of Jack, one grandchild on each knee, the ever-present frown gone briefly from his forehead as he held them close. They made him forget his sorrows like nothing else could. He had always been a quiet man, a brooding man, even when they were courting, but children had a way of easing that up in him. He was not much of a conversationalist, and Alice knew that a lot of people mistakenly thought her husband was a sullen, grumpy person, but they would have realized he was different once they saw him with kids. He seemed to feel right at home with the illogical chatter of children. He would laugh at their doings and lose track of time. It had been that way with their own kids and especially with the grandchildren.

Alice went into the living room and sat on the edge of a chair to wait. She picked up some needlework on the end table and began to do her counted cross stitch. She was making a sampler for Glenda's kitchen. She had started it in January, hoping to have it done in time for Mother's Day, but she hadn't counted on losing Jack in March. Alice's work rested in her lap as her thoughts returned to that fateful Saturday when an old friend offered him his boat to go fishing and she had urged Jack to go. She had thought it would do him good.

Alice sighed at the memory. What was the use of wishing she had done differently? A squall blew up suddenly while he was out, and all they ever found was the wreck of the boat. People kept saying to her, maybe he made it to shore, maybe he'll turn up. Have faith, they'd say. Well, Alice did have faith. She had faith that her husband, who was a good and decent man, had gone to heaven and she would meet him there one day. But she knew better than to think that a sixty-year-old man could have survived at sea. When it was your day to go, it was your day. There was no use pretending otherwise. Living on false hope took too much out of you. She had tried that before.

No, she was a widow now. One of those women who microwaved frozen dinners and didn't get invited to mixed gatherings anymore. At least she didn't have to go pleading to some other woman's husband to come put in her storm windows or help her fix things around the house. Bill was good about that sort of thing. He would call her faithfully each week to see if anything needed doing. No mother ever had a more reliable son, she reflected.

The doorbell rang, and Alice glanced, puzzled, at the clock on the mantel. Bill and his gang weren't due for a while. Besides, they never rang the doorbell. They just came trooping in, calling out to her, the kids shouting one another down to get her attention.

A little stiffly because of her arthritis, Alice rose from the chair and went to the door. Bill urged her to use a chain so she could check out any callers before she opened the door, but Alice was not about to begin living like that at her age, husband or no husband. Bayland had always been a nice town—that's why they'd picked it to bring up their family. It was still a nice town.

Alice pulled the door open and looked at the woman on the steps, smiling tearfully at her. It took a full minute for it to register whom she was looking at.

"Hi, Mom," said Linda.

Alice just stared.

"Don't you recognize me?" Linda asked.

Alice's heart was thrashing in her chest like a fish on a hook. Her face felt numb. It was Linda. Her Linda, whom she hadn't heard from or set eyes on now for— she tried to count back, but numbers wouldn't come to her. "Lord in heaven," she said. "Is it you?" It was at once a rebuke and a cry for joy.

Tentatively Linda reached out her arms and stumbled forward as Alice pulled her in, holding her close, wanting to slam the door against her but unable to let her go.

"Oh, Mom, I'm sorry," she sobbed into her shoulder. "Oh, Mom."

As if brought back to her senses, Alice disentangled herself from Linda's embrace and stared at her child, now a woman. "Where have you been?" she demanded, as if Linda were still a teenager who had walked out an hour before, promising to be back shortly.

Linda wiped the tears from her eyes and began to laugh at the sound of her mother's question. "Oh, Mom," she said. "It's a long story. Can I come in?"

Alice nodded helplessly, tears in her eyes. Linda picked up her suitcase and walked through the door. "I'll tell you everything," she said. She looked around the familiar room and sighed at the sight of it. She turned to her mother, "New drapes," she said. "They're pretty. And a different rug."

Alice and her daughter hugged sharply again, and then Alice pushed her away. "Linda Jean Emery," she said, "I ought to slap your face. Never a word from you in all these years. How could you?"

"I had my reasons, Mom, believe me."

Alice shook her head. "I don't want to hear it. There's no excuse. How we suffered!" she exclaimed.

"I'm sorry, Mom. Forgive me."

Alice shook her head and then began to weep bitterly. Linda put an arm around her shoulders and led her to her chair.

"I know," said Linda, nodding sadly. "It's so good to see you, Mom. You look the same."

"I look terrible," Alice protested. "I've had the worst year of my life. Since you took off on us, that is."

"I know about Daddy," said Linda. "I'm so sorry."

"You should be," said Alice. "How did you find out?"

"I had a subscription to the *Gazette*. In another name, of course."

Alice peered at her. "Why?" she cried. "Why didn't you at least call us?"

"I thought it was better that way."

"Better?" Alice cried. "How could it be better? To leave us hanging like that. It was torture for us. Your poor father never got over it."

Linda turned away and stared out the window as if lost in the memories of the past. "I don't blame you for being mad," she said.

"Well, thank you, Linda. I can't think, I'm so mad at you," Alice fumed.

As if she had not heard, Linda drifted away from her mother, making a tour of the old, familiar rooms, touching objects and pieces of furniture. She stopped in the doorway to the dining room. "Who's coming?" she asked, looking at the perfectly set table.

"Bill and his wife, and their two kids, Tiffany and Mark."

Linda shook her head wonderingly. "Bill has two kids? Who did he marry?"

"He married Glenda Perkins."

"His high school girlfriend?" Linda asked. "I'm surprised. I didn't think that was a big romance."

"Well, they got back together when Bill came home. He had to quit college after you left. Your father became too depressed to work. Bill came back and got a job at Shane's Sporting Goods so he could help us out. He stayed on there. He's the manager now." The accusation in Alice's tone was strictly intentional, but Linda did not seem to notice.

"He always liked sports," said Linda vaguely.

"Liked them! He planned to play pro football after college. 'Course he wasn't able to finish school, so . . ." Alice could see that her words were not getting through to Linda. Her mind seemed to have wandered off. "Anyway," she continued, "Glenda's a wonderful wife to him, and she's been like a daughter to me."

"I'm glad," said Linda.

"Don't tell me you're glad," Alice erupted. "How dare you just waltz in here like this? Why in the world did you run off and leave us like that, without a note, or a word? Weren't we good parents to you? No one could have loved you more than we did."

Linda sat down on a shabby, plaid easy chair and gazed at her mother's indignant countenance. "Mom, I was ashamed and confused. I didn't want you to know about it."

"Ashamed of what?" Alice asked warily.

"When I left, when I decided to leave, I was pregnant."

Alice flinched at the word. "Oh, Lord."

"You see what I mean? You and Dad were always so strict. You were always bragging about my grades and all. You would have been so humiliated."

Alice recovered herself. "Well, my goodness, Linda. Of course we wouldn't have been happy about it . . ."

"Worse than that," Linda muttered. "I couldn't tell you."

"We could have helped you," Alice cried. "Or what about the boy? Surely he cared about you."

"He wasn't about to marry me."

"But running off like that. It made everything so much worse than it had to be."

"I was a kid, Mom. All right? I didn't know what to do. I did the only thing I could think of. I guess I figured you would disown me anyway."

Alice sighed. She suddenly felt exhausted. All those lost years. And it could have been so easily avoided. What was the use of arguing now. It was too late to change the past. She sneaked a glance at her grown daughter. In spite of everything, the sight of her was like balm on a wound. She was still beautiful. Alice forced herself to concentrate on what Linda had told her. Pregnant at seventeen. Some boy had taken advantage of her innocence. Despite all their warnings and trying to teach her the right way. Then another thought occurred to her. She was almost afraid to ask.

"What about the baby?" she said. "What happened to the child? You didn't . . ."

"No, I didn't have an abortion. I had the baby. A girl. I gave her up for adoption."

"Oh, God," said Alice miserably.

"Well, what else could I do? I couldn't very well raise her myself. I didn't even have a high school diploma then."

"If only you had told us," Alice lamented, shaking her head.

Linda studied her mother gravely, as if weighing her next words. At last she said, "Mother, there were circumstances. . . . Look, I've come back here to . . . let's say, straighten out a few things from the past. A wrong that was done, if you will. And it's going to get pretty messy before it's over. But I promise you, you'll understand everything in time . . ."

"Don't talk to me in riddles, child. What circumstances? Girls get pregnant every day. Does this have something to do with the father? Was he married or something? I wasn't born yesterday. I see this stuff on TV and in the papers. I know these things go on. Although I wouldn't have thought it of you." Another thought occurred to her. "It wasn't some interracial thing, was it?"

"Please, Mom, don't grill me. For right now you have to trust me . . . or believe me."

Alice threw her head back and closed her eyes. "What a waste," she said.

"I didn't waste my life," Linda insisted. "I got a degree, got a pretty good position at Marshall Fields. I've worked my way up. I have a nice little apartment in Chicago."

"Chicago?" Alice said numbly. "I suppose you're married now."

"No," said Linda shortly. "And I don't plan to be."

There was a silence between them. Alice pushed herself up out of her chair and said, "Do you want some tea or something?"

"Not right now. Mom, there's something else I want to tell you."

Alice looked almost frightened. How much worse could it get? "What?"

"I've seen my daughter."

Alice dropped back down into her chair. "The baby?"

"She's thirteen years old now," said Linda proudly. "She was adopted by a couple here in Bayland. I went to see her this afternoon."

"They asked you?"

"Not really," said Linda. "But I was able to find out who they were."

"Oh, Linda, Linda."

"She's beautiful, Mom. Her name is Jenny. Jenny Newhall. They live over on Potter's Way."

"You're not allowed to do that, are you?"

"Do what?" Linda asked defensively.

"Go showing yourself to the child. At least in my day you weren't."

"Things have changed, Mom."

"Things don't change that much. There was a good reason for that. No one wants to be reminded of how that child came into the world."

"God, you have attitudes from the Stone Age. She came into the world like any other baby. Aren't you curious about her? She is your grandchild."

"Linda, for goodness' sake. I didn't even know she existed until two minutes ago. I'm still trying to get over the fact that you've shown up here after all these years. Although I see now it was probably just an afterthought."

"What are you talking about?"

"Well, you really came back here to see this child you gave up. Figured you'd drop in while you were in town."

"That's not the way it is," Linda said bitterly.

Alice turned her face away. "I don't know how it is," she admitted.

Linda sighed, and the room was silent. "Well, I'd like to wash up," she said.

"Bathroom's in the same place," said Alice tartly.

Linda went up the stairs to the bathroom, where she washed and dried her face. Then she turned and went down the hall to her old bedroom. She pushed open the door and looked in. Everything in the room was exactly as she'd left it when she was seventeen years old. Other than being cleaned and dusted, the room had not changed in fourteen years. The same pink dust ruffle on the bed, her books still in the bookcase, her posters on the wall, all the childhood mementos still crowding the bureau top.

She heard Alice's heavy tread on the stairs. Alice walked up behind her and peered in around her. "Mom," Linda breathed. "It's exactly the same."

Alice nodded and sighed. "Your father wouldn't let me change a thing. He always swore you would come back, and he wanted you to know that we'd kept it this way for you."

"Daddy," she said woefully.

"He got sick after you left. I mean, mentally," said Alice. "They gave him all kinds of medication, but he never completely pulled out of it. You were always his pride and joy. More than his son, even," said Alice in a tone that indicated her lasting bafflement at this preference. "It just drained the life out of him, little by little."

For a moment Linda's face darkened and she tensed up as if she were going to lash back at her mother's not-so-veiled accusation. Then her shoulders slumped. "I missed him, too," she whispered. "More than you'll ever know."

"Well," said Alice grudgingly, "you look like you turned out all right."

Linda shrugged, still staring at the shrine that had been her room. "It's not how I pictured my life when I was a little girl here. I guess I made the best of it." There was a hard edge to her voice.

Just then there was a commotion downstairs as the front door banged open and the high, excited voices of children spilled into the house.

"Grammy," they cried.

"That'll be Bill's bunch," said Alice proudly.

"Hey, Mom, where are you?" Bill's voice yelled up the stairs.

Alice summoned her composure and headed for the staircase. She did not want to say anything to Linda, but she was a little worried about Bill's reaction. "I'm up here," she called out, descending the steps carefully.

When she reached the bottom, Bill came over to her and kissed her on the cheek. "Happy Mother's Day."

Alice hugged him tightly. "Thank you, son."

"Happy Mother's Day, Mom," said Glenda, who was holding a pile of presents. "Where do you want these?"

"Put them on the sideboard, dear," said Alice distractedly as Tiffany and Mark rushed up and tackled her legs.

"I got you a present, Grandma," Tiffany cried.

"Me too," chimed in Mark.

"You did not," said Tiffany.

"I could use a beer," said Bill.

"In the refrigerator," said Alice.

Bill started across the room and then noticed the suitcase beside the sofa. "Hey, you got company? Whose suitcase is this?"

Linda had followed her mother down the steps.

"Who are you?" Tiffany demanded.

Glenda smiled apologetically at Linda. "Don't be rude, Tiff."

"I have a surprise for you, son," said Alice. She tried to make her voice sound light and cheerful.

Bill stared at Linda, who fidgeted under his gaze. All of a sudden recognition dawned in his eyes, and then his normally florid complexion turned ashen.

"Hi, Bill," said Linda shyly.

"Your sister has come home to us," said Alice, shooting for gaiety and missing the mark.

"Linda," he said flatly.

Alice knew her son well. He had always been her favorite, her adored boy, and she recognized the look in his eye. She licked her lips nervously and chattered on. "Imagine my shock when I opened the door. I mean, I never thought I'd have a Mother's Day like this. There she was, big as life, all grown up. Our Linda." She chose the word *our* deliberately, trying to emphasize their blood tie. That was the most important thing, after all.

Linda was gazing at her brother. "It's so good to see you, Bill. After all these years."

The children huddled up next to their mother and cast worried glances at their father. They knew enough to be quiet.

Bill's gray-green eyes were steely. He was a large man, a former college linebacker whose dark hair was peppered with gray but who retained a robustly youthful appearance. His meaty hands were clenched into fists. "What the hell are you doing here?" he demanded in a low voice that was almost a growl.

"I wanted to come back and see Mother. And see you, too," Linda said.

"Linda lives in Chicago," Alice interjected anxiously. "She tells me she has an apartment there and a good job. We've been having a long talk about the past and all that happened. She explained everything to me."

Linda said, "I know that no explanation is really going to do after all this time. . . ."

Alice turned to Glenda, who had her hands crossed protectively over the children's narrow chests. "You've heard about our Linda," Alice went on. "You may even remember her from years back."

Glenda shook her head sharply as if to say, don't suck me into this.

Alice turned back to Bill. "Didn't you and Glenda used to take Linda along to the beach sometimes when you were all kids?" Alice asked, trying to conjure up some pleasant memories. The air in the room was still and menacing. Alice rubbed her arms briskly. "I'm sure you did. You were always good about taking your little sister along. . . ."

Bill did not even seem to hear his mother. "Get out of here," he said to Linda.

"Now, Bill," Alice protested.

"No, Mother," he barked. "No."

"But don't you want to even know—"

"Why she left? Where she's been? I don't give a flying fuck about any of it. I just want her out of here."

"Bill," Glenda exclaimed disapprovingly.

Linda blanched but did not look away.

"Don't use that language," said Alice. "Not in front of the children."

"Well, I don't want to leave any doubt in their minds about how I feel about this person. Their aunt, I suppose. You're their aunt, aren't you?" Bill spat the word out like another curse.

Tears welled up in Linda's eyes, but she stuck her chin out. "Yes, I am," she said.

"You've got a lot of fucking nerve showing up here."

"Son," Alice cried furiously. "Don't use that word in this house."

Bill turned on his mother. "That's what you're worried about? My bad language? Wake up and live, Mother. Do you remember what this . . . what she did to us? Have you forgotten that?"

"It's water under the bridge now, son," Alice said, trying to soothe him. "We have to forgive and forget."

"Spare me the platitudes, Mother. I will never forget." He strode over to Linda's suitcase, picked it up, and took it to the front door. He jerked the door open and tossed the suitcase out on the front steps. "Get out of here, Linda."

"Bill, stop it this instant," Alice cried. "She came to stay for a while."

"She's not staying in this house," said Bill.

"Now, wait a minute," said Alice. "This is my house. I guess I can say who stays here."

Bill glared at her. "The only reason this is still your house is because I went to work and helped you make the payments when Dad got too depressed to work."

"I didn't realize you felt that way," said Alice in an injured tone.

"I'm sorry, Mother. I have no argument with you. But she can't stay. If she stays, I go. It's that simple. I will not be under the same roof as this selfish . . ." Bill bit back another epithet.

Alice turned and looked helplessly at Linda. She saw at once that Linda expected her to stand up to him. But Bill was the man of the family now. And what he said about the house was true. "You didn't actually say you were staying here," said Alice.

Linda's face fell, and she stared at Alice. "Mother,"

she said, "are you going to throw me out?" Her eyes filled again with tears.

Alice looked hopelessly from Linda to Bill.

"You get the picture," said Bill with grim satisfaction.

"But I came here to see you, to be with you," Linda protested.

Alice felt as if her heart were being torn apart. She could not look her daughter in the eye.

Bill was unrelenting. "You should have thought of that about ten years ago. Where've you been, in a coma all these years?"

Linda shook her head wearily. "Bill, I wanted this to be a time of healing old wounds. I thought we could try."

"You thought wrong," said Bill.

Linda looked back at her mother, but Alice was staring at the floor. "You're not being fair to me," Linda said.

Bill snorted derisively. Alice did not reply.

Slowly Linda went over to the door and looked out at her suitcase lying on the front steps. Bill drew back when she walked past him, as if afraid she might brush against him. "I'll get a room," she said shortly.

"I'm sorry," said Alice in a pleading tone.

"Don't be sorry," said Bill. "It's her own fault."

"I'll call you, Mother," said Linda.

Alice wanted to say something. I love you. But she didn't dare. Not in front of Bill. She tried to say it with her eyes, but Linda did not look at her. She wanted to embrace her again, but it would have to wait.

"Don't hurry back," Bill said. Linda looked back at him ruefully as she stepped outside, but he stared straight ahead as though she were invisible, a ghost drifting through the open door.

Chapter Four

Karen sat in the living room, an open book on her lap, staring out the front windows into the night sky. From the floor above, there was a continuous muffled thunder of rock music. Greg came into the room and watched his wife intently for a minute before he managed to summon a rueful smile.

"Enjoying that book, are you?" he said.

Karen looked up at him blankly. "What?" she asked.

"That book you're so absorbed in," he said, sitting down across from her.

Karen looked down at the book in her hands and closed it with a sigh. She placed it on an end table. "I don't know why I even bothered to open it," she said.

Greg folded his arms across his chest. "What's on your mind?" he said.

"As if you didn't know," she said.

"Well, what about her? Specifically. Maybe we'd better talk about it."

Karen stared beyond him, out the window again. You could see stars glimmering through the trees in their yard. She tried to collect her thoughts. Finally, in a dismal voice, she said, "You're going to say I'm overreacting."

"I doubt it," he said grimly.

Karen was a little surprised by his tone. Usually he did his best to minimize her worries, to explain them away. But tonight his expression seemed to mirror her own. "What if," she began. "What if this woman wants to take Jenny away."

Greg shook his head. "She can't," he said.

"You don't know that for sure."

"Of course I do," he countered. "This was a legal adoption. That woman gave up all rights to her baby when she signed those papers. Of course I'm assuming that the incompetent Arnold Richardson did have her sign the papers."

"Don't say that, Greg."

"I'm sorry. I'm sure he did."

"These days it seems as if the old rules don't apply anymore," Karen mused. "You're always seeing these women on 'Oprah' and 'Donahue' who show up years later and win their natural children back in court."

"Those are one-in-a-million situations," Greg insisted. "That's why they're on 'Oprah' and 'Donahue.' I mean, it would be one thing if we were just foster parents, or we bought her on the black market or something. But that's not the case."

"It just seems like there's no limit on how long these

women have to change their minds and decide they want their child back," Karen protested.

"There certainly was a limit, as I remember. It was in the papers, and it was something like a month."

"It was three weeks," Karen admitted.

"So, you see, you answered your own question."

Karen nodded. She could never forget the tension of those three weeks, wondering if a phone call would come from Richardson, reporting the mother's change of heart. She hardly dared give her heart away to the baby she held so tenderly, fearing the worst. And when the time was up, and the agreement sealed, she rejoiced inside all over again.

"If you want," said Greg, "I'll call Arnold Richardson in the morning and explain the situation to him. He'll tell you himself. She hasn't got a legal leg to stand on."

"I hold Arnold Richardson responsible for this mess. He let someone get into our private files."

"I'm sure he had no idea what was happening," said Greg.

"That's no excuse," said Karen angrily. "He should run a tighter ship."

Greg took a deep breath and picked up a magazine, impatiently riffling the pages.

"Now you're mad at me," she said.

"No, I'm not. I just don't want you going to pieces over this. The sky hasn't fallen. You just have to remain calm."

"Like you," she said.

Greg did not reply. He rolled up the magazine into a tight tube and whacked it into his palm absently.

"It's just that legality isn't everything, Greg."

"Meaning what?"

"Meaning what if Jenny wants to be with her? What if she chooses Linda over us . . . over me?"

"That doesn't make any sense," he cried. "Why would she choose a stranger over the family she knows and loves?"

"You saw her reaction," said Karen. "She was thrilled with the whole thing. It was as if she had been waiting all her life for this wonderful 'birth mother' to appear."

"You're exaggerating."

"Maybe I am. But I'm scared. She and I can't have two words in a row these days without a fight. I mean, we are at each other's throats. Everything I do or say is wrong. And then, whammo, along comes this glamorous, mysterious stranger who says, 'I'm your real mother and all I've done is fantasize about how wonderful you are and you turn out to be even more wonderful than I ever imagined.' " Karen got up and began to pace around the room. "So, on the one hand we have the unnatural mother, Karen, who's an old witch that makes her pick up her clothes and do her homework, and on the other we have Linda, the all-embracing birth mother, who treats Jenny like some kind of walking miracle. I ask you, which one is more appealing? Which one would you choose?"

"That's not all that's involved," Greg insisted, avoiding her frantic gaze.

"She's looking for a reason to reject me once and for all. And that reason just walked in the door this afternoon. And I can't stand it, Greg. She's all I've got. She's my only baby."

Greg banged the magazine down on the coffee table and jumped up. "Stop it, Karen. Stop blowing this thing out of proportion. Try and be rational, for God's sakes."

Karen glared at him, and then tears came to her eyes. "I'm sorry," she said. "If I can't tell my fears to you . . ."

An anguished expression rose in his eyes. He looked away from her. "Look," he said. "You are acting as if this whole thing is up to Jenny. As far as I'm concerned, we'll just tell her that she can't meet with this woman anymore. We just forbid it. She's a minor. We're her parents. And what do we know about this woman, anyway? She could be some kind of a nut. She could be unbalanced. At the very least she has poor judgment, showing up out of the blue like this."

"That's true enough," said Karen. She came back to the couch and sat down beside him.

"To tell you the truth, I don't know why you agreed to this meeting tomorrow in the first place."

Karen did not reply.

"So, it's that simple. We simply forbid her to see this Linda anymore and that's the end of it. I'll be glad to deliver the verdict to Miss Emery myself. You don't ever have to set eyes on her again."

"No," said Karen with a sigh. "We can't do that."

"Believe me," said Greg, "I'll tell Jenny too. I don't mind being the villain."

"No," said Karen. "It's not that. It's just . . . we can't deny her the opportunity to get to know her natural mother. Not now that they've made contact. It wouldn't be fair. It wouldn't be fair to Jenny. She has a lot of questions, I know. The school psychologist told me that. It's a critical age for this identity crisis business. And adopted children have it the worst. Maybe it would help her to know this woman. To find out about her. And her father. Whatever Linda wants to tell her."

"I don't get it," Greg cried in exasperation. "First you say one thing, and then, when I offer a solution, you say the opposite. I'm trying to protect you. And Jenny. Let me do this."

"It's not a solution," Karen insisted. "Don't you see that? If we make a big issue out of it, she'll just sneak off and see her. Or worse. No, we have to let her go. Or she'll hold it against us."

"You don't know what you want," he said furiously. "You're going around in circles."

"Stop yelling at me. This isn't my fault. I didn't ask for this to happen. I'm just trying to cope with it," she cried. "Why are you mad at me?"

"Because you won't let me do anything," he fumed. "You're predicting doom, and when I try to find a way to head it off . . ."

"There is no way to head this off," said Karen. "She's here. We have to deal with whatever happens. All I was doing was saying how I felt. . . ."

"Fine," said Greg. "If that's what you want to do, suit yourself."

"I was hoping for a little support from you," she said indignantly.

"You want me to hold your hand while you let this woman destroy what we've built?" he cried.

Karen looked at him in amazement. She felt dizzy, as

if the ground had dropped away beneath her. He was always the cool head, the optimist. "Is that what you think?" she asked. "Is that what you really think?"

Greg shook his head. "No," he said. "I'm sorry. It's this day. It's been a terrible day."

She felt a sudden wave of pity for him. Shame, almost, for having voiced all these dire possibilities as if she were talking to some disinterested third party. After all, Jenny was his child, too. Whatever the outcome of this showdown between mothers, it was turning his world upside down, too. "If it hadn't been today," she said gently, "it would have been another day. We just have to face it."

"I guess you're right," he said grimly.

She touched his face, which was creased with worry. "We can handle it," she said.

"That's my line," he said.

"Usually," she admitted.

He looked away.

Chapter Five

The woman seated behind the motel desk was so absorbed in her book that she did not notice the wiry, sallow-complected man enter the lobby until he was right in front of her. She started and let out a little cry, clapping a beringed hand to her ample chest. "Eddic, my God. You're like an Indian the way you sneak up on people."

Eddie McHugh checked his watch against the clock on the wall. "Those mystery books you read make you jumpy," he said.

Margo Hofsteder closed her book and looked at her own watch. "Is it eight o'clock already?"

Eddie nodded. "I mopped up around the ice machine again," he said. "But you better get somebody over here to fix it. I don't know beans about refrigeration and stuff like that."

Margo, a heavyset woman in her late fifties, sighed and slid off the stool behind the desk. "I called the appliance repair guy two days ago," she complained. "He keeps saying he's coming. I'll tell you, sometimes I wonder why I keep this place now that Anton's gone. He always had a way of getting these people to hop to it."

Eddie grunted impassively. He'd heard it all before. He came around the desk as Margo wedged her way out past her night desk man. Margo and her husband, Anton, had owned the Jefferson Motel for twenty years. In December Anton had keeled over one night at dinner and was gone before the ambulance arrived. Margo was still dickering about whether to sell or stay on. In February she'd hired Eddie as a night clerk and general maintenance man. Ed and his wife were separated, and while Margo didn't pay a lot, a free room in the motel was an irresistible part of the deal. Between the two of them they managed to keep things running pretty well in the off season, but summer was coming, with its crush of visitors, and Margo had to decide what to do. Ed was okay, but he was no ball of fire about taking care of things. And it just wasn't any fun without Anton. On the other hand, sitting around with a bunch of other widows in Florida wouldn't be much fun, either, Margo realized. It gave her a headache to think about it.

"Now you know how to work this credit card thingamajig," Margo said, pointing to a small console on the counter that looked like a child's calculator.

"I know," said Eddie irritably. She asked him that every single time she left him to work the desk.

"Well, okay," she said. "I'm going home to finish my book. Good night, Ed."

And eat a pound of candy, Eddie thought as she sailed out the door of the lobby. "G'nite," he said.

He turned on the ancient black-and-white portable TV behind the counter and began to watch the Red Sox game. He managed to get through two batters before the door to the lobby opened and he looked up to see his wife, Valerie, come striding in wearing a sweatshirt, cut-off denims, and gold, high-heeled bedroom slippers. She was dangling a lit cigarette in one hand. A cloud of carnation scent and smoke seemed to fill up the room.

"Well, well, I thought you'd be off plunging some toilet," she said by way of greeting.

Eddie's gaze returned to the game. "What do you want? Where are the kids?"

"Right out there in the car," said Valerie.

"Well, take 'em home and put 'em to bed."

"I have to talk to you," she said, picking a stray speck of tobacco off her tongue with her silver-polished fingernails and examining it.

"Didn't you ever hear of a phone?" said Eddie.

"That's just it," she cried triumphantly. "They turned the damn phone off today."

"So, pay the bill."

"With what, Eddie?" Valerie demanded, taking a deep drag on her cigarette. "I can't afford to pay it. Not with what you're giving me."

"Stop bitching. Nobody tells you to call your mother for an hour every day. That's what runs it up."

"Don't talk against my mother, Eddie. She's been

good to us," she said, pointing her cigarette at her husband. The long ash trembled, dropped, and disintegrated on the countertop.

Eddie rolled his eyes. "Use an ashtray," he said sullenly, and slid a magenta aluminum ashtray down the counter to her. Valerie squashed out her butt on the gold-leaf printing in the center that read "Jefferson Motel, Parkway Boulevard, Bayland, Mass." and a phone number.

"You always have enough money for the magazines and those cancer sticks," Eddie observed.

Valerie shook the last cigarette out of her pack, her stringy blond hair drooping around her pinched face. She crushed the pack wearily and tossed it on the floor. "Look, babe," she said, "I didn't come here to fight."

"Pick that up and put it in the trash, for crying out loud," said Eddie. "Margo will get all over me for your mess."

"Margo," Valerie grumbled, bending down to retrieve the wadded-up, empty pack. "Look," she said, "why don't you just ditch this place, come back home, and see if you can get your old job back at the water company."

"Number one," said Eddie, "they're still laying people off at the water company, and number two, if I come home, it's just going to be more bitching and complaining from you."

"I won't," said Valerie. "I promise. The kids miss you."

Eddie shook his head. He wasn't about to discuss number three—that even though it was a shit job, he liked living here, sleeping late in his own room with no one to bug him. And the job had another benefit, too, which he didn't want anyone to know about.

"Come on, babe," she pleaded. "We're still good together."

Eddie pretended to be thinking it over. Just then the lobby door opened and a good-looking, dark haired woman walked in. Eddie straightened up, composing his sharp features into a friendly expression.

The woman walked up to the desk. She glanced at Valerie, who took a seat on one of the lobby chairs and pretended to leaf through a magazine.

"I'd like a room," the woman said.

"Okay," said Eddie. "How many nights?"

The woman frowned and hesitated. "I'm not sure." She brushed her dark hair off her forehead in a nervous gesture.

"The reason I ask is, we have a weekly rate," said Eddie helpfully. He turned a Jefferson brochure around to face her. The woman read the information while Eddie's gaze traveled slowly up and down her frame.

Valerie coughed, and when Eddie looked her way he saw her narrowed eyes were riveted to his face.

The woman pushed the brochure back across the desk. "I probably will be here a week," she said hesitantly.

"It's a good deal," said Eddie. "You'd pay as much for four nights."

"Okay."

"How many people?"

"Just myself." The woman passed her plastic card across the desk.

"Okay, Miss . . . Emery," said Eddie, reading off the

card. "I've got room 173 for you. Ground floor, near the soda machine, but private."

"It sounds fine," she said.

"Ever been to Bayland before?"

Linda smiled wryly. "Not for a long time."

Valerie cleared her throat loudly.

"Well, it's a nice little town. Enjoy your stay."

"Thank you," said Linda, picking up her bag.

Eddie walked out from behind the counter and scrutinized her. "There's a lot of places to eat in the area if you're hungry."

"I'm not," said Linda shortly, taking the key he held out to her. "Excuse me."

As soon as Linda was out the door, Valerie jumped up from her seat, tossing aside the dog-eared magazine. "You scumbag," she cried. "You were coming on to her."

"I was doing my job," he said.

"Don't tell me. I know what you were up to. I know you." Valerie raised her hand as if to slap him, and Eddie grabbed her wrist and twisted her forearm.

"Let me go!" Valerie yelped.

"I'm sick of you coming in here, Val," he muttered.

"That woman wouldn't be bothered with you in a million years," she shot back. "She wouldn't spit on your ugly face."

Eddie gave her arm an extra twist until she whimpered, and then he pushed her away. "Get lost," he said.

Valerie rubbed her arm ruefully, jammed her cigarette in her mouth, and drew herself up with whatever dignity she could muster. "I'm right," she said. Slowly she walked over and pushed open the motel door and looked either way, as if expecting to see some sort of performance going on in the parking lot. Eddie knew what she was doing. She was waiting for him to call out to her to come back. It was always the same with them. When he remained silent, Valerie turned and looked at him with a haughty glare. She took the cigarette from between her lips, dropped it on the carpet in the lobby, and crushed it with her shoe. Then she hurried out the door as he yelled out, "You bitch."

Eddie picked up the still smoldering butt, Valerie's orange lipstick greasy on the filter, and deposited it in an ashtray. Then he stared at the black patch in the rug where the cigarette had been defiantly ground out. He had some spot remover in the janitor's closet. He'd better get it and clean the mess up.

Eddie went back behind the desk. The Red Sox were losing, 9–3. Disgusted, he snapped off the set and took out a paper clock with movable hands on it that said "Back in . . . minutes" around the clock face. Eddie moved the paper hand to five and hung it in the doorway. Then he locked the door and hurried down the outside sidewalk to the janitor's closet at the end of the first corridor of rooms.

He found the spot remover and closed the closet door. As he emerged from the janitor's closet his gaze was drawn to the lit room where the ice, soda, and snack machines were. A woman was in there, getting ice. It was room 173.

Eddie walked over and pushed the door open. "Hi there," he said.

Linda Emery jumped and let out a cry. Ice bounced

out of her bucket and cracked on the tile floor. "Don't sneak up on people," she said angrily.

"Sorry," he said, looking down at the puddle of water around the machine, now studded with ice cubes. "This thing is leaking. We're waiting for the guy to fix it. Here, let me get you some fresh ice."

"That's not necessary," said Linda.

"How's your room?" Eddie asked, leaning against the door frame.

"Perfectly adequate. Would you mind getting out of my way?"

Her tone was imperious, but Eddie could see fear in her eyes, which sent a pleasant sensation of excitement surging through him. "Pardon me," he said slyly, backing out the door to let her pass but leaving only enough room so that she had to stiffen up to get by him.

Linda avoided his gaze. She walked across to her room, fumbled with the key in the lock and let herself in, slamming the door behind her.

Eddie grinned, but there was a cold gleam in his eye. "I'll be seeing you," he said. Then he started to laugh.

Chapter Six

Karen pulled up in front of Memorial Junior High School, and Jenny, who was waiting on the curb, jiggling from one foot to the other and clutching a stack of photo albums and scrapbooks to her chest, slid into the car and slammed the door. She looked around furtively, like a thief in a getaway car, hoping not to be seen.

"Let's go," she urged her mother.

"Nervous?" Karen asked.

Jenny looked at her suspiciously, then shrugged. "Excited, I guess."

Karen nodded noncommittally and watched the road. Linda had called while they were having breakfast, and the two had made arrangements to meet after school at Miller's, which was a popular local restaurant. Jenny had reported proudly that Linda used to work there as a waitress when she was in high school. Linda had offered to pick Jenny up at school, but Karen had insisted, over Jenny's loud objection, on driving her. Karen was trying her level best to be agreeable and ready to compromise, but it was taking every ounce of her self-control.

"How was school today?" she asked.

"Okay," said Jenny. "I couldn't concentrate."

"I'll bet not," said Karen. There was a silence between them. Then Karen said, "I see you've got all your albums."

Jenny rested the stack on her lap and looked down at it. "Linda wants to know all about my life. I figured I'd bring some visual aids."

Karen smiled. "That seems like a good idea."

"She might like to have a picture to take back to Chicago."

Karen felt her leaden spirits rise slightly at this remark, a reminder that Linda would soon be gone. That Jenny understood and accepted it, even. "Well, that would be nice," said Karen.

"Yeah," said Jenny wistfully. "I wish she didn't have to go."

Karen stifled a sigh and tried to concentrate on driving. But she could not keep herself from pursuing something that had been bothering her since Linda called. Karen had been more than a little surprised when Linda gave Jenny her phone number and her room number and told her that she was staying at the Jefferson Motel. Greg had wanted to make an issue of it, but Karen had calmed him down. Still, she could not help wondering. She glanced over at Jenny, who was

staring out the car window, absently clasping and un-
clasping her hands over the stack of albums. Karen
tried to make her question sound casual. "Did
um . . . did Linda mention why she wasn't staying with
her family?"

"I don't know," said Jenny. "Maybe they didn't have
enough room. What difference does it make?"

"None," said Karen quickly. But she tried to imagine
that it was Jenny, coming back after a long absence.
She tried to imagine saying that there was not enough
room for her to stay. Never, she thought. I would give
her my own bed and sleep on the floor first before I
would send her off to some motel. It was something
else. Something had happened when Linda went home.
"I just thought it was strange," Karen said, "that she
wasn't staying with her mother. I mean, after all this
time, you'd think—"

"Maybe she didn't want to stay with her mother,"
Jenny said testily. "Are you going to make a big deal
about this?"

Back off, Karen thought. It's her problem. It's her
business. "There's the restaurant," said Karen.

Jenny's eyes widened with eager anticipation, as if
she were about to enter a foreign land.

Mary Miller Duncan had grown up in the dining
rooms and the kitchen of Miller's restaurant. When she
looked back on her childhood she could hardly remember a day when her parents were not working.
Sometimes Mary thought it had driven her mother to an
early grave. Mary's husband, Sam, whom she had met
in high school, started work in Miller's as a busboy,

and Mary's father had liked him from the start and taught him the business from the ground up. Two years ago her father had died a happy man, knowing that his daughter was married to a man who loved the business. Mary sighed and looked, from her post at the door, over at her husband, who was behind the bar checking the levels of the liquor bottles. It was the bartender's job, but Sam liked to do everything himself. Then Mary heard someone walk up behind her and she automatically resumed her hostess smile as she turned around.

The woman standing there gave her a lopsided grin. "Hey," she said gently, "what do you have to do to get a table around here?"

Mary's mouth dropped open and she stared. "Linda?"

Linda nodded. "In the flesh."

"Oh, Linda!" Mary cried. She tossed down the menus and threw an arm around her old friend. The two women embraced awkwardly. "My God," said Mary. "We thought . . . well, we thought all kinds of things."

"I know," said Linda.

"Come and sit down," said Mary. "Come and see Sam. He'll be so surprised. Sam!" she cried, leading Linda by the arm toward the bar. "You won't believe who just walked in."

Sam Duncan, a stout, prematurely balding man, dressed in a suit and tie he wore like a uniform, turned at his wife's bidding and frowned at the stranger. All of a sudden recognition dawned in his eyes, and the vodka bottle he was holding slipped from his hands and dropped to the floor behind the bar with a thud. "Linda," he breathed.

Linda smiled sweetly at him. "Hi, Sam," she said.

"Excuse me," he mumbled, bending down to retrieve the bottle. He displayed it clumsily for them. "Good thing these bottles aren't fragile," he said.

"You still work here," Linda observed.

"Actually, Sam and I are married," said Mary. "We got married about nine years ago."

"Oh, that's wonderful," Linda exclaimed. "How's your dad?"

"He died a few years back."

"I'm sorry," said Linda.

"I"m sorry about your dad," said Mary. "Good Lord, Linda, where have you been all these years? Everyone was worried sick about you. Your mother must have called me a dozen times to ask if I'd heard from you."

"It's a long story," said Linda. "But we can't talk right now because I am meeting someone very special here in just a few minutes."

"Okay," said Mary a little coolly.

"Don't misunderstand," said Linda. "I want to talk to you. It's nice to feel welcome somewhere. I am welcome here, aren't I, Sam?"

"Sure," Sam said gruffly, avoiding her teasing gaze.

"Your mother must be so happy," said Mary.

A flinty look came into Linda's eyes. "That's hard to say. I saw her last night, but since then I have not been able to reach her. This is my brother's doing. He threw me out of my mother's house last night, and I had to stay in the Jefferson Motel. Then, today when I tried to call my mother, there was no answer. He's stonewalling me. Punishing me, I guess, for having been a bad girl. My mother isn't at her house, and I suspect he's got her

stashed at his place, but I don't know where they live.
There's no number here in town. Do you remember my
brother?"

Mary nodded, trying to keep a disapproving tone out
of her voice. "Sure, I know Bill," she said. Bill Emery
often came into the restaurant for a drink after work or
to lunch in a secluded corner. His companions were
usually blond and barely of drinking age. Mary knew
his wife, Glenda, also. She was a nice woman who
didn't deserve to be treated that way. Mary knew where
they lived, too, in the next town over. She was tempted
to tell, but she was reluctant to get involved in this family fight. Mind your own business, Sam always said.
The customer is always right. Besides, Mary thought,
you couldn't blame Bill for being a little peeved with
his sister. She should have at least let them know she
was alive.

Linda hesitated a moment, clearly hoping for an answer, but Mary did not offer anything further.
"Anyway," said Linda, "I really do want to tell you
everything. But . . ." Her voice trailed away and her
eyes seemed to glaze over. Mary felt the old familiar
sense of annoyance with Linda. They'd been friends,
but there was always something so secretive about her,
even back then. She'd confide in you, but you always
had the feeling she was only telling you bits and pieces.
Of course that was a quality, along with her good looks,
that made her very attractive to boys. Mary glanced up
at her husband behind the bar. Sam was studying Linda
with a look on his face that Mary remembered from
days long ago.

"Well," said Mary briskly, "it's certainly nice to see

you again. Where are you living, anyway? Or is it a secret?" She immediately felt ashamed of the catty way her question sounded, but Linda did not seem to notice.

"No, no," she said. "I live in Chicago. I've been there all along. No, I'm done with secrets. This visit is going to put an end to a lot of secrets. Not only mine."

In spite of herself, Mary felt a little shiver run over her at the ominous tone in Linda's voice, the darkness in her eyes. She started to say, "Are you all right?" when suddenly Linda's face was aglow.

"Oh, good, she's here," she exclaimed. "Come with me, you two. There is someone I want you to meet."

"There she is," Jenny cried, and began to wave.

Karen had insisted on coming in to make sure Linda was there. Jenny was furious anew at the implication that Linda might leave her stranded, but Karen was adamant. Now, with a sinking heart, Karen watched Linda approaching them, her arm around the waist of a plain-featured woman with rather dry, shoulder-length brown hair. A balding man with his hands clenched at his sides was following them. Karen realized she'd been hoping that Linda would not show up. It was a terrible thing to wish for—it would have crushed Jenny. But there it was.

Linda smiled and gazed at Jenny, and then her eyes flickered with a quickly concealed disappointment at the sight of Karen. "Are you joining us?" Linda asked in a pleasant manner.

Before Karen could reply, Jenny blurted out, "She's leaving."

Linda's relief was evident in her smile. "Well, before

you go, I'd like you both to meet some old friends of mine." She gestured to the woman beside her. "This is Mary Miller, now Mary Duncan," she said, nodding to Sam. "This is Sam Duncan. Mary's parents started this place, and I had my very first job here when I was in high school. Actually, we were all in high school then. Mary, Sam, I have someone I want you to meet."

Mary smiled in the practiced manner of a restaurant owner and extended her hand.

"This is my daughter, Jenny," said Linda proudly as Mary took Jenny's hand. "And this is her adopted mother, Karen Newhall."

Karen knew that her face would not conceal her anger at the wording of the introduction. She saw confusion and embarrassment in Mary's eyes as Mary briefly took her hand and then dropped it and looked away. Sam muttered something by way of greeting but kept his eyes lowered.

Linda did not seem to notice their uneasiness. Her gaze was focused on Jenny. "I had to give Jenny up for adoption when she was born. But now I've found her again, and we're here to do some catching up. I know this probably comes as a shock . . ."

"Well, that's wonderful," said Mary, not knowing whether she was more shocked at the news or angry at Linda for the way she'd just dropped it on them. She wanted to say, "Don't you have any sense? Look how you're hurting this woman," but she wasn't about to get into it. She avoided looking at Karen's distorted expression. "We'll get you a nice quiet table and leave you to it," she said, and led the way to a table in the corner.

She handed them menus automatically. "The waitress will be over in a minute."

Before she sat down, Linda embraced Mary impulsively. Mary was stiff and unresponsive. "I want us to really sit down and talk," said Linda. "There's a lot I need to tell you about. It's important."

"Sure," said Mary, "I'll be here. You know where to find me." She turned and left.

Karen stood awkwardly by the table as Jenny nestled onto her seat. "When shall I pick you up?" she asked Jenny.

Jenny looked inquiringly at Linda.

Linda consulted her watch. "I'm not sure when we'll be done," she said.

"Well," said Karen to Jenny. "Why don't you just call me?"

"My mother can drive me," Jenny said impatiently.

Karen blinked back angry tears.

Linda blushed, a mixture of surprise and pleasure in her eyes, but her gaze at Karen was sympathetic. "Thank you so much for bringing Jenny today. We'll call you when we're through if you'd like. Although I can just run her home and save you the trip."

Karen was too shaken to argue. She did not trust her voice not to crack if she spoke. She nodded and quickly turned away, trying to make a dignified exit. She could feel Mary Duncan's curious gaze on her as she left, but she kept her eyes forward.

Chapter Seven

All the way home, Karen wiped away tears with the back of her hand. When she reached the house, her legs felt rubbery as she got out of the car. Jenny's words rang in her ears and filled her head. "My mother can drive me . . . my mother . . . my mother."

The house was dark and felt oppressively gloomy as she let herself in. She was glad she didn't have any dance classes to teach this afternoon. Her boss, Tamara, was still keeping her on a light schedule since she'd come back to work. In a way, it might have been better to be at the studio. Something to distract her, to get her mind off her daughter, who was, at this moment, eagerly offering her past up to the scrutiny of this stranger, her mother.

Karen poured herself a glass of iced tea and sat down

on a stool beside the island in the kitchen. Memories of days, events, celebrations, filled her thoughts. Silly things came to her. When Jenny was three years old she had been on a pancake kick, and Karen had made her pancakes for breakfast and lunch for weeks. The delight in Jenny's eyes as she drowned them in syrup had made it seem worthwhile.

All those years, Karen had thanked her lucky stars that she and Greg could make do without a second income, so that Karen could stay home with Jenny until she went off to school. Karen had been an only child whose parents had divorced when she was two, and her mother had always worked. Karen could still remember the loneliness of coming home to an empty apartment after school—the way her mother was always too tired and had too little time to ever do anything fun with her. And Greg had come from a large family—the baby of seven children. His mother had been too overworked and distracted to bother with him much. She died when Greg was thirteen, and his father, brothers, and sisters had scattered like autumn leaves once she was gone. Both Karen and Greg had wanted Jenny to have that security they had missed, of having a mom at home to make her pancakes for lunch, if that's what she needed.

Even these days, when she and Jenny were at odds more often than they were close, Karen still looked forward eagerly to the sound of that door opening, Jenny trooping in, dropping her notebooks on the island, rooting around in the refrigerator, dropping random, revealing remarks about her schoolmates and her teachers.

Karen washed out her tea glass and walked through the house, slowly climbing the stairs. She walked down the hall to Jenny's room and pushed open the door. It was a corner room in the front of the house, the pale-blue-striped wallpaper bright with the light of three windows. Recently Jenny had complained that the room was too babyish, so Karen had sewed new curtains and let Jenny pick out a new comforter and pillow shams to go with them. She had promised herself she would not interfere and let Jenny decide on the pattern when they went shopping, but in the end Jenny had asked her advice. They were both happy with the results. Karen gazed around the room, which seemed to vibrate with her daughter's presence. Jenny had dutifully hung up most of her clothes, but there were sneakers and shoes by the bed and her white desk was piled precariously with books and papers. The top of the bureau was laden with jars and bottles of every sort of beauty aid that could be pitched to teenage insecurities. So unnecessary, Karen thought. She doesn't even realize how beautiful she is.

In spite of herself, she kept picturing Linda and Jenny seated together, so alike in appearance it was uncanny. She looked at herself in Jenny's mirror, her blond hair and dark brown eyes completely unlike those of her daughter. She and Greg could be brother and sister, they looked so much alike. In fact, his friends had teased Greg about it when they were dating. "She's my soulmate," he would say seriously. "Of course we look alike." It had always seemed so unimportant that Jenny resemble them. But, still, it had been a shock to see how closely she mirrored the looks of her biological mother. They fit together like puzzle pieces, and for some reason that hurt.

Karen looked away from the mirror and noticed that Jenny had found a spot for the music box on the top of her bureau. Karen opened the lid, and the tune of "Beautiful Dreamer" tinkled forth. A little ballerina danced on a mirror. If I gave her that, Karen thought, she would think it was stupid. But Linda was a different story.

The sound of a car in the driveway startled her. She dropped the lid and went to the window. Linda's car was in the driveway. Jenny clambered out of the front seat, clutching her stack of mementos, and Linda got out as well. They stood for a moment, talking, and then Jenny threw her arms around Linda, and they embraced.

A dart of jealousy pierced Karen's heart at the sight. She could not remember the last time Jenny had embraced her like that. Lately she drew back if Karen reached out for her. Why? she thought as she watched her daughter cling to this woman she barely knew. Yes, she gave birth to you. But I rocked you, and nursed your colds, and made your lunches, and dried your tears. What does it mean to be a mother, if not that? You always felt like my very own to me. Didn't I seem like your very own to you?

As if sensing Karen watching them, Jenny turned away from Linda and glanced up toward her room. Seeing Karen there, Jenny waved and smiled. Ashamed of herself for her jealousy, her self-pity, Karen waved back and retreated from the window. How could she begrudge Jenny this important relationship? Why should it threaten her? she asked herself. Determined to be better, she composed her expression and headed down the hall to her own room. The front door opened and Jenny called out, "I'm back."

"I'm up here," Karen called out in that old, familiar way. She heard Jenny bounding up the stairs. Jenny stuck her head into her parents' room, where Karen was busily arranging clothes in her dresser. "Hi," said Karen. "I'm just putting some laundry away."

"Hi. Oh sh . . . oot," said Jenny. "I forgot to tell you not to put my red shirt in the dryer."

"I hung it up," said Karen.

"Oh, thanks, Mom," said Jenny.

"How was your visit?"

"Great," said Jenny. "I'm going to put these scrapbooks away." She headed down the hall to her room and, hesitantly, Karen followed. She stood in the doorway as Jenny dumped the albums on her bed and then began to shove them, one by one, into her bookcase.

"So, you had a good time."

"Yeah, it was great. We couldn't stop talking."

"Well, that's good," said Karen.

"It's incredible all the things we have in common," Jenny said. "It's weird, really."

"Did she like the albums?" Karen asked.

"Oh, yeah. She just kept staring at those old baby pictures, saying how cute I was."

"Well, you were cute."

Jenny smiled. "I don't know." She reached into her purse and pulled out a photograph of Linda holding a cat. "She gave me this. It's the only recent picture that she has of herself. This is her cat, Igor."

Karen took the proffered photograph and stared at those familiar blue eyes, slightly sad, the gentle smile.

"That's a good picture," she murmured as Jenny took it back and stuck the photo into the frame of the mirror over the bureau.

"Well," said Karen, "after you finish up here, I want you to come down and help me chop some vegetables. I thought I'd make that chicken casserole you like for supper." She walked toward the door and then turned back. "Unless you're too full from your late lunch," she said.

Jenny shook her head. "I was too keyed up to eat much. That casserole would be great. I'll be right down."

Smiling to herself, Karen went downstairs and began to assemble the ingredients for supper. She felt all right, almost as if it were a normal day. In a few minutes Jenny bounded in, humming cheerfully. "What shall I chop?" she asked.

"Slice that zucchini," said Karen.

Jenny picked up the knife and the vegetables. She had a tendency to labor over the evenness of her slices with the precision of a diamond cutter. Karen teased her a little, but otherwise they worked in companionable silence, as they often had. The shadows of twilight began to fall over the quiet, dense greenery of the land behind their house and dimmed the brilliant hues of the spring flowers. Karen looked out at the familiar sight with a renewed sense of how precious it was—the everyday sights and sounds, the smile of your loved ones, the safety of it. She did not want to break the mood, but she also felt as if she had to know. She tried to make her voice sound offhanded, but she was glad Jenny could not see her face.

"So, are you going to see her again?" she asked.

"Oh, sure," said Jenny. "Of course. I'll probably see her every day while she's here."

Karen breathed in sharply, then forced herself to smile. "Well, that'll be good. Then you two can really get acquainted."

"Yeah, and then when school's out I'll probably go and stay with her in Chicago for a while."

Karen turned and stared at her daughter. "What do you mean by that? Who said anything about you going to Chicago?"

"That's where she lives, Mom," Jenny drawled, as if pointing out the obvious to a mentally deficient person. "So that's where I have to go visit her."

"Jennifer Newhall, you will not go jetting off to Chicago just because you feel like it."

"I am not a baby," said Jenny. "You can't order me around and tell me what to do. If I want to go and see my mother, I can."

There it was again. The technically correct term that made Karen wince when she heard it. It was all she could do not to clutch her stomach, which felt as if it were being twisted inside of her. "And where do you think you'll get the money to go flying off to the midwest?" Karen demanded.

Jenny laid down the knife and narrowed her eyes. There was a note of triumph in her voice. "We already discussed it. She's sending me a ticket. She wants to. She promised."

The back door opened and Greg walked into the kitchen, laying his newspaper and the keys to the van down on the counter. "Hey, you two. How're my girls?"

Karen and Jenny glared at one another and did not reply.

Greg stifled a sigh. It was not the first fight he had walked in on between them. He pretended not to notice. "Honey," he said, "can we eat a little early? I've got to meet with some people who need an estimate tonight."

Karen maintained a deafening silence. With a note of surrender in his voice, Greg asked, "Okay, what's this all about?"

"Your daughter was just telling me about her travel plans."

"I am going to visit Linda in Chicago when school gets out," said Jenny defiantly.

"Wait a minute, hold it," said Greg, raising up his hands.

But Karen could not back down. "Let me tell you something, little girl. You do not make the decisions around here. Not while you are living in this house."

Jenny's eyes were fiery. "Well, maybe I won't live in this house anymore. Maybe I'll just go and live with my real mother."

"Don't you threaten us," Greg exclaimed.

Jenny ran from the kitchen.

"You get back in here," he yelled after her, "and apologize."

"I won't," Jenny cried, and they could hear her footsteps thudding up the stairs. Greg turned back to Karen, who was wiping her hands distractedly on a dish towel. "It's just a lot of big talk," he said.

Karen shook her head. "No," she said quietly. "This is the real thing. This is just what I was afraid of."

"You're letting her walk all over you," he said irritably, taking a beer out of the refrigerator. "It's all going to blow over. This woman will get back to Chicago and forget all about Jenny."

Karen squinted at him as if she were having trouble seeing him. "Are you listening to what's going on?" she demanded. "Are you paying attention? We're losing her. I am going to lose her."

"You're just not thinking clearly," he said. "If you weren't still depressed about the baby, you'd realize that this isn't going to amount to anything."

"I can't talk to you," she said.

"There's no reason to think we will lose her."

"There was no reason to think we'd lose the baby . . . but we did."

"That's different and you know it," he said.

"Why is it different? One day everything is going along fine, and the next day your world collapses. It happens."

Greg stared past her shoulder, out into the darkening yard.

"What are you thinking?" she asked.

Greg shrugged and shook his head. "Nothing."

"You know I'm right."

Greg took a swig of his beer and sank down on a stool beside the island. "I don't know anything anymore."

"Dinner will be ready in an hour," she said in a chilly tone.

"I'll just go wash up," he said. "Look up a few prices before this meeting."

Karen ignored him. It's my problem, she thought bitterly as he left the kitchen. I'll deal with it.

Chapter Eight

Hallelujah," said Margo Hofsteder, waddling back to the desk from the front door of the motel. "Knudsen finally showed up to fix the ice machine. His truck just pulled in."

Eddie, who was still groggy from his afternoon beers, glanced up at the clock. "Kinda late," he said. "It's nearly seven-thirty."

"Better late than never," said Margo, plucking another cookie from the box on the desk and returning her attention to the old detective movie on the TV.

"I checked about the spindles for the railing," Eddie reported. "They won't be in until next week. Is there anything else?"

Margo held out the box of cookies. "Have one of these. They're good. I got them at the volunteer fireman's bake sale."

Eddie waved the box away. "I don't want no cookie some fireman baked."

Margo chuckled and rummaged around the desk for a list. "Here," she said. "Just a couple of burnt-out bulbs."

"What's this?" Eddie complained. "I can't read it. There's grease all over it."

"Gimme," said Margo, waggling her butter-stained fingers. She put on her half glasses and frowned at the list. "That's 216, and 250. And check 160. They sneaked a dog in. Carpet stain."

Eddie made a face. "All right. I'll get it."

"Be back by eight," said Margo. "My back's bothering me."

"I'll be back," he said.

"I'll leave you a couple of these cookies just in case," she said cheerily.

Eddie started off down the open corridor to the janitor's closet to get the light bulbs, thinking about Margo. She was a pest in a lot of ways, but he'd worked for worse people. He wondered if she treated Anton the same way she treated him, always reminding him of everything twice, telling him the same things over and over. That could get to be real annoying if you were married to it.

The bulbs were in the top shelf of the janitor's closet. He got down a package of two and closed the closet door. As he walked out, he checked the parking spot for room 173. Her car was there all right. He glanced at his list, hesitated, then stuffed it in his pocket. It would have to wait. He edged down the corridor and saw a crack of light between the heavy drapes and the window frame. Transferring the box of light bulbs under his left arm, Eddie looked around, then used his passkey to get into room 171. The room was dark, and he did not turn on the light. He set the light bulbs on a chair and headed for the closet.

He had discovered the secret of room 171 by accident. Some guest had complained about the closet bar being loose, and Eddie had gone in to check on it. It turned out that rooms 171 and 173 had back-to-back closets, but some joker had put a door into the wall between them. Eddie figured that it had to be Anton. The guy had to get off somehow. It was a cinch that he wasn't doing much with Margo. Everytime Margo maundered on about her dear, departed Anton, Eddie thought about that door, and the late, lamented Anton slipping back and forth between those closets. Eddie loved the idea.

You couldn't use them that often—only when one room was occupied and the other wasn't. And you had to be very careful. But sometimes the show was well worth the trouble. And he had definitely had the adjoining closets in mind when he gave room 173 to Miss "I don't want any ice" Emery.

Eddie crossed the carpet of the darkened room 171 and opened the closet door, making sure not to jostle the empty hangers. Listening at the wall, he could tell that she was not near the closet. He undid the unobtrusive latch and pulled the door to him. He was looking into her closet. A couple of dresses hung there, redolent of a light, spicy scent. There was a pair of pants folded over the hanger, a couple of pairs of shoes piled haphazardly on the floor, and an inchwide column of light that told him he was really in luck. Her closet door was slightly ajar.

Carefully he pushed apart the clothes, blessing the plastic hangers that slid silently down the bar, and let himself into the closet. He inclined one eye to the crack where the door and the frame were separated. His heart was thumping and his mouth was dry, not from fear, but from excitement. He was already feeling aroused. If she was anything like most people, she had immediately undressed when she got into her room that evening. Any minute he would catch a glimpse.

At first he did not see her. Then he heard the toilet flush and the tap running. A few moments later she walked by the closet, still wearing a gray dress, her only concession to comfort being her shoes abandoned on the floor, and she was in her stocking feet.

Eddie felt the letdown, and pressed his lips together so as not to swear. There was still hope. She might be going out again, but on the other hand, she might decide to take that dress off at any minute. And then he could watch her shimmy out of it, which would be even better. Of course, it meant he'd have to be quick about getting out of the closet if she decided to hang it up.

While he was considering his options, the woman seated herself on one of those stiff chairs beside the window. Both the voile and the heavy drapes were carefully drawn closed. She was not one to relax like some people, Eddie thought, sprawling across the bed in their undies or less. On the other hand, the idea of spying on someone so uptight only added to the anticipation. He had a feeling that under that plain dress was something brief and lacy.

She drank a soda, smoked a cigarette, and fidgeted on the chair, glancing occasionally at her watch. All of a sudden Eddie realized that she was waiting for someone. He jumped at the sound of the door knocking, just as she did. Then she got up, stepped into her shoes, and let the guy in.

She and the visitor did not even shake hands, much less embrace. The man edged past her as if reluctant to make any contact with her.

Shit, Eddie thought, as the guy sat down on the other stiff chair. I haven't got all night to see if this thing warms up. The phone rang and she walked over and picked it up while her visitor, his arms folded across his chest, looked disapprovingly around the room.

Disgusted, Eddie backed out of the closet, quietly shut the connecting door, and walked back through room 171. He started to let himself out of the room when an old couple came walking down the corridor. His impulse was to duck back inside, but he reminded himself that there was nothing suspicious about what he was doing. Then he remembered the light bulbs. After letting himself back inside, he picked up the bulbs and looked at his watch. He'd really have to hurry to get these replaced before his shift. The hell with it, he thought. It would give him a good excuse to come back down later on. This guy had to leave sometime. And she had to take her clothes off sooner or later. The night was still young.

Chapter Nine

Y ou just keep a lookout. Make sure nobody's coming," said the man. "And turn off that flashlight until I tell you."

Obediently the woman clicked off the switch and scanned the empty parking lot, still lit by halogen lamps, in the predawn darkness.

The man lifted the rear door of the station wagon, grumbling as he hauled out overstuffed plastic garbage bags and dropped them to the ground with a thud.

"I don't think your mother threw one goddamned thing away in forty years, Jean," he said.

The woman ignored him. She'd been listening to this for three days now. They'd just put her mother in a nursing home, and now she and her husband, Herb, were cleaning out the family home so they could sell it. Herb had made a number of trips to the county dump, but it was half an hour's drive away. They'd been supplementing their wholesale trash removal with late night and early morning drop-offs in the open Dumpster bins behind some of the local stores. So far they'd put stuff into this particular grocery store's Dumpster three times without being caught. Jean felt as if they were pressing their luck, but Herb was getting tired of that drive to the dump.

"Throw in the appliances first," she whispered. "Then we can cover them up with the bags."

Herb lifted an ancient, grease-encrusted broiler over from the back of the car. "Why in the world did she keep this?" he cried. "We gave her a microwave two Christmases ago. This thing probably hasn't been fired up in ten years!"

"I don't know, honey," said Jean, trying to be patient. She couldn't blame him for complaining. It was a big job, and he'd been working like a trooper. And she had to admit, her mother had been a compulsive saver of useless items. "The Depression mentality, you know," said Jean. "I guess she thought she might need it sometime."

With a sigh, Herb lifted up the oven. "Okay," he said. "Shine it in there."

Jean climbed up on the lower rim of the Dumpster and pointed the flashlight on the piles of loose, rotten produce and broken boxes inside. On top of the pile was an overstuffed black trash bag. "We're not the only ones doing this," she observed.

"Just hold the light steady," Herb said, wrinkling his nose against the smell. He tossed the rotisserie over the side of the Dumpster. The sharp corner of the broiler oven snagged on the bag below it.

"Now get the portable TV," Jean ordered.

"Aye-aye," said Herb. He walked back to the car while Jean glanced around the empty lot. She knew these stores sometimes had security guards who patrolled. The sooner they got out of there, the better.

"One long-gone black-and-white Sylvania portable coming up," said Herb, carrying it toward the Dumpster.

Jean started to giggle nervously. "Let's keep it," she said.

"The hell we will," Herb cried, tossing the TV onto the pile. It tumbled in, fell atop the rotisserie, and then turned over. The broiler oven teetered and crashed on top of it, tearing the bag beneath it as it went. Jean shined the light inside and saw something dark and shiny oozing from the torn bag.

Herb walked back to the station wagon and peered inside. "I hope there's room in there for all this crap," he said. "What next?"

His wife did not answer.

He held up a rusted Christmas tree stand. "How 'bout this little beauty?" He turned around. "Jeannie?" he said.

Jean was staring into the Dumpster. She turned and looked at him, her face pasty white. "Oh, God," she whispered. Then her eyes rolled back in her head and her knees gave way beneath her.

Herb rushed to catch her, clutching her awkwardly under her armpits. "Jeannie, what?" he cried. Her flashlight had dropped into the Dumpster as she fell. Herb looked over the edge. In the flashlight's fixed beam he glimpsed the blood, the matted hair, and one lifeless blue eye. He sagged against the Dumpster, holding his wife, squeezing her. "Jesus Christ," he cried. "Help! Somebody help!"

Emily Ference stood in her immaculate kitchen, trying to thread her matching fabric belt through the belt loops in her dress. Her head was pounding and her hands trembled as she fumbled behind her to feel if she had missed any loops. Sure enough, she could feel one of the loops flattened by the belt. Pulling back the stiffened tongue of the belt, she tried again.

She licked her upper lip in her concentration and tasted the salty perspiration there. It was warm for May. That was part of it. The other part—well, the evidence glinted at her from the recycling can in the pantry where she had carefully deposited the empty gin bottle before she lost track of things last night. The dryness in her mouth, the roiling in her stomach, were also there to remind her of her shameful evening.

Have your coffee, comb your hair, take some aspirin, she recited to herself. You'll feel better. She had one more belt loop to achieve when a rapping on the door sent her into a panic. Not already, she thought. She's early.

Every weekday morning, Emily's sister-in-law, Sylvia Ference, came and picked her up, and the two women went to early mass together. Sylvia went off to her job at the bank after church, and Emily would return to her empty house, full of repentance and good intentions that seemed to evaporate when she crossed the threshold. As far as Emily knew, her weakness was her own secret, but it took some doing to keep it that way. She always kept herself and the house looking neat, and she tried always to be on time and act appropriately. She gave no one any cause to wonder about her. She tried to make sure of that.

Frantically Emily pulled the belt over the loop and fastened it, smoothing her hair with one hand as she went toward the door. "I'm coming," she said, trying not to let the anxiety sound in her voice. She opened the door, prepared to make a little joke about her state of unreadiness, and was surprised to see a young officer, Larry Tillman, on the doorstep.

"Good morning, Mrs. Ference," he said. He had strawberry-blond hair and freckles. Emily could remember him from boyhood. He was one of Walter's best men these days.

"Good morning, Larry. I was expecting my sister-in-law."

"Is Lieutenant Ference here?" he asked politely.

"Well, he is, but he's sleeping. It's his day off."

The young officer spoke in a somber but urgent tone. There was an undeniable note of excitement in his voice. "The chief told me to come and get him. I'm afraid you'll have to wake him up. We have a homicide."

Emily needed no further explanation. "There's coffee, help yourself," she said, pointing toward the kitchen as she hurried off to the bedroom.

Walter Ference was sleeping on his side in their bed, his hands tucked under his face like a small child. At fifty-two his skin was smooth except for the pucker of the scar on his forehead. He looked young and vulnerable. Guiltily she wondered whether he had found her in bed last night when he got home or had put her there. She hoped she had made it under her own steam. He would never mention it in any case.

Walter sighed and turned over on his back. Emily stared at him a minute, wondering if either Joey or Ted would have grown up to look like their father. Before the yawning darkness could open up inside of her again, Emily pushed the thought away and shook her husband by the shoulder.

Walter opened his eyes and looked at her alertly, although she knew he must still be dazed with sleep. It came from years of being a cop, she thought.

"Young Larry Tillman is here," she said. "Chief Matthews sent him to get you. Apparently they have a murder."

Walter's body stiffened visibly under the bedclothes, and he stared up at the ceiling. She could see he was trying to clear the cobwebs of sleep and leftover dreams from his mind. Suddenly he sat bolt upright and threw his legs over the side of the bed. He rubbed his hands rapidly over his face. "Okay," he said, reaching for his glasses on the bedside table. "I'll be right there."

"I'll pour you some coffee," she said.

Emily stopped in the bathroom, took her aspirin, combed her hair, and returned through the maze of rooms on the first floor to the kitchen. Larry Tillman was seated at the kitchen table, a cup of coffee beside him.

"He's coming," Emily said.

"Okay," said Larry, drumming absently on the table-top. "This is a nice old house. I like old houses," he said to fill up the silence.

"Thank you," said Emily. "Walter grew up here. It was quite an elegant home in its day."

"It's still nice," said Larry loyally.

"Thanks," said Emily. She knew they had let the place get run-down over the years. It was really too much house to care for, too much house for just two people, but they had been a family of four when Walter bought out Sylvia's half. At the time it had seemed the ideal house in which to raise up the boys.

A knock at the back door made Emily jump. "That's Sylvia," she said. She walked over and opened the door to her sister-in-law. The young officer stood up politely. Sylvia looked from Officer Tillman to Emily. "Isn't it Walter's day off?" she said.

"Yes, it is," said Emily. "But there's been a murder."

Sylvia made a sign of the cross over the breast of her suit jacket and then peered at the young cop. "Who was it?" she asked.

Walter came into the kitchen, knotting a tie. "Good morning," he said. He looked at Larry. "What happened?"

"A couple found the body of a white female in a Dumpster behind the Shop-Rite about an hour ago."

Emily and Sylvia gasped.

Walter's expression was grim. "How long's she been dead?"

Larry shook his head. "Not long. Overnight. Beaten to death, apparently. Dr. Jansen's there now."

"Do we have an ID?" Walter asked, filling his pockets with change from a bowl on the countertop and accepting his coffee mug from Emily.

Officer Tillman glanced down at his pad of notes. "Chicago license. Tentative as Linda Emery."

"Little Linda Emery," Sylvia cried. "That can't be. She disappeared years ago. You remember the Emerys," she said to Walter.

"He drowned a little while back," said Emily.

"That's right, he was a carpenter," said Sylvia. "Quiet fellow. They kept to themselves. And Linda used to tag along with him everywhere he went like a little dog."

Emily grimaced at the unfortunate image.

"Well, there would be nothing left to her by now," said Sylvia. "She'd be a skeleton, like that Amber girl."

"Oh, no, ma'am," said Larry. "This must not be the same person. This woman was in her thirties."

"Well, how can that be?" said Sylvia. "That girl disappeared without a trace, must be fifteen years now."

"No details," Walter snapped. "We'll discuss it on the way."

Sylvia drew herself up indignantly. "How dare you, Walter. Your own sister."

"I don't want this all over the bank before we even have a chance to sort it out."

"That is an insult. As if I were going to be telling everyone in sight," Sylvia sniffed.

"We aren't supposed to divulge the details," said Larry apologetically.

"Well, phooey," said Sylvia. "I don't want to hear all the gory details anyway."

"Are you ready, sir?" asked Larry.

Walter sighed. "Let's go."

"We've got to go, too, Emily," said Sylvia. "Did you know you missed a belt loop there?"

"Yes," said Emily distractedly. "I'm just looking for my purse."

"Don't wait supper for me," said Walter, kissing Emily on the cheek. "I'll get something out."

Emily lowered her eyes, confused. Was he trying to embarrass her? she wondered. She could not remember if she even ate something herself the night before, much less saved something for him. She glanced at him. No, she thought. That was just his way of pretending she was normal—a good wife.

"Your purse is on that chair," said Sylvia in a shrill voice. "If it had teeth, it would bite you."

"Oh, thanks," Emily whispered.

Sylvia paused in the doorway. "Good luck with your investigation. We'll light a candle for the unfortunate girl, whoever she may be," she said piously.

"You're blocking my car," said Walter. "Let's get a move on."

Chapter Ten

Karen lifted her leotards off the drying rack in the laundry room and folded them into her exercise bag. Over the sound of the local radio station playing softly in the kitchen, she could hear Jenny banging around in the cabinets.

She picked up Jenny's T-shirt and folded it, holding it close to her. "Jenny, your red shirt is dry if you want to wear it," she called out.

Jenny did not reply. Karen walked into the kitchen and saw Jenny pouring herself some juice from a pitcher in the refrigerator.

"I said your red shirt is dry," Karen repeated.

"I didn't hear you," said Jenny. "Who can hear anything over this Muzak on the radio? Do we have to listen to this station?"

"Your father needs to know the local forecast so he

can plan his day." They'd had this discussion many previous mornings.

"He isn't even downstairs," Jenny protested.

"Yes, I am," Greg said, walking in and taking a glass out of the cabinet. "Can I have some of that juice?"

Jenny poured him a glass. He sat down at the island and Karen handed him a plate with an English muffin on it.

"You went up early last night," he said, buttering his muffin.

Karen avoided his gaze. "I was tired. I read awhile in bed and went to sleep. How did it go with the new clients?"

Greg shook his head. "We didn't really see eye-to-eye. They thought my estimates were too high. I don't think I'll get the job."

"That's unusual for you," Karen said coolly.

"They'll find someone who promises to do it cheaper and faster. You know how that goes."

Karen nodded. In the course of any big construction job, there were always delays and hidden expenses. Greg tried to avoid customers who seemed impatient from the first meeting.

"Can we please put on another station?" said Jenny. "I hate these oldies."

"These are classic tunes," Greg teased her. "Your mother and I courted to these songs."

"It's the stupid news," said Jenny.

"You're in a good mood," Karen observed.

"Why complain?" Greg asked cheerfully.

" . . . the top story this morning: A body was found

in a Dumpster behind the Shop-Rite supermarket," the announcer said.

"Ugh," said Jenny.

"Police have identified the victim as thirty-two-year-old Linda Jean Emery, a Chicago resident who was here visiting her family."

The juice glass Jenny was holding crashed and shattered on the wood floor as Jenny let out a strangled cry.

"Oh, my God," said Greg.

"It can't be," said Karen. She looked at Greg, and then both looked at Jenny, who teetered back against the counter. "Honey, are you all right?" Karen asked.

"My mother," Jenny wailed. "No . . ."

"Baby, sit down," Karen pleaded, guiding Jenny to a chair. Greg was hurriedly mopping up the floor and collecting the broken glass.

Jenny looked at Karen, but her expression was dazed. "It can't be her."

"Turn it up," said Karen to Greg, who was near the radio. He turned the dial and listened intently.

"Maybe it's a mistake," Jenny cried.

Greg shook his head grimly. "I don't think so."

Jenny began to weep and shake her head. It tore at Karen to see those narrow shoulders shaking with grief.

"Oh, honey," she said, putting an arm around her. "I'm so sorry. I just can't believe it."

Jenny reared back and shook off Karen's embrace. "No, you're not," she said, sobs burbling in her voice. "You're glad."

"Jenny!" Karen exclaimed.

"You were mean and horrible to her," Jenny wailed.

"You hated her. You didn't even want her in this house."

"That's not fair," Karen cried. "It's not true, either. I did not hate her."

"Oh, no. Not much. You're glad she's dead."

Karen's first impulse was to lash back at the unfairness, the cruelty of it. But she could see that Jenny was in pain, that she was flailing out like a wounded animal. She grabbed her daughter by the shoulders and sought her averted gaze. "She was your mother. She gave birth to you. I wouldn't have seen this happen for the world."

Jenny's anger dissolved again into grief. "If only you could have given her a chance," she said miserably.

Greg, who had stood silently through this exchange, suddenly said, "That's enough."

"Well, it's true," said Jenny miserably. "You never tried to like her. You were against her from the first minute."

"Sit down there right now and be quiet."

Karen looked at Greg's stony expression in surprise. "Greg, she's upset," she said. "You know she is."

"I know she's upset, but this is important and I want her to pay attention to what I'm saying."

Silenced by his vehemence, Jenny sniffled and wiped her eyes.

"Now, listen to me," he said. "Before this day is out the police are going to hear about her connection to you and want to know about it. They're going to be over here asking a lot of questions about Linda Emery. And when they do, I expect you to keep whatever gripes you have with me or your mother to yourself. Do you understand me?"

"Greg!" Karen exclaimed.

"The truth of the matter is that whether this woman was your natural mother or not—we hardly knew her, and we don't want to be involved in this business."

"But we are—" Jenny protested.

Greg cut her off. "No, we are not. She barged into our lives two days ago with no warning, and whatever connection there might be, we are not responsible. We don't know her. We don't know anything about her. And let's just leave it at that. Now, it's terrible that she was killed, but there's nothing we can do about it. Whatever complaints you have about how your mother and I treated her, you just keep them to yourself. We'll tell the police we were glad to meet her, and we all got along like gangbusters, and that's the end of it."

"That's a lie," Jenny cried. "You hated her. You both did."

"This is not up for discussion," Greg shouted. "You will do as I say. You will not start causing us trouble with the police because your feelings were hurt. This has nothing to do with us. Is that clear?"

There was no mistaking the finality in Greg's voice. Jenny began to sob, shocked by his anger at her.

"I think you'd better stay home this morning," Karen said gently.

"Well, I wasn't planning to go to school the day my mother is murdered," she said, weeping. "I'm going upstairs." Wiping her eyes, she shuffled out of the room. Karen's heart ached as she watched her go.

Greg sighed and sank back against the counter.

Karen stood up and glared at him. "Why did you do that?" she demanded.

"What?" he asked in a dull voice.

"Can't you see she's devastated? Why are you telling her to lie about this? Just because we didn't like the woman—just because we weren't happy that she came here isn't a crime. The police aren't going to be interested in us."

Greg looked wearily at his wife. "Somebody killed the woman. The police are going to be looking into everything she did since she came to town. In their eyes, we had a damn good reason to dislike her. We might have wanted her out of the way."

"That's ridiculous," said Karen impatiently.

"Is it?" he said. "She was threatening our relationship with our daughter. People have been known to get very angry over things like that."

Karen looked at him aghast. "Not angry enough to kill someone."

"Why not?" he asked.

"Oh, for heaven's sake, Greg. The police are going to be looking for a psycho."

"Maybe. Maybe not. All I know is, when they find out that this woman showed up in town and claimed the child of another woman as her own, and then, the next day practically, she was murdered . . . Well, what would you think if you were a cop? Women have been known to lift cars off their children. Mothers . . . parents will go to any lengths. And then they hear Jenny spouting off like that about how much we hated her and all."

Karen gazed at him intently. "You're talking about

me," she said. "That's what you're thinking, isn't it? You think they'd suspect me."

"Look, I'm just saying we should be prepared for this."

"Well, that's just not . . . I mean, it's stupid. A man must have killed her. It was probably some kind of a sex crime."

"It didn't say that on the radio," he pointed out.

"Well, it had to be. What else could it be?" Karen's voice trailed off. She shook her head. "Nobody could think that. It's not possible." She turned and looked back at her husband. "Could they?"

Greg came over to her and put his arms around her comfortingly. "I don't know what they might think. And I'm not saying we have to lie. All I'm telling you is what I told Jenny. We don't have to volunteer our every feeling. There's no reason to bring up all the problems. It's not our fault that she showed up here and then got herself killed. It doesn't concern us. All I want to do is keep out of it. All of us."

Karen nodded, distracted. "It just sounds so . . ."

"What?"

"I don't know. Heartless." She shuddered.

"It's just being practical," he said.

"Maybe you're right," Karen agreed, shaken by the possibilities he had conjured. If there was a way to avoid being seen in that light . . . "Maybe that would be for the best."

Chapter Eleven

Mom, the police are here." Bill Emery stood in the doorway of his mother's bedroom. A crucifix hung over the headboard, and the crocheted bedspread was pulled up to Alice's neck. After a nightmarish trip to the morgue, Alice had insisted that Bill bring her back to her own house. Now she lay on the bed, and Dr. Martin Nolte, who had tended to their family for years, was removing a needle from her upper arm and swabbing it with cotton.

"Bill, you better talk to them. Or tell them to come back. Your mother's in no condition," said the doctor.

Bill hesitated and then said, "I'll take care of it."

"Good boy," Dr. Nolte said as if Bill were still a small child. Bill retreated from the room.

"Martin," said Alice in a weak voice.

"What is it, my dear?"

"Hand me that picture on my bureau."

The doctor brought the photograph to her bedside, and Alice gazed at it, tears running down the sides of her face, following the grooves made by the earpieces of her glasses. The photo was taken when Linda was about five and Bill was eight. Jack had refused to be in the picture. He always hated to have his picture taken. Alice could never understand it. He was such a nice-looking man. Her mind wandered back to when she had first seen him, the day he came to fix her mother's porch steps. He was new in Bayland, but a friend of her mother's had recommended him as hard working and honest. As soon as Alice looked out the kitchen window and saw him there, her heart turned over. She had never been the bashful type, but it took a lot of doing to engage him in conversation those first few times. But when he finally opened up a little, it was worth the effort.

Alice looked at the two children smiling in the photo, arms linked in hers. Her gaze focused on the little girl. "You're with your daddy, now," she said, a sob in her voice.

"That sedative I just gave you will help," said Dr. Nolte gently.

"She just came back to me and now I've lost her for good," said Alice. But already her thoughts were beginning to blur.

"Try and rest," said the doctor, picking up his bag. "I'll leave a prescription with Bill. You call me if you need anything."

"I will," Alice whispered. Her hands became weaker as the drug spread through her body. Her grip on the photograph loosened, and the framed picture slid down the covers and dropped to the hooked rug on the floor. Alice's mind began to travel—back, back, tumbling through a bittersweet twilight of memories.

Bill Emery pulled open the door of his mother's home and looked at the woman with a notebook standing on the steps, pressing the doorbell. She was in her twenties, dressed in a functional skirt and blouse and sensible flats. Her ash-blond hair was short and had no discernible style, as if she could not be bothered with it. She had good, clear skin but wore no makeup. Her tone of voice was all business.

"My name is Phyllis Hodges," she began. "I'm from the *Bayland Gazette*." She peered around Bill as he examined her press card and saw Walter Ference and Larry Tillman seated in the living room. She waved at Walter, and he nodded at her.

"I'm sorry," said Bill. "We have nothing to say."

"Are you related to the victim?" Phyllis said hurriedly, all but putting her foot in the door.

"She was my sister. If you don't mind . . ."

"I see the police are here. I wouldn't mind waiting," Phyllis persisted.

"Please, leave us alone," said Bill, closing the door on her protests. He turned back to Walter Ference, who was seated on the edge of Alice's wing chair. Larry Tillman got up and stood by the window, peeking out through the curtain at the cluster of curious people at the edge of the lawn.

"These reporters have no respect for people's privacy," said Bill.

Walter nodded sympathetically. "Now, Mr. Emery, there are a few more things we need to clarify here. About your sister. You say it was her idea to stay at the motel."

Bill nervously picked up a china figurine of a shepherdess off his mother's mantelpiece and then replaced it. "Yes, it had something to do with calling this a business trip. You know, tax deductions."

Walter nodded.

"Glenda," Bill called out. Bill's wife poked her head out of the kitchen. "We could use some coffee."

"Not for me," said Walter firmly. "And what were you doing last night?"

"What do you mean? I was working late. At the store."

"Were you alone?"

"No, actually, one of my salesgirls was there."

"Name?"

Bill looked as if he were about to protest, but then he capitulated. "Christine Bishop."

Walter made a note. "Okay. Now, the name of these people—the ones who adopted your sister's baby."

"Newhall," Bill snapped. "I told you already."

Glenda came into the living room. "Honey," she said, "excuse me. I'm going to run down to the pharmacy and get this prescription filled for Mom."

"Go ahead," Bill said irritably. Glenda glanced curiously at the police officers and backed out of the room.

"And this was the first you knew about your sister's pregnancy, or why she ran away?" Walter continued.

"Yes," said Bill. "But what has all this got to do with

finding the nut that killed my sister and left her in that Dumpster?"

Walter closed his pad and stood up. "I think we're all set for now. Thank you for your cooperation, Mr. Emery. We'll talk to your mother later."

Bill's tense shoulders relaxed as he showed them to the door. "Glad I could help you," he said.

Bill watched from the window as the two officers went down the walk and got into their car. As soon as the car pulled away from the curb, he went to the phone and dialed.

"Shane's Sporting Goods," answered the raspy voice of Trudy Kubinski, the cashier.

"Christine Bishop," said Bill in a soft, low voice.

Trudy hesitated. "Bill?"

"Excuse me?" Bill said in an unnatural, offended tone.

"Sorry," said Trudy. "Just a minute."

Bill could feel moons of perspiration spreading under his arms as he waited. Finally Christine picked up the phone.

"Christine Bishop."

"Listen, Christine," said Bill without preamble, "don't let anyone at the store know you are talking to me."

"Okay," Christine said uncertainly.

"The police may be coming to talk to you. My sister's been murdered."

"Oh, Bill, I'm so sorry. How awful."

"Didn't I just tell you not to mention my name there?"

"I'm sorry," she pleaded.

"I told them we were working late at the store last night. Together. Have you got that?"

"Sure. I guess so."

"And if they mention the Jefferson Motel, you never heard of it."

"Why?" she asked plaintively.

"Because I said so," said Bill.

There was a silence at the other end. Then a soft, sad voice said. "Okay. All right. Don't get mad."

Bill clenched his fist and silently counted to ten.

Margo Hofsteder's heart skipped a beat. Two cops were coming in her doorway, one uniformed, one in a tie and jacket. Glancing out her window, she saw that there were two more cops and another squad car in the parking lot.

"Can I help you?" she said.

Walter Ference nodded. "Are you the manager?"

"I own this place. My name is Margo Hofsteder."

"Miss Hofsteder . . ."

"Mrs."

"We understand you had a guest here by the name of Linda Emery."

Margo consulted her book, running a pudgy finger down the page. "Still do," she said. "Is she in trouble?"

Walter and Larry exchanged a glance. "I'm afraid Miss Emery is dead. She was murdered last night," said Walter.

Margo clutched her chest. "Here?" she cried.

"We don't know where," said Walter. "We'd like to see her room."

Margo's complexion became splotchy with nervous

excitement. "Oh, my God," she said, fumbling under the desk for her keys. "Not here. Not in my place. . . . "

"We don't know that," said Walter. "We just need to take a look."

"Of course, of course," she mumbled, coming out from behind the counter, her keys and her bracelets jangling. She kept up a running commentary to no one in particular as the policemen followed her rolling gait down the sidewalk to room 173. "Oh, I can't believe it. This is a family place. It'll be all over the papers. Oh, my. Horrible, horrible."

She reached room 173 and said in a hushed voice, "This is it."

"Open it, please," said Walter.

Margo inserted the key with trembling fingers, pushed the door open, and jumped back, as if expecting the murderer, still inside, to leap out at her.

Larry Tillman led the way in, snapping on the lights. Walter came in behind him and looked around.

From outside the door Margo wailed, "Is there blood?"

Larry, who walked back into the bathroom, came out and shook his head. The room was untidy, but it was clearly not the scene of the crime.

"No, everything's normal in here," Walter said.

"Oh, thank God," cried Margo, feeling a twinge of disappointment. She poked her head around the door.

"When does this room get cleaned?" Walter asked.

"Usually around one o'clock. She's slow," said Margo apologetically.

"Just as well," said Walter. "A couple of men will be

looking through her belongings. No one should touch this room until we're finished."

"I understand," said Margo knowledgeably. "There could still be evidence here you wouldn't want disturbed."

"Did Miss Emery have any visitors?" Walter asked. "Do you remember seeing anyone come here?"

Margo shook her head regretfully. "I try to respect the privacy of my guests."

"Would you remember if anyone came asking for her?"

"Well, I might remember that, but no. There wasn't anybody. You can talk to the night man, though. He might remember something."

"Where can we find him?"

"Probably still asleep upstairs," said Margo.

Eddie heard the knock at the door and rolled over in the tangled sheets, cursing the intrusion. "Go away," he mumbled. The heavy drapes made the room exceedingly dark, and he had no idea what time it was. He didn't even really register that it was knocking until he heard Margo calling out, "Eddie, open up. The police are here."

If there was a worse way to wake up, Eddie couldn't think what it might be. He stumbled out of bed, grabbed a pair of pants off a nearby chair, and turned on the bathroom light. His face had a lavender hue.

He splashed some water on his face and neck, and it splattered on the T-shirt he'd been sleeping in. Barefoot, he went to the door and opened it.

The two cops at the door peered into the darkness. Eddie's gaunt face was like a smudge on a chalkboard.

Margo frowned disapprovingly at her handyman. "Eddie," she said, "you have to talk to these men. There's been a murder."

Eddie rubbed his eyes and shook his head. "Wait a minute. What is this? I didn't do nothing."

Walter stepped into the room. "Turn a light on in here. Or open those drapes."

Obediently Eddie pulled the drapes open.

"You can go now, Mrs. Hofsteder," said Walter firmly.

"Margo," Eddie pleaded, shielding his eyes from the brightness of the daylight, "what's going on?"

"Just answer the questions, honey. Somebody killed that girl from Chicago that was staying in 173."

His eyes adjusted, Eddie looked at the two policemen, then looked sharply away, staggering back and sinking down onto the edge of the bed. He let out a little whimpering sound.

"Did you know Miss Emery?" Walter asked.

Eddie shook his head.

"Well, you seem awfully upset," said Walter.

Eddie folded his arms across his chest, avoiding the detective's eyes. "No," he mumbled. "Just surprised."

Walter indicated to Larry with a glance that he should look around, and Larry began a leisurely circuit of the messy room.

"We want to know if you saw anyone coming here to visit Miss Emery. Anyone suspicious, hanging around."

Eddie gave Walter a challenging look, "I don't pay any attention."

"So, you didn't see anyone."

"No one," said Eddie. His eyes had a strange, glittering cast, half-calculating, half fearful.

"Do you live here, Mr. McHugh?" asked Walter.

"Yeah."

"Ever been in trouble with the law?"

Eddie hesitated. "No," he said. "Just kid stuff. I didn't do anything to that woman."

Walter gazed at Eddie until Eddie averted his eyes. "Thanks for your cooperation."

"Glad to help you out," he said.

The cops left the room and Eddie closed the door behind them. For a few moments he leaned against it, staring, unseeing, at the chaos of his room. Then, slowly, a feral grin spread across his face. "Well, well, well," he said aloud. "What do you know about that."

Chapter Twelve

This'll take a few minutes, Glenda," said the pharmacist, a gray-haired man in a white doctor's smock.

"No problem," said Glenda. She walked over to a display of cosmetics and began idly brushing various shades of blusher on the back of her hand.

"Excuse me," said a young woman, approaching her. "Mrs. Emery?"

Glenda looked at the young woman curiously, thinking the girl could really use a little pink blusher herself. "Yes?"

"My name is Phyllis Hodges. I'm a reporter from the *Bayland Gazette*. I was wondering if I could ask you a few questions about the murder victim. She was your sister-in-law, wasn't she?"

Glenda looked anxiously at the pharmacist's counter.

The druggist was busy in the back. She could hear the tapping of a typewriter. "I didn't know her all that well," she said apologetically. "How did you know it was me?"

"I saw you leaving the house," Phyllis admitted, "and I sort of followed you."

"You followed me?" Glenda asked, surprised and a little flattered by this admission.

"I've been assigned to write a story about this case, and I was hoping to be able to really give a sympathetic picture of the victim, but I need some background on her. Apparently your sister-in-law has been away from Bayland for some time."

Glenda shrugged. There was no secret in that. "Yes, she has," she said. "She disappeared when she was seventeen. Of course, at the time there was all kinds of speculation. You know, about what happened to her. But it turns out she ran away."

"What a tragedy," said Phyllis. "She'd just come back, and now this."

"It's been awful hard on my mother-in-law," said Glenda, nodding. She honestly felt very sad for Alice. As mother-in-laws went, Alice was a bargain. And Bill had made this whole thing so much worse by forcing her not to see Linda. If it had been Tiffany gone missing all those years . . .

"And your husband," said Phyllis.

"Hmmm?"

"Your husband must be very upset, too."

"Oh, yes," said Glenda. She was warming to Phyllis. She seemed like a nice girl. A little naive, maybe. But being a reporter was a good job. Glenda hoped that

Tiffany would get a good job someday and not be dependent on some man to support her.

Phyllis's face was a study in innocent curiosity. "Do you know why she left Bayland?"

Glenda hesitated. What difference did it make to tell? She really couldn't see why Bill was being so close-mouthed about it. He was putting on a good show about being upset, but, really, he was more ticked off at Linda than anything else. It was all going to come out in the wash anyway. And in this day and age, it was no disgrace to have a baby outside of marriage and give it up for adoption. Heck, with all the people having abortions, it was practically a noble thing to do. Oh, Bill would be mad at her when he found out she had told. But she could probably tell it a lot more kindly than he would. Besides, Glenda thought defiantly, I believe in freedom of the press.

"Well, as a matter of fact," she said, "I do know why she left. And it's kind of an interesting story."

Phyllis leaned forward, a wolfish gleam in her eye.

Greg Newhall opened the door with an attempt at a smile on his face. "We've been expecting you," he said.

"May we come in?" Walter asked politely.

Greg ushered them into the house and pointed to the living room. "My wife and daughter are in there," he said.

Karen sat in the corner on the sofa. Jenny was slumped in the rocker, staring at the empty grate in the fireplace.

"Sit down," said Karen anxiously.

Walter sat in an armchair. Larry stood in the doorway. "We're here to ask you a few questions about Linda Emery."

Greg walked over and stood behind Karen. "We thought you might be wondering. I guess you know by now that she was the . . . that she was our daughter's biological mother," he said.

Walter smiled thinly. "How long have you known about this?" he asked.

Karen glanced up at Greg. "About two days now, I guess," he said. "Three, if you count today."

"And you had not known the identity of the child's mother before that time?"

"No," Greg said with a shade of disapproval in his voice. "I know these 'one, big, happy family' arrangements where everybody gets together and bonds are in vogue these days, but no . . . that was thirteen years ago. The mother's identity, and ours—so we thought—remained anonymous."

"So, did you seek her out, or did she find you?"

"She found us," said Greg shortly.

"Did she say how she found you?"

"She mentioned a private investigator," said Karen.

"I see," Walter murmured, making notes on his pad. "So, essentially she just called you out of the blue and said she was Jenny's real mother."

"She showed up here, actually," said Karen. "On Sunday, Mother's Day."

"Were you angry about that?" Walter asked smoothly.

Karen was finding it difficult to smile or keep a tremor out of her voice. She could feel Greg's hands pressing down on her shoulders, as if to steady her. It was a good thing he had warned her to anticipate these questions. Greg was right—she felt guilty and apologetic under police scrutiny, even though she had nothing to hide.

"Well," she said carefully, "a little notice would have been good, I suppose. But, you have to realize, this was someone Jenny had wondered about her whole life. It was a great thing for her to finally meet her biological mother."

Jenny wiped tears away from her eyes but avoided looking at her parents or the policeman.

"Is that right, Jenny?" Walter asked. "Were you happy to meet her?"

"Yes," said Jenny in a small voice. She was pushing the rocker back and forth with one foot.

"And your parents didn't mind," he said.

Jenny's eyes flashed angrily and she pursed her lips. "I guess not," she said.

"Detective, do you have children?" Karen asked. From his spot in the doorway, Larry let a little exclamation of dismay escape his lips. Like everyone on the force, he knew about Walter's tragedy. Karen looked up at the young officer, puzzled by his reaction.

Walter hesitated and then said, "No, ma'am."

"Well," Karen stumbled on, flustered by the offended expression on Officer Tillman's face, "when you have a child, you want whatever makes them happy. That becomes your number one priority."

"Even if it's someone else claiming to be their mother," said Walter.

Karen took a deep breath. "She was Jenny's mother."

"But surely this must have been very upsetting to you," Walter persisted.

"Stop baiting my wife," Greg exclaimed. "She told you how we felt. We were happy for Jenny's sake."

Walter glanced up at Greg, his eyes wide. Then he proceeded calmly. "Did she tell you who the father was?"

"She didn't say," said Karen. "We didn't ask."

Walter nodded. "And when was the last time you saw Linda Emery?"

Karen looked at Jenny, who refused to meet her eyes. "I guess when she brought Jenny home yesterday afternoon. They had lunch together at Miller's restaurant."

"Did you see or talk to Miss Emery after that?" Walter asked Jenny. "Did any of you?"

"No," said Jenny. Greg and Karen shook their heads.

Walter stood up. "I think that will be all for now. We may be back later, however."

Greg stiffly led the two men to the front door. Karen looked at Jenny, who was rocking furiously in the chair, her face dark as a thunderhead.

The voices receded, and then they heard the front door slam. Jenny stood up from the chair and met Karen's eyes for the first time. "You hypocrite," she said. "I hate you."

Greg came into the room. "I think that went pretty well," he said.

"Excuse me," said Jenny bitterly. "I think I'm going to be sick."

Mary Duncan stretched in her bed and yawned. Sometimes she thought the best thing about owning a

restaurant was that you got to sleep late in the mornings. Miller's only served breakfast on weekends, so
weekday mornings were the most leisurely time she
had. Sam generally got up first and went out for the
paper and doughnuts for them, while Mary made the
coffee. Of course, everything would change if they had
a baby. No sleeping in for them. No more late nights at
the restaurant, either. At least not for Mary.

Mary rolled over and buried her face in the pillow.
Who am I kidding? she thought. We're never going to
have a baby. With Sam it was always some excuse. The
timing was wrong, finances were tight, something.
Sometimes she could not believe that they had been together all these years and still no children. And these
days there wasn't much chance of her conceiving anyway, since they hardly ever found the time to make
love. Seeing Linda with that child had thrown her into a
blue funk. It reminded her of how the years were passing. And what did she have to show for it. Her father's
restaurant and a husband who was obsessed with the
business. She had been sure that Sam really loved her
when they got married. They were young, of course,
and Mary was inexperienced, but still. He was no
Romeo. He just announced his love for her, and that
was it. But, over the years, sometimes . . . If Miller's
restaurant hadn't been part of the bargain . . .

Mary heard the front door of the condo open, and she
forced herself to get up and out of bed. She pulled on
her bathrobe and tied it, calling out, "I'm sorry about
the coffee. I'll put it on now." She shoved her feet into
her slippers and padded out into the kitchen. The bag of
doughnuts and a newspaper were on the table. Sam was

standing by the sink, looking out the window onto their view of the harbor.

"I'm sorry," said Mary again. "I just couldn't seem to get myself out of bed."

Sam turned and looked at her, and his round face was very pale.

"What's the matter?" she said. "You look awful."

"I heard some bad news at the bakery."

"What? Sam, don't make me nervous. Tell me."

"You better sit," he said. "It's about your old friend Linda Emery."

"Our old friend," she corrected him. "She was your friend, too, back then." Sam glanced out the window again, as if pained by her remark. Mary felt a sudden chill run through her. She took her husband's advice and sat down. "What is it, Sam?" she said. "Tell me quick."

Chapter Thirteen

The Bayland Library was a Federal-style brick building, surrounded by flowers and shrubs, which sat on the corner of an intersection across from the Washington Street Park. Jenny rode up on her bicycle and lifted the bike into the rack beside a bed of geraniums alongside the building. Peggy had called her from school and offered to meet her there after school got out. Jenny jumped at the chance to get out of the house and away from her parents. She needed to talk to a friend, someone she could confide in, anyone but her mother and father. Every time she thought of that interview with the police that morning, she wanted to hit something. Or someone. It was as if she were seeing a side of her parents that she never knew existed.

She sat down on a bench under a flowering pink

dogwood tree to wait for Peggy. When Peggy called from the school cafeteria she said all the kids were talking about the murder. Of course none of them but Peggy knew about Jenny's connection to the victim. Peggy had assured her that she didn't mention anything about it. She was a good friend like that. Besides, she was someone you could really talk to. She had problems with her own parents that were pretty bad.

"Jenny?"

Jenny looked up, startled, and saw a woman she did not recognize approaching her. She had short, blondish hair and a friendly smile. Jenny frowned at her. "Yeah?"

"Excuse me, Jenny," said the woman. "I'm sorry to bother you. Your mom said I might find you here."

"Oh," said Jenny.

"My name is Phyllis, Jenny. I . . . I was a good friend of Linda Emery's from way back in grammar school days," Phyllis Hodges said, lying with practiced ease. She was counting on the fact that Jenny would not be able to judge the age difference between herself and Linda Emery. All grown-ups looked alike to a kid, she figured. Phyllis had been watching the Newhall house ever since she talked to Glenda Emery, and when she saw Jenny pedaling away, she had followed her to the library. "Linda called me the other night when she got to town," she went on in an unctuous tone, "and we had a great conversation. It was so good to hear her voice again."

Jenny smiled wanly. "That's nice," she said.

"She told me all about you, Jenny. About coming back here to find you and all."

"She did?"

"She was very proud of you. She said she wanted me to meet you, but, well . . . you know what happened. I'm just so heartbroken."

"Yes," said Jenny glumly.

"Look, Jenny, I know you're probably on your way into the library to study . . . "

"My girlfriend's meeting me here, actually."

Phyllis sighed. "Linda and I used to meet here when we were your age. We'd sit and talk, or go get a soda or something. Those were the days."

Jenny felt awkward. "Well," she said, "it's nice to meet you."

"I wonder, Jenny . . . I mean, if it wouldn't be too much of an imposition . . . "

"What?" Jenny asked warily.

Phyllis pointed to the spot on the bench beside Jenny, as if requesting permission to sit down. Jenny shrugged. Phyllis perched gingerly on the seat beside her. "Well, it's just that I never did get to see her, and I feel so bad about it. I feel like I missed my opportunity and now I'll never have another chance to see her again. If you could spare a minute, tell me what she was like, fill me in a little on her life and all that. I mean, I know this is a bad time for you, but it would mean so much to me."

Jenny glanced at her watch. Peggy wouldn't be along

for a little while yet. And the idea of sharing what she knew about Linda with this old friend was appealing. Here was someone who really cared. And Linda would want her to do it.

"Okay," she said. "Sure."

"That's great," said Phyllis. She exhaled a little sigh and sank back against the bench. Jenny gazed across the street at the park, abloom with azaleas and flowering fruit trees. Her eyes suddenly filled with tears. Sometimes she and Peggy would walk through the park and toss pebbles in the pond and talk about their deepest secret thoughts. She suddenly pictured Linda there, at her age. "Did you two tell each other your private secrets and stuff?" she asked Phyllis.

"Oh, sure," said Phyllis. "We'd talk about our fantasies, what we wanted to be and all that. I didn't even get around to asking Linda on the phone what she was doing."

"She worked in a big store, in the clothing department," Jenny said promptly. "In Chicago. She worked her way up to a manager."

"That sounds like a good job. She always liked clothes," said Phyllis blandly, taking a stab that seemed pretty likely to hit the target.

"That's what *she* said," Jenny exclaimed. Then she said warmly, "What did you become?"

Phyllis hesitated. "Well, actually, I became a writer."

"That's neat," said Jenny. "What do you write?"

"All kinds of things. I'm working on a book," said Phyllis airily. "But let's talk about Linda. Did she look the same?"

"I don't know how she looked when you knew her," said Jenny.

"No, of course not. That was a silly question. I guess I just meant did she look healthy and happy."

"I don't know." Jenny shrugged. "Everybody said she looked a lot like me. And she had pretty clothes."

"Oh, it's true. You really do remind me of her," said Phyllis. "That's how I knew who you were the minute I saw you."

Jenny smiled, pleased.

"I'll bet you were surprised to find out she was your real mother."

Jenny nodded, a faraway look in her eyes. "I'd always imagined what she'd be like. But she was even better than I'd imagined."

Good quote, Phyllis thought. This article was going to be a heart wrencher. "So," she said sympathetically, "it was a wonderful surprise for her to turn up. What did your parents think about her? Were they excited, too?"

Jenny snorted derisively. "Yeah, thrilled," she said.

Phyllis's antennae went up. Go slow, she thought. "Well, you know, parents can be touchy about certain things."

"Touchy," Jenny exclaimed. "My mother practically threw her out." She shook her head. "It really made me mad. I mean, here she was, my real mother, finally showing up, and Mom had a fit over it. She didn't even try to be nice to her."

Phyllis proceeded cautiously. "Linda didn't mention that. But, knowing her, it must have hurt her feelings quite a bit."

"It did," Jenny said, grateful for this sympathetic adult's ear. "She tried not to show it, but I know it did. Me and Linda were a lot alike, and it made me feel horrible. But Mom didn't care."

"Well," said Phyllis, "maybe she just felt a little jealous of Linda. You know, another mom on the scene."

"It was a lot worse than that," Jenny confided. "She didn't even want me to see Linda or talk to her or anything."

"She didn't?" Phyllis felt a rising excitement. A good tear-jerking sidebar was one thing, but this was something else. Jealousy and hate were better than sentiment any day of the week. This had both. And there was no telling what she could make of it with the right slant. "You know, moms can be very protective. Especially if they have only one child. Or do you have brothers and sisters?"

"No," said Jenny. "Well, my mom was pregnant, but she lost the baby."

"Was that when you were little?"

"Oh, no, it was only about a month ago. And she's been really bummed out ever since."

"That's too bad," said Phyllis. Her palms were beginning to sweat. "Women can become very depressed, almost unbalanced, when they lose a baby."

"Oh, yeah," Jenny agreed. "Having this baby was going to be like a miracle. And then when she lost it, she became like a zombie. I was really sad for her when it happened, even though it wasn't even a real person and I couldn't really understand why she wanted a baby, being so old and all. But I tried to be sympathetic and help her out around the house and everything. And then, when my real, actual mother gets murdered, my mom can't even pretend to be sorry. I almost think she was glad."

"Oh, I'm sure that's not so," said Phyllis, squeezing the girl's forearm. "Why would she be glad about such a thing?"

"I think she was afraid I'd like Linda better than her," said Jenny bluntly.

Phyllis had all she could do to keep the elation she felt from showing on her face. This was beautiful. And the kid was just dropping it in her lap.

Just then a pudgy girl with glasses rolled up on her bicycle and came to a stop in front of them. "Hey, Jen," she said, looking owlishly at Phyllis.

Jenny's face broke into a sweet smile. "Hey, Peg." She turned to Phyllis, who stood up immediately. "This is my friend, Peggy. Peg, this is Phyllis. She was a friend of my real mom's."

"Nice to meet you," said Phyllis.

"Hi," said Peggy.

"Listen, I'm going to leave you girls. I know you have a lot to talk about. Jenny, this has really meant a lot to me."

"It was nice talking to you," said Jenny.

"I'm very sorry for your loss," she said, extending her hand.

Jenny shook it and said gravely, "Thanks. I'm sorry for yours."

Phyllis felt the smallest twinge of guilt at that. But it vanished as she headed for her battered Volvo parked around the corner. A good reporter does what she has to do, she reminded herself. She could hardly wait to get to her computer. Her fingers were going to make music on that keyboard.

Chief Matthews unrolled an antacid tablet, popped it in his mouth, and indicated the chair across from his desk. "Sit down, Walter," he said.

Walter Ference sat and took out his notebook. Dale Matthews held up a form and then passed it to the lieutenant.

"Medical examiner's report," said the chief. Walter began to glance through the pages. "Let me cut to the chase," Dale said. "No sexual assault."

Walter raised his eyebrows and nodded. "So I see."

"Pending confirmation by the coroner, of course, after the autopsy. But you know what this means," Dale said.

"Well, it could mean any number of things," said Walter cautiously.

"It means our killer could have been a woman." There was a barely suppressed relish in his voice.

"It would have to be a pretty strong woman," observed Walter.

"Or a pretty desperate one," said Dale. "Now tell me more about this family that adopted the kid."

Walter looked up from the report in surprise. "You think it might be her? The Newhall woman?"

"You have to consider that possibility. This Emery girl comes to town, announces herself as the child's natural mother, and is murdered the next day. And it's not a sex crime."

"You have a point," said Walter.

"Do you know where the Newhall woman was last night?"

Walter looked in his notebook. "She says she went to bed early."

"Check it out," said the chief.

Walter made a note. "What about the husband? You don't think he might've——"

"I don't think men get as worked up about this 'biological mother' business." Dale leaned back in his chair. "It doesn't make sense psychologically."

"Probably not," said Walter. "It's just a little soon to be pointing a finger. Don't forget—this child had a father, too. Probably somebody who lived in this town."

"A point well taken," said Chief Matthews. "He could be a man with a lot to lose by now. If she made contact with him, that is."

"I just don't want to jump to any conclusions," Walter explained.

"Conclusions," said Dale portentously, "are what we are seeking in this case. The people in this town have not forgotten about 'Amber,' and the fact that we still don't even know who she was, never mind who killed her. We don't want the same thing to happen with this Emery woman. Besides, we're one step ahead of the game. We have an ID on this one."

"No crime scene," said Walter. "No weapon as yet."

"We'll get it," said Dale irritably. "This one is not going to get away from us."

"No, sir," said Walter.

The two men were quiet for a moment, each ruminating on his own concerns. Finally the chief said, "Well, it's been a long day."

Walter stood up. "I'm going to look this report over again before I go home."

Chief Matthews gave his detective an encouraging nod. Walter was not the most electrifying of thinkers, but he was thorough. Dogged, even. "We're going to nail this sucker, whoever he or she might be," Dale said, assuming his best Dirty Harry persona. But as Walter bade him good night and left his office, Dale opened his desk drawer and unrolled another Tums tablet. He tried to sound positive, but this case had his stomach roiling. Even the most diplomatic of officials couldn't get away with zero for two when it came to murder. This time he needed a winner.

Walter closed the door to the chief's office and managed a wan smile for Larry Tillman, who was still hanging around outside.

"What did he say?" Larry asked in a confidential tone.

Walter hefted the report. "It wasn't a sex crime. The chief seems to think it might have been the Newhall woman."

Larry made a face. "I don't think that. Do you? Too bloody for a woman."

Walter tossed the report on his desk and got himself a paper cup of water from the cooler. "Women commit bloody crimes, too," he observed.

Larry folded his arms over his chest and gave it some thought. Being in on a murder case was nothing short of thrilling to him. He did not want to appear naive or impulsive in his opinions. "I *didn't* think she was being completely honest," he said. "You know, about how she felt about the victim."

"No," Walter admitted, crumpling his cup and tossing it in the basket, "but then, neither was anybody else."

"So, you don't think she did it."

Walter sat down at his desk and looked up at him. "I didn't say that."

"Are we going back out there?" Larry asked, ready and willing.

Walter shook his head. "Not tonight," he said. "It's late. We need to talk to some other people. Tomorrow will be soon enough. Why don't you go home and get some sleep? I'm sure it's going to be another long day tomorrow."

"I doubt I'll be able to sleep," Larry admitted.

"Why not?" Walter asked. "Aren't you tired?"

A crimson blush, the curse of the redheaded, seeped up Larry's face. He sounded like some schoolboy playing cops and robbers, not a professional law officer. "It's just a more interesting kind of case than the usual, you know, stolen bicycles or drunk and disorderlies. Have you done many murders, sir?"

Walter smiled at the question. "Not many, no. Enough to suit me, though. I guess you just have that youthful enthusiasm," he said. "Well, you'll get over it."

Larry nodded. Yeah, he thought. Probably around the same time I get over blushing. "I'm sure you're right, sir. G'nite," he said, backing away from Walter's desk. "See you early."

Chapter Fourteen

H ow could you do this?" Greg thundered. "What is wrong with you?" He brandished the morning newspaper in Jenny's face.

Jenny sat on a dining room chair, her arms crossed over her chest, her small chin stuck out, trembling slightly.

Karen stood at the French doors, looking out at her blossoming garden, blinking back tears. Her stomach was in a hard little knot.

"I told you, I didn't know she was a reporter," Jenny cried.

"We've heard your explanation," Greg said disgustedly, banging the newspaper down on the glossy cherrywood surface of the empty table. He had literally been stalking Jenny through the house, waving the paper at her. They had ended up in the dining room.

Devoid of candles, silver, china, and food, the room had a chilliness that seemed appropriate to the mood among them.

"It's true," Jenny cried. "I didn't know."

"Are we supposed to be reassured by the idea that you would say all these things about your mother to a stranger, as long as it wasn't a reporter?" Greg demanded.

"I have to go," said Karen stiffly. "I have to teach a class. Will you drive Jenny to school?" she said to Greg. "She's missed the bus."

Jenny looked up at her mother. "I'm sorry, Mom," she said. "I didn't mean it the way that woman made it sound."

"Are you saying that she made it all up?" Karen asked coldly.

Jenny hung her head. "Not exactly," she whispered.

"Well then," she said. "You should be quite pleased with yourself. Everyone who reads the paper today will think that I killed Linda Emery. Or at least that my daughter thinks I am capable of it."

Tears trickled down Jenny's face, and for a second Karen regretted her harsh words, but the sight of the headline in the paper stared up at her, the shock and the shame of it still fresh as a bleeding wound. She turned her back on them, picked up her gym bag, and left the house. She went out to her car, got in, and slammed the door. She did not look back to see if they were watching her.

All the way to the dance studio, Karen felt as if she were going to be sick. Once she even pulled over to the side of the road, but the wave of nausea subsided and she drove on. She kept checking her rearview mirror, half expecting a police car with a siren going and lights flashing to flag her down.

That's ridiculous, she reminded herself. You didn't do anything. They have nothing against you. Just the cruel assessment of your own daughter. "I wish she had gone off with Linda Emery," she said aloud as she drove along. "Who needs this?"

Oh, stop it, she chided herself. You're just hurt. And, of course, that was it. She was so hurt by it. How could Jenny speak about her that way—her own child? It was beyond comprehension. Didn't she deserve some loyalty, some amount of faith, something for all they had shared?

Work it off, she advised herself, pulling into the parking space behind the studio and opening the back door of the building. Concentrate on the students, do a strenuous warm-up, and try not to dwell on it. A physical workout always helped her to feel better mentally as well. That was one reason she'd recovered so slowly from her miscarriage—the forced inactivity.

Karen had one hand on the door to the teacher's changing room when she saw Tamara Becker, who owned the studio, come out of one of the practice rooms and approach her. Tamara's parents were dancers in Eastern Europe, and Tamara had emigrated when she married an American. Her blond hair was skinned back off her face, emphasizing her strong Slavic features, and a black leotard encased her short, sturdy body. Karen towered over Tamara, who exuded a lot of compressed power. She made Karen feel a little bit like a giraffe or a gawky crane.

"Good morning, Karen," Tamara said. She still had a strong, guttural accent.

Karen smiled. "Good morning."

"So, Karen, come in here for a moment," said Tamara in a confidential tone. "We need to talk."

Karen was alert to danger, noting the unfamiliar tone in the dance teacher's voice. She looked at her watch. "I've got a class in ten minutes," she said. "I really need to warm up today. I'm full of kinks."

Tamara appeared not to have heard her. She gestured to the door of a practice room, and Karen followed her inside. Along one wall were mirrors and a barre. The outside wall was lined with north-facing windows that filled the empty room with a cool, white light.

"Karen," said Tamara bluntly, "I think it would be good idea if you took a little while off."

"Why?" said Karen. "I don't need time off. I've just come back, and I need to work."

"I'm just thinking," said Tamara, "maybe you come back too quickly after losing the baby."

"I know my own body," said Karen defensively. "I'm not pushing it."

"Even so," said Tamara stubbornly, avoiding Karen's eyes. Tamara was unconsciously flexing one knee, pointing her toe and then extending her leg as she spoke.

Karen's face flamed. "Is this about that article in the paper, Tamara?" she asked. "You and I have known each other for a long time. I can't believe you would take that seriously."

"No," said Tamara quickly. "I don't."

"Well, good," said Karen. "Because it's just nonsense. That reporter basically tricked my daughter into saying a lot of things . . ."

Tamara looked at herself in the mirror. Karen watched her intently. Tamara stroked her throat thoughtfully, lifting her chin. Then she turned and faced Karen, her broad, angular features set in a grim expression. "Some of the parents, though . . . I've had phone calls this morning. Several of them."

Karen's eyes narrowed. "What do you mean?"

"Calling to complain. They think you did something, to that woman. They don't want you around the kids."

"Didn't you tell them it was nonsense?" Karen exclaimed.

Tamara spread her square hands in a wide, helpless gesture. "People believe what they read in the paper. I can't afford to lose my students. You can understand. I'm not saying quit. I'm just saying take a little time off."

"Well, I might as well quit," Karen cried. "It's as good as admitting I have some reason to hide. Surely you can see that?"

Tamara folded her arms over her chest and looked down at her extended foot. "Don't make me insist," she said.

"Tamara," Karen protested, "I thought we were friends. I thought I could count on you."

"We are friends, personally," Tamara insisted. "But this is my business."

"Business," Karen said bitterly.

"I'm sorry, Karen. Truly. When this whole mess is cleared up . . . "

"Never mind," said Karen. "I get the picture."

Karen opened the door and left the practice room. One of her students, a five-year-old named Marilyn, was seated on a bench outside, suited up in a tie-dyed leotard. "Hi, Mrs. Newhall," she caroled. "I'm ready."

Karen felt the sorrow bubbling up beneath her anger. "I'm not teaching today," she said gently, and her voice cracked. Before the child could ask why, Karen slung her gym bag over her shoulder and fled to the parking lot.

Once inside the car, Karen wanted nothing more than to lower her head to the steering wheel and cry. But there was a chance that Tamara might see her. She would not give her the satisfaction. With trembling fingers, Karen managed to insert the key into the ignition. She had to concentrate on getting home.

Jenny stood at the open door of her locker and pitched books into the narrow cabinet. Peggy stood by her side, eyeing the river of leather-, spandex-, and denim-outfitted students that flowed sluggishly past them in the hall.

"I can't believe it," said Peggy. "That woman at the library was a reporter?"

Jenny nodded.

"How did she know where to find you?"

"I don't know. She said my mom told her, but she didn't. I guess she followed me from my house."

"I'm sorry," said Peggy.

Jenny sighed. "It's not your fault. My mom is really mad at me, though."

Peggy nodded. Her father had read the article aloud to her stepmother at breakfast. And they both quizzed

Peggy about the Newhall family. "Did you tell your mom what happened?" Peggy asked. "How that woman pretended to be a friend of your real mother's?"

"I told her, but it didn't help."

"Hey, Newhall," called a loud voice. Jenny and Peggy turned and saw a wiry, acne-ridden kid with greasy brown hair grinning at them slyly. Two guys stood behind him, watching curiously. Mark Potter was well known around the school as a bully.

"What do you want?" said Jenny belligerently.

"Is it true your old lady is a murderer?" he taunted.

"Shut up," said Jenny, feigning a weary tone.

"Hey, you said it. I didn't," he persisted. "Read the paper."

"I did not say that," Jenny cried. "Some man did it. Some maniac."

"Some maniac," he mimicked. "Sounds like your mother's the maniac," he said.

Jenny panicked as she felt tears forming in her eyes. It was her own fault for saying those things about her mother. She wished she could fall through the floor and just disappear.

A few kids had begun to gather around them at a distance. Jenny felt trapped, as if they were all just waiting for her to break down in front of them. All morning she felt as if people were staring at her curiously. It was as if she knew this awful moment was coming. "My mom wouldn't hurt anybody," she said. To her complete humiliation, she heard her voice crack as she spoke.

"Oh, poor little girl," Mark crooned, reaching out as if to pat her hair. "Did her mommy do a berry bad thing?"

Jenny smacked his hand away furiously, which caused a burst of laughter from the other boys and murmured comments designed to goad them on.

Peggy, who had remained steadfastly by Jenny's side, spoke up in a high-pitched voice. "Leave her alone," she insisted. "Why don't you pick on somebody your own size?"

Mark turned his attention to Peggy, his eyes filled with malicious glee at the prospect of another victim. Before he could launch his attack, a girl's voice spoke up from the sidelines.

"He is her size."

The group surrounding them broke out into laughter. His eyes narrowed, Mark whirled around to confront the kibitzer. Angela Beeton, a pretty, languid, blond goddess snapped her gum and stared impassively at Mark Potter.

Jenny felt with relief that the attention of the group had turned to the two of them.

Mark, thin-skinned about his height, glared at the coolly self-confident Angela, scanning her for the physical flaw he could use for ammunition. Instantly it was obvious to all that he was outmatched. Any further remarks on his part might cause Beeton to draw more attention to his short stature, and effective retaliation was out of the question. "Get bent," he said wearily, throwing a rude gesture at Angela. Then he signaled to his henchmen and did his best to swagger away.

Jenny gave Angela a quavery smile. "Thanks," she said.

Angela shrugged off the gratitude. "I loathe that little

twerp," she said. Surrounded by her own friends, Angela glided off in the opposite direction.

Once the crowd had dispersed, Peggy gazed at Jenny solicitously. "You don't look good," she said.

"I don't feel good," said Jenny. "I think I'm going to go to the nurse. I want to go home. Even that's got to be better than this."

"I'll walk you over there," said Peggy.

"You'll be late for class," said Jenny.

"I don't care," said Peggy loyally.

"I hope I don't throw up on both of us," Jenny said.

"You better not," said Peggy.

Sam Duncan nudged his wife, who stood in the archway between the dining rooms, a sheaf of menus clutched tightly to her chest, a vacant look in her eye.

"Hey," he said. "Look alive. We've got customers."

Mary looked at her husband as if awakened from a trance. "What?"

"Earth to Mary," he said, waving a hand in front of her face. "Did you hit your head somewhere?"

"Sam," she said, "I can't stop thinking about what I said to the police." Walter Ference and Officer Tillman had come by earlier in the day to ask about Linda's meeting with Jenny at the restaurant.

Sam sighed and then smiled placatingly at a pair of elderly ladies who were hobbling into the dining room and talking in the loud tones of the hard-of-hearing. "I hate this early bird special," he grumbled. "We don't make enough off of it to make it worth all the trouble."

"Miller's has always had the early bird," said Mary defensively. "It's a goodwill thing."

"We don't need goodwill. We need profit," said Sam. "Besides, what is this sudden concern for the tradition of Miller's? You're the one who's always complaining about too many hours. . . ."

"Sam, did you hear what I said about the police?"

"You answered all their questions," said Sam. "What's the problem?"

"You know perfectly well what the problem is," said Mary. "I didn't tell them everything I knew."

"They're not interested in idle speculation, Mary. Or thirteen-year-old, warmed-over gossip."

"It's not gossip," Mary insisted. "It was a confidence. And it might be very important. I think I should go down to the police station and tell them."

"That's ridiculous," said Sam.

"Why is it ridiculous?"

"Look, Mary, you can't just leave. You're the hostess. Number two, you know that going to the police station is like going to the Emergency Room. You'll be there all night. Besides, you'll be getting yourself involved in something that is none of your business."

"It is my business," Mary protested. "Linda was a friend of mine."

"That was light-years ago," said Sam. "We were just kids. . . ."

"So what? She was murdered, for heaven's sake. What difference does it make how long ago I knew her? Somebody killed her and stuffed her body in a garbage bag and left it in a Dumpster."

"And," said Sam, "you don't really know anything about it. All you know is a little piece of girl talk from thirteen years ago. Look, face it, Mary. Some sex pervert picked her up and killed her. Probably the same guy that killed that little girl they found last fall. What'd they call her . . ."

"Amber," said Mary irritably.

"Right. Her. Now, I admit, it's no fun to think about some nut on the loose here in town, but it makes more sense than what you're saying. Read the papers, Mary. This stuff happens every day. Some drooling creep goes crazy and kills some poor woman. The police know how to handle this stuff. What do they need you sticking your nose in?"

Mary leveled a cold gaze at her husband. "You don't care who killed my friend. All you care about is whether or not I'm manning the desk. You don't have a life, Sam. You don't have friends, you don't have a family. All you have is this restaurant. Well, years ago my friend entrusted me with a secret that could have everything to do with this murder. And, if you think I'm going to let you bully me out of telling the police. . . . "

Sam waved a hand angrily. "Do what you want," he said.

"I will," she said.

An old man leaning on a cane clumped up to them and poked Sam in the side, apparently ignorant of the tension between them. "Sonny, where do I sit?" he demanded.

With an effort, Sam managed not to glare at the customer. "My wife will show you to a table," he said with a false smile.

Mary shoved the menus at him. "No, she won't."

"Mary," he hissed.

But she ignored him as she headed for the door.

Chapter Fifteen

Greg pulled the car up onto the shoulder of the dirt road that overlooked the local beach. The sun was almost down, although the sky still clung to the pink-and-gold lights of the waning day. Through the latticework of an old gazebo near the path, the last rays of the sun splashed a grid of shadows and light.

Jenny was curled up on the backseat, her face small and pinched-looking. She had stayed in her room most of the afternoon. "Why are we stopping here?" she asked. "I thought we were going out for pizza."

"I thought you were too sick to eat," Greg teased her gently. "I thought you were just going to sip a Coke."

"I'm not faking, Dad," she said. "I feel horrible."

"I know you're not, honey," he said. "We're going soon. I just wanted to watch the sunset."

Karen shifted in her seat and said nothing. She felt a positive dislike for these long, long days with their endless twilights. She wanted the darkness to come. She had had enough of this day.

Greg turned to her. "Do you mind?" he asked.

Karen shrugged. "I don't care."

She and Jenny had hardly spoken all afternoon. The school nurse had called, and Greg went to pick up Jenny. But once they got home it was obvious that Jenny was not really sick—just a bundle of nerves. Instinctively Karen felt sympathetic, but it was hard to sustain it after that article this morning and the fallout from it. She was still angry and hurt about being dismissed by Tamara. And she found herself reluctant to do the errands she needed to do around town, for fear that people would be looking at her, pointing her out. Plus, she spent most of the day expecting the police to turn up at her door. The last thing in the world she wanted to do was go out for pizza and have people stare at them, but Greg had insisted.

"If you want pizza, why don't we have one delivered?" she had said, but she knew very well that he wanted to get them out and doing something together. And he was not about to let it go. So she had agreed, reluctantly, to come.

"I love this beach," said Greg. "It's still so unspoiled."

"It's pretty," Jenny agreed in a small voice. Karen stared dully out the window.

"Yes, it is," said Greg. "You see that gazebo over there. When your mother and I were young we used to meet there, or leave each other messages."

Jenny knew the old story by heart, but it still appealed to the romantic adolescent side of her. "Your parents didn't want you to see each other," she said, reciting the next line by heart.

"Well, they thought we were too serious. And too young to be serious," he said. "But I had known from the first minute I set eyes on her that she was the one for me. I didn't care what anybody said."

"Did you get in trouble for it?" Jenny asked, knowing the answer.

"All the time." Greg chuckled. "But it was worth it. I didn't have any choice, you see. I had to follow my heart. And your mom here, she owned it. Always did."

Karen felt tears fill her eyes. It wasn't so much from the old story, although she loved the way he told it. It was just that she was so hurt inside. Tears were very close to the surface. "Don't tell her that," she said coldly. "She doesn't need any more encouragement to defy her parents."

Greg was undaunted by her angry tone. "I'm not sorry I did it," he said. "I'd be a liar to say otherwise. What about you? Any regrets?"

She could feel his smile without looking at his face. He knew very well that she could trace her whole adult life from those passionate meetings in the gazebo. All the good days and the bad days; their home, their life, their fights, their child. Every bit of it. She shook her head. "No," she said. "None."

Her words seemed to reverberate in the silence of the car. After a minute Karen felt Jenny's touch, light as a butterfly, on her shoulder.

"Please don't be mad at me, Mom," she said. "I'm really, really sorry."

"It's all right," said Karen stiffly. Her words did not sound warm, even to her own ears, but they all knew, from their lifetime together, that her icy crust was a thin one. Now that it had cracked, it would break up quickly.

"I know you'd never hurt anybody. I don't know why she made it sound that way."

"Look," said Greg sternly, turning around in the seat and pointing a finger at her. "You better learn a lesson from this. You can't blame this on anyone but yourself."

"I know," said Jenny.

"This is a free country, and people can say any old nasty thing they want if you give them the opening. That reporter just took what you said and ran with it."

"I wish I could take it back."

"Well, that's the oldest story in the world." Greg sighed and squinted into the distance. "But, everybody makes mistakes. Now we have to make the best of it. And we have to do it together. We're a family. We stick together. No matter what people say about us, we just hold our heads up and ignore them."

Easier said than done, Karen thought, but she knew he was right.

"Okay," said Jenny solemnly.

Karen did not say anything. After all, she was the one they would be talking about. Not Greg. Not Jenny. She could feel them waiting for her, for some indication of solidarity. She thought it over for a minute.

What was the use of being stubborn with them? Greg and Jenny were the most important people in her world. What did it matter what other people said?

"All right," she said.

"Now, I could eat some pizza," Greg said, relieved. "What about the rest of you?"

"I could," Jenny cried.

"Even if people point at us?" he asked.

"I'll point back," she said seriously. "Sticks and stones can break my bones, right?"

"How 'bout you, Mom?" he asked.

Karen nodded. "I'm ready."

The sun was gone now, the sky darkening rapidly. Karen smiled at him but shivered in spite of herself. Once that sun was gone, you would never know it was almost summer.

"You," Margo Hofsteder cried as Knudsen, the man from the appliance repair service, came through the door in the lobby. "Don't you dare send me a bill. I've had nothing but trouble with that ice machine since you fixed it. My man has had to mop up five times a day since you were here."

"What!" Knudsen protested, hands flattened on his chest. "I don't know what you're talking about. I never touched it."

"Well, that's the damn truth," Margo snorted.

"I just come to fix the thing tonight. I couldn't get here any sooner."

Margo, who was prepared to continue her tirade, sat back down on her stool, deflated. "You couldn't?"

The man grimaced. "I'm sorry about this," he said. "My wife got the flu and I had to stay with the kids. I figured you might have called somebody else, but I thought I'd come check anyway."

"No," said Margo, taken aback. "No, I thought . . . " A puzzled look came into her green eyes as she began to calculate.

"How 'bout that murder?" Knudsen asked. "I read in the paper she was staying here."

"Mmmm," Margo mumbled. She pointed her pencil at him and examined him with narrowed eyes. "You didn't even stop by to look at the thing? The other night? The night she got killed?"

"Nope," said Knudsen. "So what do you say? You want me to work on it?"

Margo frowned in his direction, but she was looking through him. Then she said, "Okay, but fix it right this time."

"I told you," Knudsen cried, "I never touched it."

"Okay, okay," said Margo. "How come you're here so late?"

"I've got another day job, lady. You need two jobs these days to make ends meet."

Margo nodded and waved absently as Knudsen headed out the door and down to the room with the broken ice machine. She sat back and tapped the pencil against her teeth. An idea had come to her. After all, hadn't the police asked if she'd noticed anything unusual that night? Well, she had noticed something. She just didn't realize it at the time. She wished Anton were here. He would really have appreciated this. Actually, he probably would have beaten her to it. Nothing got by that man. He was a born observer. They often used to read the same mysteries, and they would jot down the page number when they had figured it out and who they thought the killer was. He always beat her by at least fifty pages. Margo sighed. She always missed him, like a dull ache in her heart. But at a moment like this, she would give anything . . . Oh, well, what was the use of wishing. Picking up the phone, she started to dial Eddie's room. Then she hesitated. Maybe she should wait until morning. She didn't want to blow this out of proportion. No, she told herself, shaking her head. She knew from a million mysteries that the police didn't want the trail to get cold in a murder investigation. There was actually not a minute to waste. She resumed dialing Eddie's room. When he answered, she did not bother with small talk. "Eddie, I need you to help me out. Can you get down here right away and mind the desk for me? There's something I have to do."

Eddie agreed grumpily, and Margo hung up the phone. Then—she could not help it—she hugged herself with glee. A clue, she thought. I have a clue. It was a mystery lover's dream come true. She took out her compact mirror and began to touch up her makeup while she waited for Eddie. She wanted to look good for her appearance at the police station.

Chapter Sixteen

Karen came up behind her husband and put her arms around his waist. He was wearing his T-shirt, pajama bottoms, and an old plaid bathrobe, and he was studying the contents of the refrigerator.

"You can't be hungry," she said. "I've got a soggy mass of pizza in my stomach."

"Actually, I'm looking for something carbonated, for that very reason," he said.

Karen smiled and rested her cheek against his broad back. "That was a good idea, tonight," she said.

Greg leaned over, took a bottle of seltzer off the door, and chugged some down from the bottle. "I'm full of good ideas," he said.

"Well, I enjoyed it. I feel better."

"That was the object of the game," he said. "That,

and giving our little waif a chance to redeem herself. She looked so pathetic when I picked her up at school today. You never saw a sorrier sight."

Karen smiled. "I know," she said. She released him and walked over to the back door, locking it. "I think I'm going up to bed. What a day."

"It has been quite a day," Greg admitted. "I feel like we're going to be all right, though."

Karen tied a knot in her bathrobe belt and nodded. "Me too," she said. "And in the end, I guess it was a lot of fuss for nothing. The police obviously didn't put much stock in Ms. Hodges's article. They never did show up here."

"What's that?" Greg said. He frowned and cocked an ear toward the outside.

Karen heard it, too. She tried to smile. "Famous last words," she said.

"Mom, Dad," Jenny cried, clattering down the stairs. She came down the hall to the kitchen and stared at them, her face dead white. "There's three police cars in the driveway."

Karen's heart began to race. Stay calm, she reminded herself. You have nothing to hide. "I was just saying to your father that I didn't think they were coming," she said, attempting a self-deprecating tone.

"I'm sorry, Mom," Jenny said miserably.

"It's okay," she said to Jenny. "I just wonder why they had to wait until the middle of the night."

Karen and Greg walked down the hall hand in hand and peered out the front window from behind the curtains. Two black-and-white cars and an unmarked sedan were parked behind Greg's van in the driveway, their radios squawking. "God, do you think they brought enough manpower?" Karen joked weakly.

"These are storm trooper tactics," Greg exclaimed. "It's outrageous, showing up here at this hour."

"All right," said Karen. "Let's just talk to them, and get this over with." She walked over to the front door and opened it. Walter Ference and Larry Tillman stood on the front steps. There were several officers with flashlights on the lawn behind them.

"Good evening, gentlemen," said Karen calmly. "Are you looking for me?"

Walter glanced from Karen to Greg and Jenny, who had walked up and flanked her. "May we come in?" he asked.

"Sure," said Karen, stepping aside. Walter and Larry entered the house, leaving the other officers talking in low tones outside. As she followed Officer Tillman into the living room, Karen had the thought of offering them something to drink, then remembered that she was not feeling especially hospitable.

"I think we should talk privately," Walter said, glancing at Jenny.

"Jenny, why don't you go on up," said Karen.

"This is all my fault," Jenny cried.

"Never mind," said Karen. "Go on." As soon as Jenny left the room, Karen turned to Detective Ference. "Look, I know what this is all about." Her heart was pounding, but she was proud of the steadiness in her voice. "My daughter said a lot of misleading things to that Hodges woman, but she was under a lot of stress. . . . "

"We don't pay much attention to newspaper articles, Mrs. Newhall," said Walter.

Karen looked at him in confusion. "You don't? Well, then, I don't . . . "

Walter turned from her and looked at Greg. "We'd like to ask you a few questions, Mr. Newhall."

Greg rubbed his mouth nervously with his fingers. "Okay," he said.

Karen frowned at them and sat down gingerly on the edge of the sofa.

"How long have you known the deceased, Linda Emery?" asked Detective Ference.

"Well, as we told you, she showed up here Sunday night."

"And you never met her before Sunday night?"

Greg frowned, as if trying to concentrate. "I don't think so . . . no . . . I mean, I may have . . . you know . . ."

Walter Ference remained impassive, but Karen thought she saw the redheaded uniformed officer smirk in a way that made her feel furious.

"Did you visit Miss Emery in her motel room on Monday night?" asked Walter.

"Of course not," Karen cried. "What are you talking about? He was with a client."

Greg stared at the detective, his expression blank. Sweat started to bead around his hairline.

"Mr. Newhall," said the detective. "This is not a fishing expedition. You may want to call your attorney. We have a witness who saw your van at the motel."

"That's stupid," said Karen. "There must be a million trucks like his."

"It happens that she was looking out for a van at the time. She gave us an exact description."

Karen turned to her husband. He was staring at the floor. "Greg?" she said.

He did not meet her inquiring gaze. "All right," he said. "All right. Yes, I did go there."

"Why?" Karen exclaimed. "You never said anything to me about it."

"Let me caution you of your rights, Mr. Newhall," Walter interjected.

"His rights!" Karen exclaimed.

"Never mind," said Greg to the detective. "There's no need. It's just that I never mentioned this to my wife. That I had seen Miss Emery. But, yes, I did. I won't deny it."

"And why did you go to see her?" Walter asked calmly.

"Well, Karen and I had been talking, you know, since she showed up like that, so unexpectedly. Karen was convinced that she was trying to come between us and Jenny. We weren't exactly straight with you about that. My wife was very upset about that. Not like they portrayed it in the paper," Greg said hurriedly. "But upset. Worried. You can understand that."

"Certainly," said Walter.

Greg was rubbing his knuckles with the palm of his hand as he spoke. "I kept reassuring Karen that there was nothing to worry about," he went on. "But I guess, deep down, I wasn't comfortable with her explanation, either. I . . . wanted to know why she had come here. I thought maybe she had some other agenda in mind. You know, maybe that she was going to try to . . . I don't know what. Try to take Jenny away from us or something."

Walter nodded.

"Anyway," Greg went on, "I just thought I would seek Miss Emery out and make sure that she was . . . you know . . . on the level."

"Greg," Karen cried, "I can't believe you didn't tell me this."

"Honey, I didn't want you to worry."

"And after your conversation?" Walter prodded.

"I . . . uh . . . I was satisfied," said Greg, "that her intentions were fairly innocent. Pretty straightforward. She just wanted to meet the child she had given away."

Walter tapped on his pad with his pen. "So, you talked this over, and then you left, and came home."

"Yes."

"Mrs. Newhall, do you remember what time your husband arrived home?"

"I don't know," Karen said distractedly. "I went to bed early. Very early. I mean, I don't usually."

Walter turned back to Greg. "And once you got home, you decided not to tell your wife about this meeting with Miss Emery. Wouldn't your information have been reassuring to her as well?"

"Well, after I talked to her, there didn't seem to be anything to be concerned about, so, you know, I thought, let sleeping dogs lie. . . ."

Karen did not know what was making her more angry—the fact that Greg had done this and not told her or the detective's insinuations that because Greg had seen Linda Emery he was somehow a suspect. She couldn't work up too much anger at Greg—this was typical of him. Always trying to protect her, as if she were still a schoolgirl in knee socks. Still, why did he have to keep it a secret?

"Mr. Newhall," said Walter, "does your wife know about your previous relationship with Miss Emery?"

Greg's complexion turned ashen. "What previous relationship?" he asked cautiously.

"Isn't it true that you had an intimate relationship with Linda Emery fourteen years ago?"

"Stop it," Karen blurted out. "That's ridiculous. He told you he'd never met the woman before."

No one looked at her. There was a silence in the room. Karen felt as if she were in some sort of bad dream where everything familiar had become suddenly strange and distorted.

She turned to her husband. Greg glanced at her and then away. In that split second she knew. Her world was about to topple. She stood up, as if by standing she could somehow stop him from speaking, make everybody leave.

Greg put his face in his hands for a moment. Then he looked up. "All right," he said softly. "I was afraid of this."

Chapter Seventeen

L et me remind you, Mr. Newhall," said Walter Ference. "You may want to call a lawyer before saying anything more."

"A lawyer?" Greg mumbled. He sat, lost in thought for a moment. Then he shook his head. "How did you find out?"

"A friend of Miss Emery's came forward," said Walter briskly.

Greg looked dazed. "She swore she never told anyone."

Walter gave Greg a thin smile. "People often tell you what you want to hear. Do you wish to wait for counsel, Mr. Newhall?"

"No," Greg whispered. Then he said more firmly, "No, I can't do that to my wife. I can't leave her hanging like this. Anyway, I haven't done anything wrong . . . well, not legally, anyway."

"Suppose you tell us all about it," said Walter.

Karen was staring at Greg. She felt as if someone were squeezing her heart so tightly that it might explode. "You knew her?" she said. It was hard to catch her breath, as if she had been running.

"I'm sorry," said Greg. "She said she never told a soul."

"She lied," said Walter. "Did you kill her?"

Greg ground the heel of his hand against his forehead. "No, no, of course not. But when I heard she had been murdered, I panicked." He looked at Karen beseechingly. "I was afraid to tell the truth. I knew how it would look for me. I didn't think I had to say anything. No one knew about it. . . . "

"About what?" said Karen. Her hands were trembling in her lap.

Greg looked away from her. "Our relationship," he muttered.

"You had an affair with her?" Karen whispered.

Greg nodded.

It was as if someone had tilted the room. Karen grabbed on to the arm of the sofa to keep her balance. She suddenly felt cold. Freezing.

"The only person who knew, or so I thought, was Arnold Richardson. Our attorney. And that was privileged information."

Karen peered at her husband in disbelief and confusion. "Arnold Richardson? Why would you tell him?" She felt a sudden blast of comprehension. "Were you planning to divorce me? Good God! Is that what you're saying?"

Greg shook his head and spoke in a dull voice. "Not divorce. You'll probably think it's worse than that. There's something I . . . never told you," he finished weakly.

Karen did not reply. Greg glanced at Walter.

"Go ahead," said Walter.

"Karen, it all happened around that time when we were trying so hard to adopt and getting nowhere with it. You were so depressed. Do you remember?"

Karen stared at him as if she were in a trance.

Greg cleared his throat. "I met Linda at Miller's. She was waitressing there. I was having lunch there most days. Sometimes dinner, too. You didn't seem to want me to come home in those days. I don't mean that as an excuse. There's no excuse, really."

"How could you?" Karen breathed, shaking her head. "How could you do that?"

"I'm sorry," Greg said again. "She and I . . . we fell in with one another in a way. She was very lonely and . . . messed up, and I was . . . I don't know. You didn't want me. You kept telling me our life was ruined 'cause we couldn't have kids."

"Oh, it's my fault," said Karen furiously.

Greg shook his head. "No," he said. He looked up at Walter Ference. "Could I talk to my wife in private?" he asked.

"No," said Walter bluntly. "It's too late for that."

The detective's words seemed to snap Greg around. "You're right," he said. "I had years to tell her . . . and I didn't. I was a coward. I was afraid. . . . " He looked at

Karen. "I don't know if you can forgive me," he said, "but in a way, it will be a relief to be rid of this secret." He took a deep breath and then he continued. His voice was flat, without emotion. "We only had a brief relationship, but Linda got pregnant."

Karen covered her face with her hands and shook her head. "No," she cried.

His droning voice drowned out her cry. "She was only seventeen. I thought she was older, I swear it. I never knew until . . . Anyway, she was Catholic, and didn't want to have an abortion. I pleaded with her to let us have the baby. She finally agreed that would be best. We arranged it with Arnold Richardson."

Karen leapt to her feet. "You're lying!" she shouted. "This isn't true." She walked over to where he sat, his hands clasped tightly in front of him.

"Yes," he said. "Linda is . . . was . . . Jenny is my child by Linda Emery."

As hard as she could, Karen slapped her husband across the face. Greg's head snapped back, but he did not flinch or cry out. He did not look at her.

"Take it back," she demanded, and her voice broke.

Larry Tillman took Karen by the arms and forcibly guided her back to the sofa. "Sit down, ma'am," he said. "I'm sorry, but we're not finished here."

Greg rubbed his face. Then he spread his hands wide and shrugged. "There's not much more to tell," he said. "Linda used the money we gave her to go away, to have the baby and start a new life. That's what she wanted. I never heard from her or saw her again until she showed up here on Sunday."

"And threatened to blow your life sky high," said Walter.

"I was afraid of that," Greg admitted, "but when I went to talk to her she said she had no grievance with me. She had no intention of telling our secret."

"But how could you be sure of that?" Walter asked. "She was a grave threat to you."

Greg looked at the detective defiantly. "I believed her."

"Mr. Newhall, you might as well know that based on the statements of our two witnesses, we have obtained a warrant to search these premises."

Greg waved a hand absently. "Go ahead," he said. "I have nothing more to hide. I didn't kill her."

Walter nodded to Larry, who walked to the front door and called to the uniformed officers outside. One came into the house, tipping his hat politely to Karen. Two more entered behind him. The rest stayed outside. "Start upstairs," said Larry to the officer as he left the room. He called out the front door. "Search the van, and the garage."

Karen sat on her sofa and stared at the man she had loved since she was fourteen. He looked like an old man. The side of his face was pink where she had slapped him, but his complexion had a grayish hue. He kept his eyes focused on some point on the floor in front of him. He would not meet her gaze. In a way, she was glad. She did not know how she would ever look in those eyes again. Those traitorous eyes, in which she had always seen honesty and love, through a lifetime of lies.

"This cop wants to come in my room," said Jenny, appearing in the doorway.

"It's okay, honey," Greg said automatically.

Karen turned and looked at Greg's daughter, as if seeing her for the first time. Karen used to tease Greg that Jenny took after him in certain inborn traits and tastes, and they would laugh because, of course, it was impossible. And all the time he knew. He was always quick to say that even dogs began to resemble their masters when they'd lived together long enough. Married people came to look alike. Everyone knew that. And all the while, he had a secret. Jenny was his own flesh and blood.

"What's he looking for?" Jenny asked. Greg did not answer. Jenny looked at Karen. "Mom?"

That single, questioning syllable had its customary effect on Karen. "It's all right," she managed to say.

Jenny turned to Walter Ference. "My mother didn't do anything wrong," she said.

"We know that," said Detective Ference.

Jenny seemed surprised and a little taken aback by this. "How come you're still here, then?"

Before Walter could frame an answer, the front door opened and Larry Tillman stepped back inside. "Lieutenant?" he said. He was holding a plastic bag. Inside the bag was what appeared to be a key—with a large plastic disc on the key chain.

Walter rose and walked over to his officer. He examined the contents of the bag through the plastic.

"Jefferson Motel, room 173," Larry confided. "We found it behind the passenger seat in the van."

Greg jumped to his feet. "That's impossible," he

protested. "She was never in my truck. I spoke to her in her room and then I left. That's it. That's all that happened."

Larry did not look at Greg. He continued to speak to Walter, who was still peering at the contents of the bag. "It's splattered with something. Could be blood."

"Get it to the lab," said Walter. He turned and faced Greg. "Mr. Newhall, we're going to have to take you in."

"No," Jenny howled, grabbing on to the sleeve of her father's bathrobe.

Larry called the officers down from the upstairs and ordered one of them to take in the evidence. Then he turned to Greg. "You have the right to remain silent . . . "

Karen watched in numb disbelief as Officer Tillman droned on through the Miranda rights. Jenny was shaking her as if to try to awaken her. "Do something, Mom. What's going on?" Her voice was frantic.

For a moment Karen and Greg looked at one another. Then Karen looked away. "I don't know," she said.

Officer Tillman took out a set of handcuffs and gestured for Greg to raise his wrists.

"Handcuffs?" Jenny howled. She tried to bat them out of Larry's hand, but Walter caught her wrist and held it.

"Take it easy," said Walter.

"Wait a minute," said Greg. "I'm in my pajamas. Can't I even put my clothes on?"

Walter hesitated. "All right," he said.

Jenny knelt down in front of Karen and grabbed her

arms. "Mom, why don't you help Daddy? Why are they doing this? Stop them!"

Karen felt as if she were encased in a layer of cold, transparent gel. "There's nothing I can do," she said.

Greg walked up the stairs like a man mounting a scaffold. Officer Tillman, who was accompanying him, did not speak as Greg pointed out the bedroom. He followed Greg in the room.

"Sorry, no privacy for you," he said in a clipped voice.

"I understand," said Greg. He crossed the room to the armoire and opened the door. Carefully he slid the hangers down the rod, examining the pants that were hanging there.

"Don't take all day," said Larry. "You're not going to a fashion show."

"No," Greg agreed in a shaky voice. He put on a clean shirt and a pair of pants, scooping his wallet, keys, and change off the bureau and into his pockets.

"You won't need that stuff," Larry observed.

Greg shrugged. "Force of habit," he said. He tucked in his shirt and buckled his belt. "Okay," he said. "I'm ready."

Larry motioned for him to cross in front of him to the door. Greg did as he was told. In the hallway outside his bedroom he turned and walked toward the stairs. To his left, at the head of the staircase, was a pine table holding a blooming white cyclamen plant. Above the plant was a window. Greg took hold of the staircase bannister and took one step down. Larry Tillman followed. Then, with one swift, well-considered motion, Greg turned, grabbed Larry under the armpit, and jerked him forward. Taken by surprise, Larry tumbled down half a dozen steps and broke his fall only by grabbing on to the bannister as he cried out. In the time it took him to scramble to his feet and rush back up the stairs, Greg had mounted the top step, leapt up on the table, and hurled himself out the open window, kicking the table and potted plant over as he went. He broke through the screen and landed on the eaves below the window.

"Hey," yelled Officer Tillman, drawing his gun. "Stop him!"

But Greg had worked on every inch of that house and knew his way down off the roof like a cat in the dark. By the time the startled officer had galvanized the others and managed to fire a shot out the window, Greg had rolled down the pitch, dropped, with the aid of a tree branch, to the ground below, and disappeared into the darkness of the woods behind the house.

Chapter Eighteen

Chief Matthews glared at the redheaded officer who stood before him, turning his hat in his hands. "Jesus Christ, Tillman, how did you manage this?"

Larry did not need reminding or reprimanding. He would never forgive himself for making such a colossal mistake on the most important case of his brief career. It was all he could do to keep from crying. "I'm sorry, sir," he muttered.

"Yeah, well, you're going to be sorrier." The chief straightened out the front of his trench coat with a jerking gesture and snorted with disgust.

"He took us all by surprise, sir," said Walter Ference. "I've been a cop for a long time and I never saw it coming."

Chief Matthews shook his head. He had arrived at

the Newhall house only moments before. He had driven
back to Bayland from Boston, where he'd been attend-
ing a seminar on law enforcement administration at
Boston University. He had come back to his hotel after
a pleasant dinner with a chief from the Jersey shore,
and another from Minnesota, only to find the message
about Greg's escape waiting for him. The drive back
was a blur. He felt as if his blood pressure was off the
charts. "I don't want to hear excuses," he said. "There
are procedures, and you didn't follow them. Tillman,
until we find this guy, we're going to need every avail-
able hand. Once he's apprehended, you're busted.
You're walking the beat again."

"Yessir," Larry mumbled miserably.

Mentally Dale Matthews counted to ten. He didn't
want to light into Walter. He was the most experienced
man he had, and besides, it would be like berating his
own father. But he was tempted. "All right," he said.
"It's spilt milk." He glared at the uniformed officers in
the room. "Let's not waste any time." He began to in-
struct the other officers on their next move.

Walter leaned over the back of the sofa. "You might
want to call a doctor, Mrs. Newhall. You've had a
shock. He could give you a sedative or something."

"No," said Karen shortly. She was already numb. In
the hours after Greg's escape her house had been be-
sieged by police, some with tracking dogs, technicians
who put a tap on her phone, reporters, cameramen, curious neighbors, and onlookers. Her front yard looked
as though somebody had set up a macabre carnival
there in the middle of the night.

Through it all, Karen sat in the living room like

someone in the eye of a hurricane. She answered questions funneled to her by Detective Ference. She gave them the names and addresses they requested—friends, family, places Greg might have gone. She agreed without argument to the surveillance methods they wanted. She made no effort to resist them or correct their impressions. She was dimly aware of Jenny, flailing out at the invasion, cursing the intruders in their house, but she made no effort to stop her or join her. She just sat.

Finally, now, after hours of this, the last of the swarming interested parties were retreating from her property. "We'll be going, then," said Walter. "Don't get up."

Karen almost laughed at that. As if she could get up. Her legs felt as if they belonged to somebody else.

Walter Ference handed her a card with his name and two numbers on it. "This is the police station," he said, "and this is my home number."

Karen looked at it blankly.

"Mrs. Newhall, the sooner we apprehend your husband, the better it will be for all of you. You and your daughter are caught in the crossfire here. You're going to be made to feel like criminals because of his actions. As long as he is at large, you will not have an unobserved moment, a private telephone conversation, nothing."

"Yes, I know," said Karen.

"If you have any information, give me a call. I'll treat you fairly. We have no quarrel with you or your daughter."

"Thank you," said Karen. She stared at the card and then put it in front of her on the coffee table.

The police had gathered up their things and, led by the chief, were straggling out through the front door like the last revelers at a party. "Good night," said Walter. He followed the rest of his men outside.

Karen heard Jenny slam the door on the departing detective. After a moment, Jenny came into the room and stood in front of her mother.

"Is it true?" said the girl.

Karen looked up helplessly at their daughter, whose face was bright pink. "They found the room key in his van. With blood on it. They seem to think—"

"I'm not talking about that," said Jenny impatiently. "I want to know if it's true that he's my real father."

Karen felt the question pierce through the numbness that enveloped her. "Yes," she said in a flat voice. "Apparently, it is."

Before she could say more, Jenny turned on her and ran out of the room, clattering up the stairs.

"Jenny," Karen called weakly after her. But there was no answer. You should get up, she thought. You should go after her. This is a terrible shock for her.

But she couldn't. Her own feelings overwhelmed her. She kept seeing Greg's face as he admitted to their accusations. Every time she pictured it she was stunned all over again. She would have been less surprised if the coffee table had suddenly started to speak.

She knew him. They had been together more than twenty years, and she knew him inside out. For all these years they had shared their thoughts. In bed, in the morning, they described their dreams. At night, if they couldn't sleep, they told one another their fears. She had never doubted his love, never suspected his actions. Because she knew—she was the center of his world. He was the center of hers—it was a given. They would never let anything threaten that. They had promised. It was written in stone.

Karen looked over at the club chair where he always sat in the evening, his feet on the footstool in front of it. He never changed chairs. When she offered to buy him a new one, he demurred. "I love this chair," he would say. "Why would I want another one?"

Once, when he went on a camping trip with some buddies, she'd had it reupholstered. He'd agreed reluctantly that it looked nice, but it took him weeks to get it comfortable again, and she knew that although its worn arms and frayed back had bothered her, he never saw it as shabby. It was his chair. He was not put off by imperfections—his affections increased with time. That was the way he was.

She squeezed her eyes shut, and tears rolled down her face. Her heart felt as if it were being hammered into something small and dented by the pain inside of her.

"I hate you," she said aloud to the chair. "How could you lie to me like that? Not you. Anyone but you. . . ."

Her thoughts reeled back to the time he mentioned. When she found out they could not have children. When they had begun to understand how difficult adoption would be. It was true, she had been depressed. It was true she didn't want to make love. She could barely speak, or get out of bed, or get a meal together. The last thing she'd wanted was to frolic in bed. It was beyond imagining.

I understand, he would always say. Once in a while,

she would worry—would he turn to someone else? But it was more of a worry for form's sake. Because magazine articles and talk shows said it happened that way in normal marriages. But they were not like other people—they were special. He was hers, for better or for worse.

And he was always reassuring her. It's not important, he would say. You're everything I need. It's just a phase. He never got mad. He never complained. And when she had the strength, she would thank her stars for such a husband. And all the while . . . he was deceiving her. He was living another life.

I'll go mad if I sit here, she thought. But she couldn't move. Outside her window, the moon was pale and translucent as a thin slice of lemon. The same moon they had admired at its rising only hours ago. She and her husband. And their daughter.

Jenny shuffled into the room, clutching a white afghan from her bed. "I can't stay in my room, Mom," she said. Her face was as white as the blanket. "Can I sit here with you?"

Karen looked gratefully at her child. She raised her arms up to her. Jenny came over to the couch and curled up against her mother's side like a kitten. It seemed to Karen that they had not sat that way since Jenny was a weary little toddler. The warmth of her child resting against her side was inexpressibly comforting. Karen wrapped one arm around her gently, afraid to spook her, to drive her away. But Jenny did not resist. She snuggled closer to her.

They sat silently like that for several minutes, each

lost in private fears. Then Jenny whispered, "He didn't do it. He never would."

Jenny was talking about the murder. Karen realized with a start that she had hardly given a thought to that, so consumed was she by the knowledge of his betrayal, the secret he had kept from her all these years about Jenny. She tried to focus on the question of murder—she tried to picture Greg, driven to such an act. "No," she whispered. "No, not your . . . father." But even as she said it, she felt a shiver of doubt. She had never imagined him betraying her, either. If anyone had asked her, she would have said that she knew him completely.

"So why are they trying to blame him, Mom?"

"He told a lot of lies," Karen said. "A million lies."

"He had to," Jenny protested.

Tears welled up in Karen's eyes. "He didn't have to," she said furiously. "Nobody has to lie like that."

"But, you know Daddy would never do that. Hurt someone."

A bitter laugh escaped from Karen. "Oh, no?" she asked.

"You know what I mean," said Jenny stubbornly. "I mean, you know, hit a person, a woman like that. Kill her."

Karen took a deep breath. "No," she said. "He wouldn't . . . he couldn't do that. But the police—"

"You have to tell them that," Jenny cried. "That he would never do it."

"Jenny, the police don't care what I might say about it. Besides, innocent people don't run away," she said.

Jenny tensed up and drew away from her. "Mother, you just said he didn't do it."

Jenny was staring at Karen, demanding consistency, reason, answers. Karen didn't know whether to laugh or cry. I have no answers, she wanted to wail. But instead she focused on her child's face. Your world has been turned upside down, she thought. You are trying to hold on for dear life. She searched for some words of comfort that would ring true. All she could think to say was, "There has to be some explanation."

"That's right," said Jenny defiantly. She sat forward on the sofa, her back to Karen. "Are you mad that he kept me?" she asked.

Karen pressed her lips together and blinked back tears. The pain in her heart made it hard to breathe. The truth came readily to her lips. "I love you more than anything in the world," she said.

Jenny's tense shoulders seemed to relax at this. After a few moments she eased herself against her mother's side. Karen pulled the edge of the afghan over her. "Rest," she said. She reached up and turned off the lamp above her shoulder.

"I can't," said Jenny, her voice small and scared in the darkness.

"Try," Karen urged her.

They sat together in silence. After a while Karen heard the rise and fall, the rhythmical breath, of sleep. She curved her arm gently around her daughter and clung to her sleeping child. Their child. She wished she could hate him. Only hate him. Make him gone from her heart the way he was gone from their house. But loving him was an ancient habit of hers. She tried not to picture him, out there somewhere, in the night chill. But it was useless. He was as familiar as herself. Greg,

who couldn't wait to get home each night to his chair
by the fire, the warmth of his bed, the embrace of his
wife, his little girl's kisses. We're the Three Bears,
Jenny had said when she was small. And they had
laughed. It seemed so true. And now Papa Bear was out
there, alone in the dark, chased by hunters. And here,
by the cold hearth, their fairy-tale world was in ruins.
How could you do this to us? she wanted to cry out. I
thought you loved me. But there was no one to hear
her. No one to explain. Flames of anguish licked at
Karen's heart, burning like home fires.

Chapter Nineteen

While Emily searched in the bedroom closet for her rain bonnet, Walter stood at the kitchen sink, washing up his few breakfast dishes. His sister, Sylvia, was seated at the table, waiting for Emily.

"Walter, you need a dishwasher," she advised. "And a microwave. And look at this floor. The linoleum is worn through in places. Well, what do you expect? Mother had that put down the year Father died. That's going on half a century now. Time flies."

Walter dried his coffee cup and put it up in the old cupboard. Sylvia grimaced as the cupboard door creaked on its hinges. "I don't know how you can stand this old place. Look at these old Currier and Ives prints. They're going to fall off the wall any day now. Why don't you take two minutes and fix them?"

Walter put away his saucer and closed the cupboard door. Sylvia sighed. "I don't know how you can stand this old place," she said. "Now, I like living in Seaside Village. Everything is new. If something breaks, somebody comes in right away and fixes it. I mean, if you're not handy," she said, looking pointedly at her brother, who was cleaning off his glasses with a paper towel, apparently oblivious of her, "you've got no business in an old place like this."

Walter held his glasses up to the old hanging light fixture and squinted through them to be sure all the smudges were gone. "Tell you the truth," Sylvia went on, "I never wanted to set foot in this place again after Mother died. It seems like there was nothing but sickness and gloom in the house. . . ." She shuddered.

"You're the most morbid person I know," Walter observed calmly, replacing his glasses on his nose. "Why else would you be going to this funeral today, except that you like the idea of a murder victim's funeral?"

Sylvia drew herself up indignantly. "For your information, I have known the Emerys for years through the church. They have no other family, to speak of. If you were more active yourself in your parish . . . "

"You know Emily doesn't do well with funerals," said Walter.

"Nonsense," Sylvia sniffed. "It doesn't matter whether Emily goes to a funeral or a garden party. Emily has a constitutional weakness. You know it as well as I do."

Emily's voice wafted to them down the hall. "I'm just looking for my gloves. I'll be right there."

Sylvia stood up and adjusted her skirt. "You should

be going to this funeral, Walter. Seeing who shows up. They say that killers often can't resist turning up at their victims' funerals."

"I'll leave the crepe hanging to you," said Walter.

"Rather irresponsible," said Sylvia. "In light of the fact that you were the one who let the killer get away."

Walter did not reply. He put on his jacket and walked to the back door. He stood there for a second, looking out at the rain. "Well, you enjoy the festivities, now," he said to his sister. "You've got a perfect day for it."

"Mother," said Bill Emery, "are you ready? The limousine is outside."

Alice Emery stared into the hall closet crammed with bags, boots, and winter coats. From the top shelf she extracted a black, beaded evening bag and stared. "Do you remember the year Linda gave me this for Christmas? She saved up her baby-sitting money for it."

Bill looked at his watch and then glanced at the bag in his mother's hand. "I don't know," he said. "All those Christmases run together in my mind."

Alice smiled wistfully. "I never had anywhere to wear it. Your father wasn't one for going out fancy." She shook her head. "I don't know why she picked this. She knew we never got dressed up like this. Probably something she saw in a movie made her think of it."

"Maybe," said Bill. "I don't know."

"I think I'll carry this," Alice said.

"Mother, that's an evening bag. It's not meant for a funeral."

"I know that," said Alice stubbornly. "But I'm going to carry it."

"All right," said Bill. "Fine. But we'd better hurry."

Alice's hands trembled as she fumbled with the clasp on the bag.

"What are you doing?" he said.

"I have to put my things in here," said Alice. She pointed to her worn, brown pocketbook, which sat squatly on top of the console TV. "Hand me my other bag, will you?"

Suppressing a sigh, Bill walked over and pulled the bag off the TV by its strap. A lipstick tube, a half-eaten roll of Life Savers, some coins, and a couple of wadded tissues spilled out onto the floor. Bill knelt and stuffed them back inside. He stood up and held out the bag to his mother. "It's just that people are going to be waiting," he said.

Alice began to sort through her brown pocketbook, extracting items and placing them in the evening bag. "Let them wait," she said. She lifted out the pocket date book and examined it thoughtfully.

"I don't think you'll be needing all that stuff, Mother. Besides, it probably won't all fit in there," he said tactfully.

Alice continued methodically to repack her purse. She did not look at Bill. "I should never have listened to you," she said. "I'll regret it for the rest of my life."

Bill's eyes flashed, but he spoke in an even tone. "No one forced you to do anything."

Alice's voice was thick with emotion as she pressed her ubiquitous tissues into the corners of the black bag.

"I turned her out. My own daughter. I never even got a chance to speak to her again."

"We had no way of knowing this was going to happen," said Bill.

"You were so determined to have your way," said Alice, stuffing a tiny change purse into the black bag. "I felt like if I didn't do what you wanted, you would turn against me, too."

Bill clenched his fists and walked over to the front window, pulling back the curtain. Glenda had stepped out of the car and was signaling him to come. "We have to go," he said.

Alice looked up at him, shaking her head. "Don't you even care? Your own sister?"

"I don't care to be your scapegoat," he said.

"Bill," Alice exclaimed, "that's an awful thing to say."

Bill walked over to the front door and called out, "We're coming."

Alice put on her hat and pulled the black veil down over her forehead and glasses. "Are the children in the car?" she asked distractedly.

"I told you twice already," Bill snapped. "They're with a neighbor. They're too young for this."

"They never even knew their aunt Linda," Alice said, awkwardly fishing a tissue from the cramped black bag. She wiped her eyes and tucked the bag securely under her arm, cradling it there.

"Whose fault is that?" Bill muttered.

"What?" Alice asked, turning back to him.

"Nothing," he said. "Let's go."

*   *   *

Considering how long she had been away from Bayland, Linda Emery drew a substantial crowd to her funeral. Few of those who gathered, however, were actual mourners. There was a clutter of reporters and an assortment of the morbidly curious. Many had come hoping to see the reaction of Linda's long-lost child—the child whose father had been accused of Linda's murder and escaped. Those who did were disappointed. Karen had forbidden Jenny to attend for just that reason—that her presence might result in circus antics at the solemn occasion.

Because of the rain, the graveside service was brief. Mary Duncan, shielded from the weather by an umbrella held by her husband, dabbed at her eyes with a handkerchief as the priest intoned the final words of interment. She could see Linda's mother looking dazed and bewildered as she threw a rose onto the casket. Mary could scarcely imagine the sorrow of losing her daughter and her husband, all in a matter of months. Mary's gaze traveled to Bill Emery, who dutifully threw in a flower after his mother, his face impassive. Mary had already noted the coltish, honey-haired young girl in dark glasses who seemed to be following Bill's every move like an ardent fan at a sporting event. She wondered if Glenda had noticed. How could she not? Mary thought, feeling a little sick. Well, sometimes the wife was the last to know.

Sam nudged her, and Mary looked up at him. "You ready to go to the car?" he asked. He hadn't wanted to come, but she'd shamed him into it. She looked at him tenderly. "Remember the fun we used to have with Linda in those days?" she asked.

Sam nodded. "Sure I do. Come on."

Mary ran one finger over the soft petals of her rose. Then she stepped up to the casket and tossed it on. "Good-bye, old friend," she whispered.

As she turned away from the grave, huddled beside her husband, she was accosted by a young woman dressed in a damp tweed skirt and a rumpled jacket. "Excuse me, Mrs. Duncan?" she asked.

Mary wiped her eyes. "Yes," she said.

"My name is Phyllis Hodges. I'm from the *Gazette*. I've heard a rumor that you are the person who identified Mr. Newhall to the police as the killer."

Mary's mouth dropped open. Before she had a chance to speak, Sam took her by the arm and stepped between her and the reporter.

"What's wrong with you?" he demanded. "This is a funeral. People are mourning here."

"I'm just doing my job," said Phyllis.

"Mrs. Duncan doesn't know what you are talking about," he said. "Come on." He hurried Mary along toward their car.

"Sam," Mary complained, wriggling out of his grasp. "Why did you do that?

Sam opened the door and virtually pushed her inside. Then he came around and jumped onto the driver's seat. "Lock the door," he said. "She might follow us."

"What's gotten into you?"

"That's all we need," said Sam. "She'll write in the paper that you blew the whistle, and the Newhall man will come back looking for you. I knew you shouldn't have gotten involved in this."

"Oh, Sam, for heaven's sake," said Mary. "He's miles from here by now." She locked the door.

Chapter Twenty

M om, what are you doing?" Jenny cried, kneeling beside the wastebasket and staring at its overflowing contents in horror.

Karen continued to rifle the jewelry box and the top drawer of her bureau. "I'm cleaning out," she said, pelting a pair of earrings onto the pile.

Jenny lifted necklaces and bracelets, bottles of perfume, and scarves out of the trash and stared at them. "Mom, this is all your good stuff. Presents from Dad. You can't just throw this stuff away."

Karen ignored Jenny's protests. Last night she had cried herself to sleep, hugging Greg's pillow, and at dawn she had been jolted awake by a dream of him making love to a woman with dark hair, white, freckled skin, and swollen breasts. In the dream they tumbled in sweaty sheets, his hand traveling over the woman's

rounded belly and disappearing between her legs, while
they chuckled at the mention of Karen's name. The
memory of that humiliating image made her scalp
prickle.

The phone began to ring on the bedside table. "Don't
answer it," said Karen sharply. It was the day of
Linda's funeral, and their phone had not stopped ringing. Seeing the stricken look on Jenny's face, Karen
said more gently, "It's just more trouble." She had re-
solved not to answer it again today. A few calls had
been friends, offering support, but Karen had refused
all visitors. Behind every offer of help hovered a flock
of unanswered questions, ready to swoop down on her.
More than anything, Karen did not want to tell the story
again. The rest of the calls had been reporters and
clients of Greg's calling to cancel their business with
him. How they were going to live with no income was
beyond Karen's fathoming right now.

The phone stopped ringing, and Karen lifted the silver locket out of its box on her dresser. She had not
even worn it yet, and she could tell that it had been ex-
pensive. The shop where Greg bought it was a pricey
antique store downtown. She pressed her lips together,
seeing again that cautious, hopeful look in his eyes
when he gave it to her. A present was not just something he bought because a day rolled around on the cal-
endar. It was an opportunity to please her. He puzzled
over each gift, studied what she liked. He rarely missed
the mark. A fresh ache seized her heart as she recalled
how he loved to describe the selection process—
baubles considered, then rejected; salespeople parading
their finest wares before him until he, like some benign

pasha, finally seized upon the perfect gift, clapped his hands, and it was wrapped.

"That's so pretty," said Jenny wistfully.

Karen snapped the locket open and dislodged the little picture of Jenny. She slipped the photo back into her jewelry box and then dangled the necklace by the chain. You will need the money, she told herself. You have to be practical. You could return this to the store. Then she shook her head and tossed the necklace on the heap of mementos in the basket. I'll find another way to get the money, she thought.

Jenny reached into the basket with a cry. "Can I keep it?" she said.

Karen looked coldly at the locket in Jenny's hand. "I'd rather you didn't," she said.

Jenny did not look up at her. "I want it," she said stubbornly. "You threw it away. What do you care?"

"I don't want to have to see it," said Karen.

Defiantly Jenny stood up and hooked the chain around her neck. She dropped the heart under her sweatshirt. "I'll wear it inside my shirt," she said.

"Do as you like."

"I will," Jenny snapped. "You're being horrible."

Part of Karen knew it was true. These gifts were lovingly given, over a lifetime together. Each one had a memory attached to it. She held up a blue-enameled pin with a gold moon, sprinkled with tiny diamond stars. That particular Christmas morning she'd opened her box from him to find a teakettle, to replace one that had cracked. She could remember thinking, with a sinking heart: A teakettle! The romance is over. And then he'd urged her to look in the kettle, and Karen had found the jewel box inside. She softened at the memory of his beaming face, pleased with his surprise.

And then her husband's smiling face changed into the lustful grimace of the faithless lover in her dream, blotting out everything else, leaving her weak and clammy with only a blaze of hatred where her heart used to be.

The sound of a car in the driveway interrupted her thoughts. "It's probably just our watchdog," said Karen. The rain and the gray skies had driven most of the curious to find shelter somewhere other than their front yard. But the unmarked police car had remained parked in the driveway, the bulky silhouette of the cop assigned to them just visible behind the wheel.

Jenny went over to the window and peered out. "No, it's someone else."

Karen walked up behind her and looked out. A black BMW had rolled up and parked in front of the house. A man with a briefcase got out on the driver's side.

"Who is it?" Jenny asked.

Karen did not answer but began to mutter angrily as she marched out of the room and down the stairs. She grabbed the front doorknob and rattled it to be sure the door was locked against the man who rang the bell. Jenny crept down the stairs behind her.

"Karen," the man called out. "I need to talk to you. Open the door."

"Go away, Arnold," said Karen grimly. "I don't want to talk to you."

"Don't be stubborn," said Arnold Richardson impatiently. "I haven't got time for this."

"So leave," Karen cried. "Who asked you to come here?"

"Who is it?" Jenny whispered.

"Our lawyer," said Karen.

"Let him in," Jenny pleaded. "Please, Mom. Maybe he can help us."

"You've got a lot at stake here, Karen. Open the door."

"You could just see what he wants," Jenny pleaded.

Karen hesitated but could not deny the desperation in Jenny's eyes. She opened the door. Arnold Richardson shook out his black umbrella and came into the foyer. He was only a few years older than Karen and Greg, but he had the sleek, paunchy appearance of a much older man.

"Jenny?" he asked gravely.

Jenny accepted his coat and his umbrella, studying him with big eyes.

"You ought to know, Arnold," said Karen shortly. She turned to her daughter. "Honey, will you hang up Mr. Richardson's coat in the back hall? It's dripping."

"Sure," said Jenny. "Are you going to be my father's lawyer?"

"I am his lawyer," said Arnold.

"He didn't do it," said Jenny.

"Jenny," said Karen.

Jenny disappeared with the coat. Karen offered Arnold a seat, but nothing else. She found it hard even to look at him.

"Karen," he began, "I know what a shock it was for you to find out about Jenny. I hope you understand that

I could not tell you before. It was a matter of privileged information."

"It was a conspiracy."

Arnold sighed. "What a mess."

"Well, I agree with you there."

"I can't believe Greg blurted this story out in front of the police, without calling me. What was he thinking? What a stupid thing to do."

"I know. It's strange," said Karen bitterly, "for such an accomplished liar."

Arnold ignored her remark. "He hasn't contacted you. . . ."

"My phone is tapped."

"I assumed so. I haven't heard from him, either," said Arnold.

"So, what are you doing here?" Karen asked.

"You're going to need financial advice, legal advice about the business. I'm offering to help in any way I can. And, of course, when Greg returns or . . ."

"Is caught," Karen finished his thought.

"I want to help."

Karen regarded him with a cold eye. Greg had always been Arnold Richardson's biggest booster. To Karen, he seemed like any other lawyer, but she took her husband's word for it. Besides, she had always been inclined to like him—he was the one who had arranged their adoption.

"Well, I know you were a big help to Greg in the past, Arnold," she said sarcastically. "I mean, if it weren't for you . . ."

"He would have found another lawyer to do it," Arnold said firmly. "He was hell-bent on that adoption.

He was like a man possessed at that time. The Emery girl had agreed to give up the child, and he was determined that you would have that baby."

"That he would have her, Arnold. Let's not twist everything around now."

"I'm not twisting anything. I remember it perfectly. I remember because I advised him in the strongest possible terms not to do this. I warned him that if he did this thing, and he didn't tell you the truth, sooner or later it would come back to haunt him. Of course, I never imagined anything like this."

"No, I guess not," Karen muttered.

"Anyway, he was adamant. He said that he had to give you a child. That your marriage depended on it. That God or fate, or whatever, was giving him a chance to make it all up to you."

"And you agreed with that?" Karen demanded.

"Frankly, it seemed crazy to me," said Arnold. "I've always liked Greg. Always admired his head for business, but everyone has his Achilles' heel. This was his. He saw his chance to give you the baby you wanted so badly."

"Stop it, Arnold," Karen cried. "Let's stop pretending that he did this for me. Did he have the affair for me, too? Did he sleep with another woman for my sake?"

"I'm not here to defend him to you. Whatever happened, that's between you and your husband. I'm just telling you what I know."

"Maybe you're just worried that I'll report what you did and you'll be disbarred for it."

"You do whatever you feel you have to do," Arnold said calmly. "Right now you have other problems that are a little bit more overwhelming."

Karen shook her head. "Maybe if he had just told me the truth."

"You would have understood?" Arnold asked skeptically.

"He didn't give me a choice."

Arnold shrugged. "None of us wants to admit to our failings. We'd all rather be heroes."

"My hero," said Karen bitterly.

There was a silence in the room. Finally Karen said, "It's not your fault, Arnold. I know that."

Arnold sighed. "Do you have any idea where he might have gone?"

Karen shook her head. "I feel I don't even know the man we're talking about."

Arnold stood up. "If he contacts you, tell him to get in touch with me immediately before he does anything else."

Karen nodded.

"I mean it, Karen. Your . . . Greg is in a great deal of trouble."

"No kidding," said Karen. She glanced at the lawyer warily. "Is there any chance of him getting off?"

Arnold shook his head. "I'm not privy to what they have. Not until he is back in custody and claims me as his counsel. He's got the motive; he was with her on the night she was killed. It's bad. You know, if he'd only waited before blurting out that story, we could have claimed that you knew already. . . ."

"Oh, you mean I could have lied for him," she said.

"Would you rather see him go to jail for a crime he didn't commit?"

"What makes you so sure he didn't do it?" she asked bitterly.

"You think he did do it?" Arnold asked incredulously.

Karen turned away from him.

"Karen?"

"No," she said in a small voice.

"Well, that's more like it. At least you haven't gone completely around the bend. Not that anyone could blame you. . . ."

"Why don't you leave," she said.

"I'm leaving," Arnold said, picking up his briefcase.

"Jenny," Karen called out, "can you bring Mr. Richardson . . ."

Before she could complete the thought, Jenny appeared with the attorney's coat and umbrella.

"Karen, any questions you have, you can call me."

"I can't afford you," she said dully.

"We'll worry about that later," he said. "Good-bye Jenny, keep your hopes up."

"I will," said Jenny. "Good-bye."

"Thanks for coming, Arnold," said Karen. She opened the door without looking at him. Arnold popped his umbrella open and stepped onto the front steps. She felt as though she were being rude, ungrateful. But he had conspired to deceive her, along with Greg. All these years, he had known. She watched him walk to his car and get in, ready to drive away from this house, from their sorrows. For a moment she wished desperately that she could be in his place, be the one leaving this unbearable situation in the rearview mirror. She closed the door and turned back inside.

Chapter Twenty-one

Phyllis Hodges unwrapped a plastic drinking cup on the motel vanity and dropped a fistful of ice into it. Then she poured some diet Sprite over the ice and slurped it down. She unzipped her tweed skirt, let it drop to the floor, and stepped out of it. She pulled the oatmeal-colored jersey off over her head and kicked off her shoes. It felt good to be out of those soggy clothes. She had spent most of the drizzly day outside, between the funeral and then following the police around as they tried to track down some trace of Greg Newhall. She hadn't really noticed how damp her clothes were until just now. She'd been far too interested in the chase.

In a way, this story was too good to be true. She had been working on the *Bayland Gazette* ever since she dropped out of graduate school, and it wasn't the place she intended to stay. But she was still too inexperienced for the big city dailies, and though she would never admit it, she was a little intimidated by the idea of moving to a city and trying to crack the well-known papers anyway. But she needed something to catapult her into the big leagues, and she had a sneaking feeling that this story was the one. Crime stories were her favorites—probably because her dad had been a cop—but there was precious little in the way of intriguing crime in a town like Bayland. She thought she was on to something with Amber. Her story about the remains of the girl found in the bird sanctuary was the talk of the town for weeks. That name she'd picked, Amber, had really stuck. But nothing ever came of it. It was frustrating. Now this was different. This story could really turn into something. Maybe even a book. That would be the best thing. A book. Then she could write her own ticket.

Exhilarated by the possibilities, Phyllis poured herself another glass of soda, padded over to the TV and turned on the news, and then stretched out on the bed to fantasize a little bit about her future. A nonfiction bestseller that would be compared with *Fatal Vision*. Or a Pulitzer for her series in the *Gazette*. She pictured herself accepting the prize, people whispering about what an amazing accomplishment it was for a reporter from such a small paper. She would thank her editor, of course, who had believed in her, and her mom, and she would mention her late father, Stan Hodges, who had always encouraged her interest in police work and set her on the road to investigative reporting.

Phyllis closed her eyes and sighed. She could hear

the applause inside her head, feel the warm glow of the admiration of her peers. All right, she finally chided herself. That's enough. Lying here on this bed isn't going to win you any prizes. Time to get to work. She set her cup on the night table and sat up, staring at the TV, which had a brief story on the funeral and the fact that Greg Newhall was still at large. Then she looked around the room.

It had been a job convincing Margo to let her take the room. Margo had all kinds of worries about whether the police were finished with it or not, whether it was bad luck or not. "It's not a crime scene," Phyllis had pointed out, biting back the word *stupid*. Phyllis knew that being insulting would not help her get her way. Finally Margo had agreed, assuring her that the room had been thoroughly cleaned and that no trace of the murdered woman remained. Well, Phyllis hadn't told the manager this, of course, but she was hoping that some traces did remain. She intended to go over this place with a fine-toothed comb since she'd paid a night's price for the privilege. She couldn't help but be a little concerned about her cats. They weren't used to staying in the apartment alone. She almost never spent the night away from home. But cats were pretty self-sufficient, she reminded herself. That was a good thing about them.

Phyllis slid across the bed, picked up the phone, called information, and then dialed a pizza chain and ordered a delivery. It was a little like a holiday, spending the night in a motel in your own town. It was kind of fun. She got up and changed the channel on the TV, to see how the case was being covered on other broadcasts, and then started thinking about Linda Emery.

Linda had been in this very room on the night she died, although the police knew that the murder had not occurred here. Still, as Phyllis looked around she started to formulate her story in her mind, putting herself in Linda's place on the night of her death. Phyllis liked to get the atmosphere right. She would have preferred to steep herself in the ambiance of a crime scene, but until they found one, this motel was the next best thing. In her mind she was sketching out a chapter where she described Linda Emery on the last night of her life. It was important to get the details right—to pick up on the vibes of the place.

Phyllis switched on her small tape recorder and tried to formulate her lead. "When she checked in here, Linda Emery did not know that room 173 in the Jefferson Motel would be the last place she would ever rest her head." Phyllis spoke aloud into the machine, her voice full of portent. "She had come to this room, in this time, to try to make peace with her past, to meet the child she had given away at birth, to confront the man who had fathered that child. She could not know in those last hours in this spare, sterile room, that she was about to meet a violent death."

As she dictated, Phyllis idly went into the bathroom and began to search for some tiny speck of overlooked evidence, some scrap of information the police might have missed.

"What were her thoughts?" She came out of the bathroom and placed the tiny tape recorder on the vanity. She crouched down and opened the vanity drawers, peering inside them. "How did she feel as she waited for her old lover, Gregory Newhall, to arrive at the door to room 173?" She took out the empty vanity drawers and shook them. She ran her hand into the empty space behind them. Nothing. "Was she girding herself for an argument? Preparing to defend her actions? Or maybe"—Phyllis straightened up and paused dramatically—"just maybe, there was a romantic streak in her that was hoping the spark between them might reignite, as it had so many years ago."

The closet, she thought. There might be something there. Abruptly she turned, walked over to the closet, and pulled the door open. Her eyes locked with those of a man standing in the darkness.

Phyllis screamed and tried instinctively to cover her underclothes with her hands. The man turned and bolted back through the door behind the closet. Through the aperture, Phyllis could see the dim gray light of the room next door. "You son of a bitch," she cried. Forgetting her modesty, she lunged after him.

Chapter Twenty-two

Karen heated up a can of soup and put two bowls on the table, along with a plate of corn muffins that she'd had in the freezer. She knew she would have to go to the grocery store tomorrow. They were running out of staples. She dreaded the public exposure, pushing her cart down the aisles, feeling as though all the shopping and shelving stopped as she went by. But there was no way around it.

Jenny and Karen ate in silence. All of a sudden Jenny said, "I'm thinking of going to school tonight. Will you drive me?"

Karen frowned at her. "What for?"

"It's Thursday, Mom. I have choir practice. Just like I do every Thursday," she said with exaggerated patience. "I'm not going to be allowed to sing at graduation if I miss practice tonight."

Karen got up from the table and went to the refrigerator. She pulled out a pitcher of iced tea and poured herself another glass, stalling for time. She felt as if Jenny were testing her, and she felt an undeniable flurry of panic in her chest. "I don't see why they have graduations from junior high school. It seems silly to me," she complained.

Jenny was not about to be put off or distracted. "Will you drive me?" she demanded.

"You didn't even go to school today," Karen protested.

"Because of the funeral."

"Well, if you didn't go to school, then you don't belong at choir practice."

"You're the one who said I shouldn't go to school. Or the funeral."

"I was trying to protect you."

"You were probably right," Jenny conceded. "But I can't miss this rehearsal. I called my music teacher. He said I should come. Besides, I *am* going to school tomorrow."

Karen recognized the stubborn expression on her daughter's face. She had no choice but to admit to her anxieties. "Look, if you go over there, people are going to be staring and talking behind your back."

"I know it," said Jenny. "But Dad said to hold your head up and ignore what people say—"

"If it weren't for your father," Karen snapped, "we'd have nothing to be ashamed about. We wouldn't be the main subject of gossip in the entire town."

"I'm not ashamed of my father," said Jenny stoutly.

"Well, that's great," said Karen sarcastically. "I'm happy for you."

Jenny got up and took her bowl to the sink, letting it drop with a clatter. "You're just being a coward and blaming it on him. I'm not going to hide in the house and be afraid of what people say. This could go on for a long time. I have to get used to it. I've thought about it all day, and I've decided. Maybe you're afraid of them, but I'm not. Now will you drive me or not?"

A weariness in Karen made her want to just get up and walk away. But, at the same time she felt amazed by Jenny's attitude. She had expected her to be devastated, to be curled up in a ball after all the emotional blows of the last few days. But Jenny seemed to have some sort of inner strength that she lacked herself. Jenny's accusation was right on the money. It was cowardice. She could feel it in the pit of her stomach, and there was no use in arguing that it was anything else. Still, if a child could face it, what choice did a mother have?

"If it's that important to you," said Karen.

"We've been practicing this for months. I want to be in the concert."

Karen sighed and pushed her bowl away. "Okay," she said. "I'll take you."

It was all she could do to get her hair combed, to get some makeup applied. Jenny was ready, for once, before her mother.

Karen emerged from the downstairs powder room to find Jenny waiting impatiently in the foyer. Karen picked up her car keys from the table in the hall. "Let's go," she said.

Driving to the school, Karen was painfully aware of the unmarked police car that was following them. It made her feel sick at heart, dirty almost, as if she were some sort of undesirable being watched.

She parked the car, and Jenny said, "Do you want me to call you when we're done?"

Usually Karen waited for her during the evening choir rehearsal. It was a long drive back and forth, and it was easier, and more pleasant, just to stay. Many of the parents waited, either reading or doing needlework, scattered through the seats in the auditorium. It was pleasant to hear the young voices earnestly practicing the music. The time went quickly. Tonight, Karen did not want to go inside the school building, but she was being shamed into it by her daughter's show of grit. "No, I'll wait," she said.

The bright fluorescent lights in the school vestibule gave their faces a sickly tone. Their steps echoed on the shining surface of the floors. A young boy who was entering the auditorium turned as they came up behind him. He started at the sight of Jenny. Behind them, at a discreet distance, Ted Ackerman, their police sentry, hovered.

"Hi, Dave," said Jenny boldly.

"Hi, Jenny," the boy said. He held the door open for Jenny and Karen, studying them both curiously as they entered the dimly lit auditorium. The burly cop relieved him of the door handle and ushered the boy in. A number of students were gathered on the stage. One plunked at the piano keys while others flirted and conversed on the apron of the stage.

"I'll sit here," Karen whispered, indicating a seat a

few rows from the back. Jenny nodded and began the long walk down the sloping, carpeted aisle.

The teasing exchanges of the choir members stopped and they fell silent as Jenny marched toward them. Karen felt as if her heart were breaking inside her at the sight of her daughter's straight back, the smile fixed on her face, as she greeted the people she knew. A few students returned her greeting as an excited buzz seemed to rise in the cavernous room.

Other parents, scattered throughout the rows of seats, turned and looked at Karen seated near the back. Out of the corner of her eye, Karen could see Ted Ackerman stationed at the double doors at the head of the aisle. She wanted to yell out, Stop looking at me. What do you expect to see? But she would not do that to Jenny. Instead she squirmed in her seat, trying not to meet any of their eyes.

The music teacher breezed in through the doors at the front, brandishing sheet music. "Everybody, places on the risers, please."

The thunderous clumping of dozens of pairs of boots and running shoes drowned out the murmurings in the room as the students ascended the wooden risers, assembling by height. Karen forced herself to sit back and try to relax her tense posture as curious eyes around her gradually turned back to the front.

The teacher gestured to his student accompanist, and the bright young voices began to climb and descend the scales in warm-up exercises.

As the students began to practice "Amazing Grace," the simple hymn that would open the concert, Karen felt a lump in her throat. The swell of those earnest voices pierced her. It was true that kids were much more sophisticated these days, more knowledgeable about life than when she had gone to school. But the purity in their voices seemed to say that they still had the innocent hearts, the righteous beliefs, of all children before they become disillusioned by life. Karen watched her daughter's face, the concentration as she followed the conductor, as she gave her best to the music. Even in all this ugliness, cynicism had not won her yet.

Half an hour into the rehearsal, when she felt as if her presence had been accepted and she could safely leave her seat without causing a stir in the room, Karen walked up the aisle and opened the auditorium door. Officer Ackerman, who had taken a seat at the back, jumped up and followed her outside.

"I'm going to the bathroom," she said angrily.

Ted Ackerman, not much more than a kid himself, accompanied her stiffly down the hall and pushed open the lavatory door, banging on it and calling out, "Anyone inside?" He went in, made a perfunctory check, and then stepped aside as Karen entered the lavatory. She almost wished that he had surprised some woman and sent her screaming from the bathroom, just so he could share some of this humiliation. But she said nothing. Ted glanced up and down the hall before returning to the auditorium.

Karen checked herself in the mirror as she washed up and felt defeated by the dismal sight of her face— gray circles around her eyes and a lifeless complexion. The patches of blusher on her cheek looked like clown makeup. It's almost over, she thought. Tonight's ordeal, anyway. There was still tomorrow to dread.

She tossed away the paper towel, opened the lavatory door, and sighed. Back to the fray. She started back down the empty hall to the auditorium, her footsteps echoing as she walked. The words of "Amazing Grace" ran through her head. A wretch like me, she thought. That's about right. As she reached the classroom three doors and a corridor away from the assembly hall, she heard the creak of a door opening behind her. She started to turn, startled by the sound in the lonely hallway, when she felt herself suddenly grasped from behind and a hand clapped over her mouth before she had a chance to scream.

Chapter Twenty-three

I t's me," a familiar voice whispered as she was
pulled backward into one of the dark classrooms.
She bumped up against a desk as he hauled her inside and shut the door.

Only the moonlight illuminated the desks, chairs,
and blackboards, the pictures and projects pinned haphazardly to bulletin boards. Karen stared into the hag-
gard eyes of her husband, feeling the pressure of his
hands gripping her arms.

Her relief at the sight of him was immediate, complete. She sagged against him with a groan, and he
enveloped her. She pressed her face against his chest,
her fingers clutching handfuls of his shirt and arms
the way a gasping shipwreck survivor might claw at a
blessed, sandy shore. She could hear his heart beating
madly. You're alive, she thought. You're all right. My

life can go on. There's still hope. She had not admitted, even to herself, how afraid she had been for him. The feeling of his arms around her again was the most comforting sensation she had ever known.

And after a moment of blissful solace, it made her furious.

She jerked away from him suddenly, remembering everything. "Let go of me," she cried.

"Please, honey," he said. "Don't scream."

"Get your hands off me."

He let her go abruptly and held his outstretched hands wide apart, like someone who had just pushed off an unsteady child on a two-wheeler, as if willing the bike to balance in the space between his arms.

"Please," he whispered. "Please listen to me."

Her arms felt hot where his hands had been. She could not sort out the raging confusion of her feelings at the sight of him.

"You bastard," she said. She didn't know where to start. Which betrayal. She was like someone drowning in anger. "God, I hate you," she said.

Greg did not flinch. He looked at her steadily, his dark eyes shining like onyx in the dim moonlight. A kind of desperate resignation was etched in the lines of his face. Instinctively she expected him to beg her forgiveness. His next words brought her around like a slap in the face. "Karen," he said, "I don't have time for apologies. I don't have time to feel anything. There's a cop who's going to come looking for you in a few minutes. I need you to listen to me."

She was stunned, amazed at his audacity.

Seeing that he had captured her attention, he hurried

on. "We can't talk about Jenny now, or what happened back then."

"How dare you—"

"I did not kill Linda," he said, refusing to allow her to interrupt. "I need to tell you what happened right now, so listen to me. Someone has framed me. Someone who knew about me and Linda. Our past history. I did go to her room that night. I pleaded with her to keep our secret, and she agreed. I asked her if she wanted money. She said she did not intend to blackmail me. She told me that she thought Jenny was a lovely girl, that we had raised her well, that she had made the right decision in giving her to us."

"Isn't that great!" Karen exclaimed. "Jenny and I were like little checkers that you and Linda moved around the board at will. And she made the right move. That's wonderful. That's . . . that's so . . . gratifying to know."

"I said I can't talk about that right now, and I won't," he insisted. There was a furious urgency in his voice that silenced her again.

Greg put his face close to hers and searched her flinty eyes. "Karen," he said, "I know there are a million things you want to say to me. And you have the right. If I were you . . . I don't know . . . the urge to kill would probably be putting it mildly."

"Don't tell me what I'm thinking," she growled. "You've stuffed words back in my throat before I get a chance to speak them. What are we doing here, anyway?"

"It's Jenny's choir night. I took a chance that you would come."

"I didn't mean that, and you know it."

"I need your help," he said.

Karen looked at him incredulously. "I can't help you."

"You're the only one who can. You are my best friend in this world," he said.

No, she thought. No friend would do what you have done. "Greg, if you care anything about us, you'll give yourself up so that we don't have to be hounded night and day and have our house torn apart by police every time we turn around because of you. Stop torturing us."

"Karen," he said, "somebody planted that bloody room key in my van so the police would find it and accuse me. I have to find out who that someone is or I don't have a prayer. You know. You said yourself you thought there was more to Linda showing up here than met the eye. You were right. I asked her why she came back. She said she came back to settle a score. While I was in her room, someone called her, and she arranged to meet this person at a bar that night. The night she was killed. I heard her say the name of the place. When she hung up, she said, 'Speak of the devil.' That was all. I didn't ask who it was because it didn't matter to me. At the time, all that mattered was that she didn't intend to destroy my family."

Karen looked at him coolly, as if she didn't care what became of him. And at that precise moment, she did not. "So, tell the cops and they'll find this guy."

"Do you think anyone would believe me, after all these lies?"

Karen made a sound that was somewhere between a laugh and a sob. "No," she said, shaking her head.

"And if I don't get back right away, that cop is going to be joining us."

"Karen," he pleaded, "please, wait. I need to find out who the person was she met that night. But I need that photo of Linda that Jenny has in her bedroom mirror. It's a recent picture. The one that was in the paper was her high school graduation picture. It doesn't look a thing like her. I need to show that picture to some people. I need to find someone who saw them that night."

"That's insane," said Karen. "You'll be caught."

"I have to try."

"And you want to involve Jenny in your crimes? As it is, she'll probably spend half her life on a psychiatrist's couch trying to sort through all the lies you told her."

Greg's face looked tortured. "Does she hate me?" he asked.

Karen hesitated and shook her head. "No," she answered truthfully. "Amazingly enough, she doesn't seem to. She's being incredibly tough about it all."

She saw his eyes well up. "What a kid," he said hoarsely.

Karen turned away from him. Her husband. Her mate. He looked ill, tired. In spite of herself, she had the urge to enfold him in her arms and make him better. She fought off the temptation. I must be crazy, she thought. Finally she said gently, "What are you hanging around here for? Why don't you run away? They're going to catch you. If you're not going to turn yourself in, why don't you get as far from here as possible? Go to Canada. Where are you staying, anyway? Do you have food? Or a roof over you?"

"I keep moving," he said. "And as for going away, I can't. Everything worth living for is here. I just want a chance to clear myself. That's why I need the picture."

Karen's expression hardened.

"If you decide to get the picture for me, leave it in our secret place in the gazebo. I'll check there every day."

He walked over to the window and put one foot on the sill. "I love you," he said.

She heard him drop to the ground outside. She did not turn around. She opened the classroom door and walked back to the auditorium. As she reached the doors, she nearly collided with Officer Ackerman, who was coming around the corner.

"Where were you?" he demanded.

"The ladies' room," she hissed.

"I checked there when you were gone so long."

Karen felt steely inside. "That dispenser was out of sanitary napkins," she said. "I went to another one. Okay?" She was amazed at how readily the lie came to her lips.

The young cop reddened.

"Excuse me," she said frostily. "Can I get back inside?"

Officer Ackerman let her pass. Karen walked to her seat on rubbery legs and sank down, her mind reeling. She hated herself for protecting Greg. She should have screamed. She should have called for the cop. It was insane even to listen to him. She looked around the auditorium. She could not let Jenny know she had seen him.

She had to hide it. She had to act normal. She wondered how she would be able to sleep that night. She doubted she would sleep at all. She wondered if, over the swell of young voices singing, anyone could hear the hammering of her heart.

Valerie McHugh, wearing black tights and a Day-Glo—decorated T-shirt, shuffled into the police station behind the stout, sweatsuit-clad figure of her mother. Both women were smoking. Ida Pence shook her grizzled gray head and rummaged in her pocketbook for the paperwork from the courthouse, then handed the cop on duty the receipt showing that Edward McHugh's bail had been paid.

"I swear, I don't know why you want him," said Ida wearily to her daughter. "He's nothing but trouble. Never has been any good, never will be."

"Where else is he gonna go, Ma?" Valerie whined. "Besides, the kids love him."

"Just a minute," said the officer, examining the papers and then passing through some closed doors to where the cells and the rooms for questioning were situated.

"He doesn't even live home anymore," Ida protested. "I don't know why I help you. I should just let him rot in there."

"He'll live home now," said Valerie with grim satisfaction.

Ida rolled her eyes. "Big deal. I'm really getting my money's worth."

"We'll pay you back, Ma. Cross my heart."

"Yeah. Not in this life," said Ida.

Phyllis Hodges, who had been seated on a stiff-backed bench ever since they'd arrested Eddie and brought him in, watched the women without much interest. She did not realize that the prisoner they were discussing was her peeper—the motel employee who was her new favorite suspect in the murder of Linda Emery. Walter Ference had promised to speak to her after he questioned Eddie, and she'd been waiting there obediently ever since. Now her mouth dropped open as the officer on duty at the desk emerged with Edward McHugh in tow, followed closely by Detective Ference.

She leapt up from the bench at the sight of the pasty-complected night clerk and yelped in protest. "Why are you letting him out?" she cried. "This man is a murder suspect."

Valerie, Ida, and Eddie all turned and stared at her. Eddie looked away first. Ida sized up Phyllis with a long-suffering expression. "This is what he was look-ing at?" she asked shrewdly. Valerie looked peevish. Ida shook her head.

"Don't forget, Eddie," said Walter. "Don't go far. We're going to need your testimony."

Eddie looked at the ground and nodded. "I know," he said.

"This is an outrage," said Phyllis.

"Come on," said Ida wearily. "I'm parked near a hydrant. I don't want a ticket to boot." Valerie tried to take Eddie's arm, but he shook her off as he followed his mother-in-law's wide figure out the station door, all three enveloped in a cloud of cigarette smoke.

Walter came over to Phyllis and sat down on the bench, motioning for her to sit down beside him.

"I don't want to sit down," said Phyllis like a recalcitrant child. "I want to see justice done. That man had access to Linda Emery's room and was probably peeping at her, too. It could have gotten out of hand, turned violent. An innocent man could be taking the blame for his crime."

"Phyllis," Walter said patiently, "make up your mind. First you were sure Mrs. Newhall did it, then Mr. Newhall, and now Mr. McHugh."

"Don't patronize me, Walter," Phyllis warned. "I'm not just Stan Hodges's little girl anymore."

"I know that," said Walter.

"You have to admit, that little pervert was probably spying on her."

Walter looked around the nearly empty vestibule of the police station. "Sit down," he said. She stuck out her chin defiantly, but Walter persisted. "I'll tell you something, off the record."

Phyllis immediately perched on the edge of the bench. She made a bargain with herself. Maybe I won't put it in the paper, she thought, but it can go in the book. "What?" she asked.

"He was peeping at her all right. He saw Newhall in the room."

This was gratifying, a confirmation of her flawless reporter's instincts, but not enough to appease her. She folded her arms across her chest. "Newhall admitted he was in the room. That's nothing new."

"Yes, but he said he didn't lay a hand on her."

Phyllis felt a sudden surge of interest. "McHugh saw him hit her? Or drag her out or something? How do you know he's not just saying what he thinks you want to hear?"

Walter stood up. "Let's just say that Mr. McHugh has testimony that will seal our case against Newhall."

"Don't leave me hanging, Walter."

"See you in court," said Walter with a brief smile. "Once we apprehend Mr. Newhall, that is."

Phyllis sat back against the bench, her mind racing, as Walter waved and returned to his office. A witness. The peeper who saw the crime. It was too good. It couldn't wait for the book. She mentally examined the "off the record" agreement she had made for technicalities. There had to be a way to say this in the paper without actually saying it. It was all in the way you phrased it. She decided to go home, and feed the cats, and see if she had a brainstorm in the process.

Chapter Twenty-four

T he waitress slapped two eggs, toast, and coffee down on the paper placemat in front of Bill Emery. Bill stared at Phyllis Hodges's article in the morning paper and did not seem to notice the food in front of him.

"Is that it?" she asked. "Buddy, yoo-hoo?"

Bill looked up from the paper, a dazed look in his eyes.

"You want anything else?" she asked.

Bill looked around the booth as if he had lost something there. "Someone's joining me," he muttered.

"Well, give me a holler when your friend arrives," she said, moving on toward the next customer.

"Sure," said Bill. He turned back to the paper.

After a few minutes he was joined by a slim young woman wearing dark glasses and her hair in a ponytail with loose, gold tendrils waving around her face. She slipped into the booth across from Bill and swept the diner with a guilty gaze, like a mole meeting a contact. Bill looked up and studied her attractive face and frame dispassionately.

"Do you want to order something?" he asked.

She shook her head. "I can't eat," she said. "I've been too upset."

Bill pursed his lips and nodded.

"I see you're reading that article," she said. "About the guy who was peeping in your sister's room at the Jefferson. Unreal. It sounds to me like he saw her with the killer."

"It sounds to me like this Hodges woman is just spinning theories."

"I don't think so," said the girl. "I think she knows something."

Bill rubbed his face with his hands. "Christine, what did you want to talk to me about?"

"Don't take that tone with me, Bill. I have a right to be upset." She removed her dark glasses. Her blue eyes were bloodshot and puffy. "I have not been able to sleep or eat for days."

"Is that why you haven't been coming to work?" he asked. "Your mother has been giving me the runaround when I call. I hope you haven't been crying on her shoulder about me."

"I haven't been at work because I didn't want to see you," she hissed. "And of course I haven't told my mother. She'd be ashamed of me."

Bill picked up a fork and poked it into his eggs. The yolk ran down in a river across his plate. He had hired

Christine Bishop as a salesgirl three months ago. Their affair had begun almost the day she started work.

"Do you want to tell me about it?" he asked.

"This is wrong, Bill," she said. "I mean, I've known all along that it was wrong, but this is different. Lying to the police . . ." She scanned the diner nervously again.

"Keep your voice down," he complained.

Christine hung her head, and her voice was small and squeaky when she said, "If my parents ever knew what I did . . ."

"Well, they won't know unless you tell them," said Bill.

She pulled a paper napkin from the dispenser and dabbed at her eyes. Then she began to shred the napkin. "Why in the world did you want to meet at the Jefferson when your sister was staying there?"

"I didn't know she was staying there. It was a mistake."

"This whole thing is a mistake," Christine said quietly.

They sat in silence. Bill glanced at the newspaper again, then back at the girl. "Look," he said, "I'm as sorry as I can be. I never meant to get you involved in something like this. But the best thing we can do is just keep it to ourselves and let it blow over."

"Bill, I've been doing some serious thinking."

"About what?" he asked, his eyes narrowed.

"About us."

Inwardly Bill recoiled from the word. Why did women always want there to be an "us"? There was no "us" in his mind. Even with Glenda, where "us" was official, he didn't feel it. He had never felt that with any woman. Then a strange thought struck him. Maybe he had, once, long ago, when he and Linda were kids together. . . .

"Bill," Christine said in a shrill voice, "are you listening to me?"

"Yes," he said. "What about us?"

"I think it might be best if we didn't see each other anymore."

Bill looked at her warily. "Well, that would be difficult," he said. "I mean, we see each other every day. We can't just deny our feelings. . . ."

"I took that into consideration," Christine said archly. "I think it would be best if I got another job."

Bill frowned. "Christine, listen, I don't blame you for being upset. Let me make it up to you. I know you're mad at me right now, but . . ."

Christine shook her head and wiped away a trickle of tears. "No, I'm . . . it's not that. I think this whole thing with the police is God's way of telling me that I shouldn't be doing this. Well, I mean, I knew I shouldn't be sleeping with a married man, but this is kind of like a big warning. You know . . . to stop doing this. To start living the right way again."

Bill pressed his fingertips together until they whitened. "Are you thinking . . . do you feel like you have to tell the police about . . . you know . . . us being there, at the Jefferson?"

Christine looked at him in amazement. "Do you think I want everyone in the world to know that I was meeting a married man at a motel like some tramp?"

"No, of course not," he said.

"Besides," she said, "you didn't kill your sister, so what difference does it make if we were there?"

"Exactly," said Bill.

"You will give me a good reference, won't you?" she asked, glancing over at him.

"What?"

"For a new job."

"The best," he said hurriedly. "You write it, I'll sign it."

She looked at him indignantly. "That's not fair. After all of this, you're too lazy to write me a letter?"

"It's a figure of speech," he crooned soothingly. "All I mean is, you couldn't dream up a better reference yourself than the one I'm going to write."

Christine sat back against the seat. "Okay," she said huffily. She tapped the shreds of napkin together into a little pile in front of her.

Slowly Bill exhaled. "Okay," he said.

Chapter Twenty-five

Somehow, Karen had managed to get through the day. She had forced herself to keep her encounter with Greg a secret from Jenny, both last night and in the morning, before Jenny went to school. She had run the gauntlet of the supermarket like a zombie, scarcely noticing what went on around her. And the entire day, until Jenny came home from school and retreated to her room, Karen did not know what she was going to do.

Now, as she stood outside the closed door to Jenny's room, she heard the tinkling melody of "Beautiful Dreamer" emanating from within. She was still not sure what she was going to say as she rapped gently on the door and asked, "Can I come in?"

Abruptly the music stopped, and after a second, Jenny's voice said, "Come on in, Mom."

Karen pushed the door open and saw Jenny returning the music box to its place on the dresser.

"It's a pretty melody, isn't it," Karen said gently.

"I guess so." Jenny opened a notebook on her bed and leafed through it.

Karen hesitated and then sat down on the bed. "How was school?"

Jenny shrugged. "Okay."

"Did anybody give you a hard time?"

"Most kids were pretty nice."

"That's good," said Karen. "How's Peggy?"

Jenny pushed her hair back off her forehead. "Peggy's great," she said firmly. "She's the best friend I ever had."

"I'm really glad to hear that," said Karen. For a moment her thoughts traveled to Jackie Shore, her old best friend from way back in grade school. Jackie's husband had been transferred last year, and they'd moved to Seattle. Jackie had called when she heard about Greg, and for the half hour of their conversation, Karen had felt safe and cared for, but once she hung up, the yawning distance between them made Karen feel even more lonely. "A friend like that is hard to find."

Jenny looked at her mother out of the corner of her eye. "I thought you'd be mad about Peggy," she said.

Karen looked at her, surprised. "Why would I be mad about Peggy?" she asked.

"Well, you know, about that thing on Mother's Day."

Karen sighed. "Honey, I've got a lot of things to think about these days. . . ." She didn't like the way that sounded, so she changed her tack. "I'm just glad that Peggy is sticking by you through all this."

"She is."

There was a silence for a minute, and then Jenny said, "You know, I've been wanting to tell you about that. About what happened on Mother's Day."

Karen felt slightly defensive. "What about it?"

"There was a good reason why I didn't show up for lunch."

"Well, I assumed there was." Karen wished they could change the subject. She didn't want to talk about it. She didn't want to be reminded of the hurt. She had enough to cope with as it was.

"No, really. You see, Peggy's mother died two years ago. I didn't even know her then."

"Oh, that's too bad. I didn't know."

"Yeah, and her father got married right away to some woman from his office."

"Well, you said she had a stepmother."

"Peggy doesn't like her. Anyway, she got all bummed out because it was Mother's Day and she kept thinking about her mom dying and how she missed her and all. And I could really see how she felt. That's how I would have felt if I was her, and something happened to you. So, she wanted to get out of the house, and I felt bad for her and I said I'd go to the movies with her. I didn't want to leave her alone, all upset like that."

Karen's heart seemed to lighten, to spring up like a parched plant that had finally been watered. She didn't realize how deeply the hurt had lodged there, even with all the other things that had happened since. "I understand," she said solemnly.

"I didn't do it to make you feel bad, Mom. You just never gave me a chance to explain."

It was such a simple explanation, but it eased such a pain. "My feelings were hurt," Karen said truthfully. "I thought you just didn't want to come."

"No. It was just that I thought Peggy needed me more right then."

Karen managed a tremulous smile. "I think you were right."

"I shouldn't have given your present to . . . Linda. I guess I was mad because you jumped all over me, and I'd been trying to do something good. And lately, with losing the new baby and all, I thought you didn't care that much about me anymore."

"Oh, Jenny, I didn't mean to make you feel that way. You're the most important thing in the world to me."

Jenny looked embarrassed but pleased.

"Anyway," said Karen. "Maybe it's just as well you did give that present to Linda. You didn't have very much time with her. Believe it or not, I'm really sorry about that."

"I believe you."

"You've been through so much these last few days. I really admire the way you are handling it."

Jenny fiddled with the chain around her neck. For the first time, Karen noticed she was still wearing the locket under her shirt. "You know, she said something funny to me when we talked."

Karen was immediately alert. "What was that?"

"Well, I thought she was talking about her own parents, but now when I think about it, she might have been trying to warn me about Dad."

"What did she say, exactly?"

"She just said that sometimes mothers and fathers

kept secrets from their children, and they do it because they think it will prevent them from being hurt, but in the end it can hurt them worse."

"How true," Karen murmured. She pictured again Greg's face as he confessed his involvement with Linda, his paternity of Jenny. The pain seared through her again, brand new and stunning.

"But you know," Jenny went on, "she was wrong about that. At least for me. I mean, at first I didn't know what to think. I was mad and hurt about it. But now, when I think about it—that Dad is my real father—I feel really happy about it. It means he really wanted to keep me. He really loved me."

Even through her own devastation, Karen felt grateful for Jenny's reaction. One thing had not gone utterly wrong. One good thing had emerged from the wreckage of their lives. But she could not just let it be. He was not a hero.

"He lied about everything," she reminded Jenny.

"I know he did," said Jenny stubbornly. "But it was just because he didn't know how else to keep me."

What about me? Karen wanted to cry out. He betrayed me. In every way. But she couldn't say it to Jenny. Because if it weren't for his betrayal, she would not be sitting here with her daughter, her Jenny, the light of her life, made possible by his deception.

"It's not that simple for me," said Karen.

"I know it," Jenny said gravely.

"You have to be able to trust someone. . . ." Karen's voice trailed off, and she pictured again his face in the moonlight in that empty classroom. She could still hear his voice, pleading with her.

"I trust him," said Jenny.

Karen squeezed Jenny's hand and forced herself to think of immediate things. The question was, did she believe that he had killed Linda Emery, no matter what else he had done?

"What are you looking at, Mom?"

Karen stood up and walked over to the bureau. The photograph of Linda with her cat was stuck in the mirror. That face, so like Jenny's, smiled sadly at her.

"I'm just looking at your picture," she said.

Jenny shifted uneasily and then said with a trace of defiance in her voice, "I think it's a nice picture."

Karen's mouth felt dry and her throat threatened to close up on her. "It is a nice picture," she agreed. "Why don't you let me take it to the Photo Gallery and have it framed for you?"

Jenny's face lit up with a combination of relief and pleasure. "That would be great."

Carefully Karen removed the photo from the mirror frame. More lies, she thought. But she couldn't tell Jenny about her meeting with Greg, about his request. It was too much to ask of a child that she keep such information to herself. This is how it goes, she thought. One lie just naturally leads to another. She held the photo carefully in her hand. Amazing, she thought, how something so weightless could be such a burden on your heart.

Chapter Twenty-six

"W hy do you have to go?" Valerie wailed.
"Look," Eddie said, throwing socks and underwear into a duffel bag, "I'm leaving you the car."

"I don't care about the car," Valerie protested. "Besides, it hardly runs."

"Get it fixed."

"With what?"

Eddie moved silently around the darkened bedroom. He had insisted on keeping the Venetian blinds closed all day in the dreary row house they rented.

"You can't just skip out on your bail," Valerie cried. "My mother will lose her money."

Eddie peered into the dresser drawer. "Where's that olive-colored shirt?" he said.

"You mean that brown one? I don't know. It's in the hamper, I guess."

"Shit."

"I'm not your maid," Valerie flared up. "How often do you expect me to get to the Laundromat with those two kids underfoot?"

"Never mind," said Eddie, tossing a few other shirts into his bag.

"I'll go tomorrow," she promised.

"I won't need it tomorrow."

"Eddie, come on. You've got to testify. You have to tell what you saw—you saw that Newhall man beating up on that woman."

Silently, Eddie strapped his watch on his wrist.

"You saw him, right?"

"Maybe I just said what they wanted to hear," said Eddie.

"Come on, Eddie. You didn't lie about that, did you? It's in all the papers that you saw the murderer."

"Don't I know it?" said Eddie. "That Hodges dame really hung me out to dry."

"I don't get it," Valerie whined. "So what?"

"Mama," pleaded the two-year-old, toddling in and clinging to her bare legs. Valerie picked him up and patted his backside absently.

"At least tell me where you're going," she said. "Or take us with you."

"I can't do that," he said.

"Yes, you can. We can be ready in no time. We'll take the car. We'll all go."

"No," Eddie barked. "I have to go by myself."

Valerie pretended not to hear him. "I'm sick of this place anyway. We'll just drive until we find someplace we like."

Eddie started to argue with her, and then he stopped. "Okay," he said. "You get the kids' stuff ready. I'll go out and check on the car."

"Really?" Valerie cried. "Can I just call my mom?"

"You better not," said Eddie.

"Okay. Okay. This will work out good. You'll see."

"Sure," said Eddie. "We'll go together."

He was somewhat amazed by her happiness. Not every woman would be so happy to pack up and leave town, he thought. Well, Valerie had always had that reckless side. That's what he'd liked about her in the first place. She was a little bit wild. Of course it was a rented house, and the truth was she'd be able to stuff most of the things they actually owned into a couple of paper bags.

"You're a good girl, Val," he said as he passed by the door of the kids' tiny, narrow room. She was emptying the dresser drawers into a beat-up suitcase, and she gave him a dazzling smile that made him look away. The two-year-old was making airplane noises and had picked that moment to rummage through the toys she as trying to collect.

Eddie carried his bag down the steep stairs. The baby was lying on a dingy blanket on the floor, flailing his arms and legs in the air. "See you, slugger," Eddie whispered. He opened the front door and stepped out into the twilight.

He checked up and down the street, then hurried down the sidewalk to an alleyway that let out behind the house. It was best this way, he thought. She'd never realize he was gone until she came down looking for him. He couldn't afford to travel with the whole bunch of them. It was too dangerous. All day he had been thinking about it. He knew what he had to do. He had to get far away, as fast as he could. He had not really formed much of a plan. He had no money to speak of, but the trains that rumbled behind the house had given him an idea. He would hop a freight. That was what hoboes did. At least that's what they used to be called, before there were so many of them and people started calling them the homeless. Somehow "hobo" sounded better. But however you sliced it, that was him now. And all because he'd had to go back and have another look at that Emery girl.

Eddie tossed his bag over the wooden fence behind the house, then climbed up and dropped down to the scrubby, trash-strewn embankment that led to the tracks. Obviously the best place to try to hop aboard a train was near the station, when it was slowing down. Never mind how guys jumped on top of speeding boxcars in the movies. Eddie had no desire to get himself killed that way. No, the idea was to follow the tracks down near the station, which was about a mile away, and try to slip aboard as the train was easing through the Bayland station. After that it was just a matter of keeping a sharp eye out for the trainmen until he got as far away from here as he could.

In the distance, Eddie heard a whistle and began to make his way through the brambles. He'd never catch this one, he thought. It would be long gone before he got near enough to the station. Still, the sound of the whistle was like a prod. Hurry, he thought. There was no telling how far away it was. He peered down the tracks. The light from the engine was a tiny glimmer in the distance. Besides, he thought, this might be a passenger train, not a freight. A passenger train would be more comfortable, but it would be hard to stay ahead of those conductors, constantly asking you for a ticket.

Eddie quickened his pace. He didn't know anything about trains, didn't know how long it took to stop one of those babies when it was really steaming along. He crunched a potato-chip bag underfoot and released his pant leg from a rusty piece of wire it was caught on as he scrambled along the slope.

The whistle blew again and Eddie stopped and looked back. The light was pretty well visible now. What the hell, he reassured himself. If you miss this one, there will be another. From the way the house was always shuddering, and the number of times a day you had to shout to be heard, there was always another train on the way. He hoisted his duffel up and walked a little farther.

Suddenly, from behind him, he heard the crunch of that potato-chip bag. It was weird. It was as if he had turned into Superman and he had X-ray hearing. That thunderous, clanging metal dragon shimmying down the tracks seemed silent as a *whoosh*ing monorail. All Eddie could hear was the crushing chips, the crackling cellophane. There was someone behind him. He didn't need to turn around. He knew who it would be.

"I'm going out for a little while," Karen called up the stairs to Jenny.

"Okay," Jenny called back.

Karen's heart pounded as she put the snapshot of Linda in an envelope and stuck the envelope in the waistband of her shorts, under a sweatshirt. She walked out to the car and got in.

As she pulled out of the driveway, her ever-present police escort turned on his engine. Karen drove slowly through the peaceful twilight, her hands sweaty on the wheel. Finally she turned in at the entrance to the town beach, drove down near the picnic grounds, and parked her car.

A man and his dog were returning to the parking lot as she got out, the dog frisky and panting after his romp. Karen gave the man a brief, automatic smile as she passed him by. Look normal, she thought. You're a woman out for a sunset stroll on the beach. There's nothing odd about someone needing to take a walk, to collect their thoughts.

The soft sand sank under her sneakers as she picked her way down to the water's edge, and then she began to walk briskly along the wet sand. There were several other people out for just the same purpose, to enjoy the waning day. A little group of teenagers sat smoking cigarettes on a rock wall behind the dunes. An old man and his equally elderly wife walked hand in hand in Karen's direction. Karen stuck her hands in her pockets and kept her head down. The corners of the envelope in her waistband bit tiny gouges into the bare skin of her stomach.

She could remember being a teenager, coming here to meet Greg, as if it had been last week, not twenty years ago. She could recall poring over the clothes in her closet, wanting to wear just the right combination of soft lace and faded denim to make his heart stop when he saw her. They would each make excuses to their parents, arrangements with their friends, all aimed toward that moment of encounter. Karen felt hot, tingling, even after all these years, remembering how the sight of him was like a blow to the chest, how they were shy when they met, how every brushing touch was torture, and bliss. Everybody said it was lust, and it wouldn't last. And it was lust, but it was tenderness, too. And giddy laughter. And deep peace, and desperate promises, and more, that she had never even dreamed of.

"Good evening," said the old man, and his wife nodded as they passed by.

"Evening," Karen mumbled without looking up.

She had always assumed she would get old with him, walk the beach like those two, hand in hand. It had always seemed the best way to prove to all those doubters, most of whom were long gone by now, that young love could be the real thing. Well, maybe the cynics would have the last laugh on her after all.

She reached the last jetty and turned around. As she looked up the beach, the weather vane atop the gazebo was visible in the distance. The irony of her mission struck her again. Here she was, doing as he asked. Trying to help him. After all that had happened. For a minute she thought about just turning around, getting back in the car, and going home.

No, give him the picture, she thought. Let him take it around to people. He's bound to get caught. And it will serve him right. She pictured again his gaunt, weary face in the moonlight. And she felt afraid. But how dare he come to her for help? After all the lies, the betrayals. Still, in the seething pit of her stomach, she knew that he would never trust anyone else but her. The unfairness of it all made her weak.

She was walking like a robot, approaching the gazebo, and as she reached it, she saw that there was a woman and child sitting inside. Panic filled her heart. It would not make any sense to go in and sit down when it was already occupied. That in itself would look suspicious. She knew that the watchdog cop was observing her from wherever he had stationed himself. No, she would be forced to walk by, to return to her car.

Just as she was about to pass the gazebo by, she heard the woman say, "Sara, it's time for your supper." The woman lifted up the protesting child and walked down the steps on the other side. Karen did not hesitate. She pretended to stumble. She climbed the two steps, entered the gazebo, and sat down on the bench. She pulled her shoelace loose and then retied it. Then she sat back against the bench and looked out at the sea, rippling with gold, the horizon glowing blood orange and purple.

You don't deserve any help from me, she thought. Her knuckles were white as they gripped the edge of the bench, and her eyes filled up with angry tears. She wiped them away with the back of her hand, and then, as she lowered her hand, she reached under her sweatshirt, pulled out the envelope, leaned forward slightly, and quickly slipped it beneath the bench. For a few moments more she sat, staring sightlessly at the sunset. Then she stood up and returned to her car.

Chapter Twenty-seven

Walter Ference stared at his wife, who sat slumped against the closet door in their bedroom. Her mouth hung open, and her head was tilted back, her eyes halfway shut. The neck of an empty bottle jutted out from beneath the ruffled organza skirt of her dressing table. Sylvia, dressed in a business suit and sensible shoes, was crouched down beside her, slapping Emily's limp hand.

"It's about time you got here," she said indignantly. "I stopped by on my way home from work and this is how I found her."

"I'm sorry. I came as soon as I got your message," said Walter. "I am working on a murder investigation, you know."

"Oh, fiddlesticks," said Sylvia. "There's nothing left

to investigate. You're all just waiting around for somebody to catch your escaped suspect."

Walter sighed and crouched down beside his wife. He tapped her cheek. "Emily," he said. "Em, can you hear me?"

Sylvia sat back on her heels. "Walter, this is a disgrace. The time has come to stop pretending and do something about this. . . ."

"Help me put her on the bed, Syl," said Walter, lifting his wife under the shoulders. "Get her feet."

Sylvia bent over with a grunt and took her sister-in-law's turned-out ankles in her hands. Together Walter and Sylvia hoisted Emily up onto the bed.

"Walter, I mean it," Sylvia continued as Walter arranged the pillows behind Emily's head. "Now enough is enough. This woman needs help."

"She's going to be upset that you found her like this," said Walter.

"Well, you certainly don't seem surprised to come home and see her passed out on the floor. How often does this happen?"

"Once in a while," Walter admitted. "You insisted on going to that funeral. I knew it would be too much for her."

"Don't blame me for this," Sylvia cried.

"Look, I'm sorry you had to walk in on this, but she's never been right since the accident. This is how she copes."

"You call this coping?" Sylvia exclaimed. "That accident was fifteen years ago. You can't let her go on and on like this. She needs to be in some kind of treatment for alcoholism."

"I've tried," said Walter. "She won't go. She's too shy."

"Make her go. What kind of a man are you? You make her go."

The phone began to ring on the bedside table. Walter picked it up. He listened for a minute and then closed his eyes and shook his head. "Oh, my God," he said. "When . . . Okay. Okay. I'm on my way."

Walter turned back to his sister. "I've got to go. My eyewitness just got himself run over by a train."

"You're just going to leave her like this?"

Walter looked ruefully at his wife, snoring slightly on the bed. "There's not much I can do for her right now."

"Don't be ridiculous. Pack a bag for her. We have to take her to a hospital. She belongs in a detox center."

"I'm afraid that's not possible, Sylvia," Walter said evenly.

Sylvia glared at her brother, who avoided looking at her. "What's the matter with you, Walter? Are you just going to stand by and let her drink herself to death?"

"I have to go. I'll deal with this later."

"I doubt that," Sylvia sniffed. "If you haven't dealt with it in all these years . . . Very well, go ahead, abandon her. I'll take charge of it. If you're not going to do anything, I will."

"She's not going to thank you for it," he said.

Sylvia shook her head. "I'm used to that," she said bitterly.

Walter backed out of the room, then hurried out to his car.

* * *

"I don't know what happened," the engineer protested tearily, wiping sweat from his grimy forehead. "One minute the track was clear, and the next minute this guy was jumping out in front of the train. . . ."

"Did he jump or was he pushed?" Larry Tillman asked. Behind them, the train's engine sat, its dark shape menacing in the moonlight. Police cars, clustered on the road above the tracks with their lights flashing and radios squawking, looked like little pups yapping at a great bear. The passengers were being escorted off the train, up the embankment, and through the guarded opening in the chain-link fence, to be put onto buses bound for Boston.

The engineer looked at the officer in desperation. "I don't know. How am I supposed to know? I didn't even see him for more than a second." The man began to cry.

"All right," said Larry, "calm down." He turned to Walter, who was crouched beside Valerie McHugh. A neighbor had gone to stay with the children while another fetched a blanket to throw around Valerie. She was shivering in spite of the warmth of the night.

Walter motioned for Larry to leave them alone. He spoke gently to Eddie's wife. "Did he say why he was leaving?"

Valerie shook her head and continued to sob. "He promised to take us with him," she wailed. "He said he had to get away. He didn't say why."

"You know he had a court date pending," said Walter.

"Of course I knew," Valerie cried. "My mother

bailed him out." She looked up at Walter, her eyes wide, her face streaked with mascara.

"Did he seem depressed or anxious?"

"What do you mean?" she asked suspiciously.

"I mean, did he indicate that he might be thinking of taking his own life for some reason?"

"He didn't kill himself," Valerie insisted, holding the blanket tightly around her.

"Okay," said Walter. "Take it easy."

Chief Matthews slid sideways down the embankment, shaking his head. "These reporters are driving us nuts," he said, gesturing to where the photographers and reporters were crowded on the other side of the fence, held back by an officer. He turned to Walter. "Is this the widow? I'm very sorry for your loss."

"Thanks," said Valerie, and then started sobbing again. "But what are you going to do about this? Somebody killed my Eddie."

"Somebody killed our witness," Walter said in a low voice to the chief.

Dale Matthews kneaded his forehead and sighed. "Jesus. Are we sure it wasn't suicide? Or he just slipped and fell on the tracks?"

Valerie leaped to her feet and began flailing out at Dale with her fists, landing little pelting punches on the back of his suit jacket. "I told you, no," she began to wail.

Larry Tillman and another officer grabbed her arms to restrain her.

"Let her go, boys," said the chief. "This woman is distraught."

"I'm not dis . . . anything," Valerie cried. "I'm pissed

off. Why didn't you people protect him? You put his name in all the papers as a witness, and now look. . . ."

"All right, calm down, Mrs. McHugh. Is there somebody who you can go to, who can take care of you?"

"My mother's coming," Valerie sobbed.

As if in response to her daughter's cry, Ida Pence, wearing a gray-and-purple jogging suit, a cigarette hanging from her lips, came toward them down by the hill, supported under one arm by an officer.

"Valerie, my baby," she cried.

Valerie flung herself onto her mother's ample bosom.

"That good-for-nothing Eddie," Ida said wearily, enveloping her daughter's shuddering frame in her arms.

Karen made a few stops on her way back from the beach. She went to the Giant Discount Store in the mall and bought some plant fertilizer and a new garden hose. Greg had been talking about replacing the one they had before summer. She felt guilty even spending that little bit of money, but she wasn't going to let her garden dry up and wither away. Then she went to an all-night convenience store and got a pint of Jenny's favorite ice cream.

It was dark by the time she headed for home. She was driving along at the speed limit, preoccupied with thoughts of the photograph, when suddenly she noticed the traffic slowing to a crawl. Up ahead, when she craned her neck out the window, she could see a glow of lights and a cluster of TV vans, police cars, and buses. All at once the traffic came to a dead stop. There were people hurrying up and down the crowded street on foot and kids weaving through the cars on bicycles.

"What happened?" she asked an older woman who was walking by pushing a sleeping child in a stroller.

"A guy got hit by a train," the woman said.

Karen nodded and drew her head back into the car. She wished she could get home. She felt claustrophobic in the car. There was no telling how long she might have to sit here. She glanced over at the seat beside her and thought about the ice cream, melting there in the bag as she sat.

People on foot were streaming by the car, chatting and calling out to one another. Karen sighed and turned on the radio, fiddling with the buttons to try to find something she wanted to listen to.

"Well, well," said a voice near her ear.

Karen cried out, turned, and saw the head of Phyllis Hodges poked in her car window.

"If it isn't Mrs. Newhall!"

"Get away from my car," Karen exclaimed. "What do you want?"

"Did you hear about the guy who got killed by the train?" Phyllis asked.

"Yes, I did," said Karen frostily. "Now stop leaning on my car."

"Did you know that it was Edward McHugh? The man who was going to testify against your husband? The cops think somebody pushed him in front of that train."

Karen felt a chill run through her. She tried not to let it show.

"Oh, you didn't know that," said Phyllis with satisfaction in her voice.

Karen felt trapped and unable to come up with any

rejoinder that didn't sound defensive. She tried to roll up the window, but Phyllis put her hand on top of the glass, and Karen was forced to let go of the button. "Leave me alone," said Karen, and was embarrassed by the plea that sounded in her voice.

"No problem," said Phyllis, straightening up and peeping ahead into the darkness. "I think they're going to let you go."

Karen kept her eyes straight ahead as the traffic started to move again. Gratefully she pulled away from Phyllis, who was leaning against a parked car, speaking into a little tape recorder. She snapped off the radio, locked the car doors, and started to drive home. She followed the familiar roads automatically, her mind reeling from this latest piece of news. When she was forced to stop at a red light, she searched the darkened streets around her with nervous glances. She reminded herself that there was a policeman following not far behind her, but it did not make her feel safe. The police were the enemy, too. They did not want to protect her and Jenny. They only wanted to find Greg. She felt like a stranger in a hostile country whose very survival depended on understanding a language foreign to her. The harder she tried to comprehend it, the more frightened and frustrated she became. Karen had heard about McHugh's arrest, had heard the scuttlebutt that he was going to be a witness. But why would anyone want to kill him? Except for Greg. And it couldn't be Greg. Her certainty wavered and then returned. He was trying to clear himself. He would never push a human being in front of a train. If there was one thing their infuriating encounter in the dark schoolroom had shown her, it was that he had not somehow changed into the leering monster that the press was picturing. He was still the same Greg. No, she promised herself. A liar, maybe. But not a killer. But if it **was**n't Greg, then who? Only one thing was settling firmly into her mind. There was someone out there with a vicious plan for her and her family.

She was relieved when she reached home, and she rushed into the house, locking her door behind her. Jenny appeared at the top of the stairs.

"Mom," she said, "I just heard on TV about that guy from the motel—"

"I know," said Karen.

"Are they going to blame Dad?" she asked fearfully.

"I don't know," said Karen. "Come down. I got you some rocky road."

Jenny came down the stairs and joined her mother in the kitchen. She climbed up on a stool and twirled her spoon absently in the dish of ice cream. "Where do you think Dad went?" she asked.

Karen put the ice cream back into the freezer. She did not want to convey her fears to Jenny. "If he has any sense," she said tartly, "he went far, far away."

"I hope not," said Jenny. "I want him to come back."

"Honey," said Karen, "if he comes back, they're only going to put him in jail."

"He'll show that he didn't do it," said Jenny.

Karen looked through the kitchen door down the dark, gloomy hallway. The house seemed cold and desolate tonight. "You better finish that and do your homework," she said.

"It's hard to concentrate," said Jenny.

"I know."

"Don't you miss him?" Jenny asked.

Karen frowned. The yawning emptiness inside her told her what she would not admit. "I'm too mad at him," she said.

"But what if we never see him again?" Jenny cried.

Karen thought of the photo in the envelope. She wondered if Greg was retrieving it at that very minute. Find your answer, she thought. For Jenny's sake. So she can have you back.

"You have to think positive," Karen said, rubbing her daughter's shoulder. It was the best she could do.

Chapter Twenty-eight

A small powerboat with two men in it bobbed on the peaceful, sparkling surface of the ocean as the golden, unhurried dawn broke across the sky. The two fishermen had come out in the dark, leaving their families to slumber. They sat companionably, without speaking, each thinking his best thoughts of the day, waiting for that little tug on the line that would send a rush of pleasure through the veins.

Neither man watched the beach. Neither one saw the crouching figure scuttling crablike, behind the dunes and the rocky retaining wall, heading in the direction of the gazebo.

But Greg kept his eye on them. He thought he had gotten here so early that he would be the only living soul around, but the fishermen had preceded him. Carefully he made his way toward the dome-shaped frame structure where his hopes were focused. When he got close enough, he checked the fishermen, who seemed oblivious to him, and then hurled himself flat to the gazebo floor and crawled across it to the bench.

With trembling fingers, he groped around under the slats until, with a stifled cry, he felt the paper crackle beneath his fingertips. Carefully he pried out the envelope. Crouched there, Greg nervously tore at the envelope and reached in. He pulled out the photo of Linda, smiling, then fumbled around inside, searching for a note, for some word of blame or encouragement. Anything, as long as it was a communication from his wife.

The envelope was empty except for the picture. Greg's spirits sank a little, but then he forced himself to look on the bright side. She'd brought the picture. Whatever else she might be thinking about him, she'd gotten it and she'd left it there for him. That was no small triumph. Maybe she had not included a note. Surely an endearment was too much to hope for. But this picture said something. It said, I believe you. I am willing to help you. Right now, there was nothing more he could ask from any friend, from any partner. She had agreed, by this token, that his crimes were only personal. It was something. It was a start.

His eyes filled up as he ran his hand along the bench, like a carpenter checking for smoothness. She had come here, to their old place. She must have had memories as she sat here. He was overcome by memories. Hunger and weariness seemed only to increase their vividness.

Stuffing the picture back in the envelope, he tucked

it away in his pocket. He had to get out of here before
the sun was officially up and the joggers and maintenance workers began turning up for the day. He knew
shortcuts from his youth, back ways around town, but it
was dangerous in the light. Even this early.

When he was a kid he loved the old thriller *The
Invisible Man*. Now he wished that it could happen to
him, so he could move freely. He worked at making
himself invisible. At night he stayed at construction
sites that he was familiar with. He chose new construction over renovations, to be sure that no one was living
there. But at least there would be a plastic tarp over the
wooden frame to make a roof over his head. And the
construction workers usually left something behind that
he could eat or drink, even if it was the last inch of a
soda with a cigarette butt floating in it or the last, two,
Sheetrock-dusted bites of a bagel or a Big Mac someone had for their breakfast or lunch. No one ever really
cleaned up a job site until the work was all finished. He
knew from long experience that workers seemed to set
their stuff down and never give a thought to throwing it
away. Of course, they had big appetites because of their
hard labor, but there was usually something left, something he could scavenge by night. By day he hid in the
uncleared land near the sites, the long hours passing
with a slowness he could not have imagined. He did not
dare to sleep. He watched birds and squirrels making
their progress through the trees, watched a spider spinning her web, observed, far more closely than he
wished to, the blooming of spring.

But today would be different. Today he had a goal.
Today he would plan for the night. He knew where the

Harborview Bar was, a honky-tonk joint in a neighboring seaside town that catered to teenagers and underage drinking. He had been working on the story he would tell about the picture, a story that would earn him sympathy and trust. He nurtured his hope, however slim, that he would find the information he needed. A plan was what enabled you to survive, to keep going, to stay sane.

Greg spotted a crumpled wrapper by a tree and went over to investigate. It contained the half-eaten remains of a candy bar. There were ants crawling on it. He brushed the ants off as best he could and greedily stuffed the candy in his mouth. Sometimes he wondered if he *was* still in his right mind, considering the diet he had been subsisting on.

On the other hand, some people would wonder if he had been in his right mind in the first place. To just bolt out of the confines of the law and run. It wasn't something he had thought a lot about. All his life he'd been law-abiding. He couldn't imagine living any other way. It was more of an instinct that made him run. A realization that all of his lies of the past were adding up to make him look completely guilty. And then, when they'd brought in that blood-spattered room key, he knew he was up against something more sinister than the police. Someone had set the stage, had hung this murder around his neck. And he couldn't just go willingly, like a lamb to the slaughter. He had to try something.

Finished with the candy bar, Greg stuffed the wrinkled wrapper in his pocket. He'd throw it away when he spotted a trash can. For a second he was struck by the ludicrousness of being concerned about littering, considering his situation. No, he thought, it's not stupid. I have to remain civilized. One day I will be a normal person again. I will get my family back. And my home. I have to keep that in mind.

The photo in his pocket seemed to glow against his leg. Karen had believed him. No, maybe that was too strong. She had given him the benefit of the doubt. All their years together counted for something. When he found out who his tormentor was—when he was free again—he would make her understand. He would spend the rest of his life trying to make it up to her. But he couldn't think about it right now. He had to think of practical things. He had to get cleaned up. He had to get a shave. He had to figure out how to get to his destination.

For the first two problems, he had an idea. There was a kitchen renovation going on at the Kingman house in a secluded, wealthy enclave. Very often, those who could afford it moved out temporarily when the kitchens or bathrooms were being redone. It was too inconvenient to stay. Greg's plan was to head that way and to observe the house while the men were working. Once they were gone, he might be able to get in there and use the bathroom. He focused on this possibility and forced everything else out of his mind as he walked along. There was no room for fear or doubt. He was too weak to withstand it.

Through the branches of the trees he spotted a trash can by the side of the road. He made a mental calculation. He was going in that direction anyway. Fumbling in his pocket for the wrapper, he peered both ways up and down the lonely backwoods road. No one was coming. He came out of the brush and hustled across the street. He tossed the wrapper in the can, and as he did so, he caught sight of the headline on a newspaper in the basket. WITNESS HIT BY TRAIN was all he was able to glimpse when suddenly he heard the sound of a car turning onto the road behind him.

His first impulse was to dart into the trees, but he knew instantly that would only draw suspicious attention. He did not look up at the car but started to amble down the road. His heart was hammering, and he cursed himself for not just leaving that infernal candy wrapper in the woods. Silently he prayed that it was not the police. The car, a midsize sedan, passed him by and then slowed down. Greg could feel the blood drain from his face as the car pulled up and stopped just ahead. Don't panic, he thought. Don't run. He tried to keep walking at a steady pace, although his legs were wobbly. The passenger was rolling down the window as Greg approached.

"Excuse me," said a heavy-set, elderly woman leaning out the window. "We seem to be lost. Can you tell me where the Bayland Inn might be?"

Greg licked his cracked lips and was keenly aware of his malodorous clothes, his unshaven face. A flicker of apprehension crossed the woman's face. At close range she clearly did not like the looks of him. "Sorry," he said, barely slowing his pace. He did not want to give them a chance to study him. He heard the woman rolling up the window behind him, even though it was a beautiful, cool morning. Greg did not glance at them as they pulled away. As soon as they made the next turn, he dived back into the wood like a deer who had inadvertently grazed his way out into the open.

Careless, he berated himself. A few more like that and they'll catch you.

Meanwhile, as the old woman rolled up her window, she turned to her husband in the driver's seat. "My eyes aren't what they used to be, but I'll swear I know that man's face from somewhere. . . ."

Her husband was not paying attention. He was too busy looking for a way back to the center of town. "I didn't notice," he said absently.

"I'm sure of it," she said. She chewed her lip and peered through the windshield, searching for the connection.

Chapter Twenty-nine

Karen knelt in her blooming flower beds, yanking out the weeds that didn't belong. She had come outside hoping that some time spent in the garden might take her mind off the dark thoughts, the fears, that had kept her awake most of the night. It had taken every ounce of her strength to get on her gardening clothes and gather up her tools. For a long time she had stood in the kitchen, staring out at the sunlit yard, feeling like a vampire, wanting to hide in the gloom all day, panicked at the idea of being out in the open, exposed to the sun. Once she finally got out among the flowers and got to work, the time passed quickly. She waved to Jenny when Peggy's father dropped her off after lunch at the mall, and she kept on working. Once she stopped and went inside, she knew she would feel enervated again and might not get back outside for weeks.

A car pulled into the driveway and Karen looked up and shaded her eyes as she squinted across the lawn. An older woman she did not recognize was walking slowly toward her. With a sigh Karen clambered to her feet and put down her trowel. She put her canvas-gloved, dirt-covered hands on her hips.

The woman approached her haltingly. She was dressed neatly in dark pants and a gray cardigan, even though the day was warm. She carried a plain brown pocketbook and a small shopping bag. "Mrs. Newhall?" she said.

Karen nodded warily.

"My name is Alice Emery," said the woman. "I'm Linda Emery's mother."

"Oh," said Karen in surprise. She felt completely unsure how to respond. "Oh."

"I know you didn't expect to see me here," said the older woman. "I wondered if we could talk?"

Karen had a sudden impression of great fragility in the other woman. She felt fearful that the woman might faint, being so overdressed for the weather. "Of course," she said hastily. "Please, come in the house."

Karen removed her gloves and gathered up her tools. She gestured to the house, and the woman followed her as she hurried toward the open doors of the patio. Karen led her through the dining room and into the kitchen. "Please, sit down," she said. "Can I get you something to drink? Some lemonade, maybe?"

"That would be nice," said Alice.

Both women were silent as Karen went about getting

the glasses and pouring out the lemonade. Karen kept thinking about the older woman's loss—her daughter had been murdered. It was hard to imagine such grief. And, as far as anyone knew, Karen's husband was the killer. Why would she ever want to come here?

"I'm sure you think it's strange my coming here," said Alice as if reading Karen's thoughts.

"It's . . . I feel . . . a little uncomfortable," Karen admitted.

"Yes, so do I." Alice sipped her drink and, for a minute, seemed to get lost in her own thoughts. There was silence again in the kitchen. Then Alice placed her glass on the table. "That's delicious," she said.

Karen felt no hostility from the older woman, although she kept expecting to. She was utterly confused. She decided to bring up the unspoken specter between them.

"I'm sorry about your loss," she said.

Alice met her gaze, and Karen wanted to look away from the pain she saw in those eyes. Grief and regret mingled in crushing proportions. For an instant, as their eyes met, they were just two mothers, united in understanding. Alice looked away, and Karen felt wary again.

"Thank you," said Alice with dignity. "I have many regrets."

The woman's words made Karen feel uneasy, angry even. Surely this woman was not hoping to unload her grievances on Karen, already stumbling under the weight of her own. Linda Emery had not been her friend—she had been her husband's lover. Nothing could change that. There was only so much sympathy that Karen was willing to feel.

As if prompted by Karen's belligerent silence, Alice began to speak. "When Linda came to see me, my son convinced me to send her away. After nearly fourteen years. And I did it."

Karen had expected some reference to the murder, to Greg. She felt a certain relief, followed by revulsion at the woman's bald admission. At the same time, it answered a lingering question she had—why Linda had been staying at a motel. Karen had wondered about it often enough. She felt oddly grateful for the information.

"Well," Karen said, groping for some appropriate platitude. "I'm sure she understood."

Alice shook her head. "I don't think so."

Once again Karen felt that suffocating uneasiness. Why are you telling me? she wanted to cry out.

Alice peered at her. "I don't want any more regrets," she said as if in answer to Karen's silent question.

"No," said Karen cautiously.

"She told me I have a granddaughter," said Alice.

Karen started at the word. Of course, it was true. This was Jenny's grandmother sitting before her in the kitchen. For a second Karen was glad that her own mother had not lived to see this day. All men are cheaters, her mother always told her, never more so than when Karen had announced that she was going to marry Greg. You'll pay in the end, her mother had said. It's not that she would have gloated about all this. No, it was more that her knowing sympathy, now that the inevitable had finally occurred, would be too much to bear.

Karen forced herself to concentrate on the woman before her. Alice looked almost defiant—as if daring Karen to deny it.

"Yes," said Karen. "It's just . . . I didn't think . . ."

"I'd like to meet her," said Alice.

"Of **course**," said Karen hastily. "I just assumed you wanted to talk about . . . you know, my husband."

Alice waved a hand wearily, as if to say it was beside the point. She hesitated, as if sorting through her thoughts, and then said, "That's a matter for the police. Whatever happens, it won't bring her back."

"No," Karen agreed ruefully.

Alice took another sip of lemonade and cleared her throat. "I've given this a lot of thought, Mrs. Newhall. I searched my heart before I came here. Linda was all excited about seeing her daughter. She wanted me to meet her. Your daughter is all I have left of mine, if you see what I mean."

"Yes," said Karen hastily. "Of course I do."

"So here I am. I decided that I wanted to meet her, and I hope you will allow it."

Karen felt a certain admiration for the woman, for the courage it took to come here. "It's all right with me," she said carefully. "But you understand, it's up to Jenny. . . ."

"Certainly," said Alice. She sank back in the chair as if relieved not to have to explain further.

"I'll just go and tell her you're here." As she was about to leave the room, Karen turned back and said to Alice, "I should warn you. Jenny bears a strong resemblance to your . . . to her mother."

Alice looked at once pleased and a little flustered by this. "Thank you for telling me," she said.

"I'll be right back."

* * *

Karen briefed Jenny on the way down the stairs, marveling to herself at how willingly Jenny had agreed to meet this stranger, her grandmother. It was as if this whole horrid experience was making the girl ever stronger and more resilient. Jenny smiled shyly at Alice as she came into the room. "Hello," she said.

Tears formed in Alice's eyes as she looked at the girl. "Oh, my," she said, "you do look like her. Oh, my." Alice got up from her chair, walked over, and cupped Jenny's face gently in her hands, shaking her head.

Karen started to object to this familiarity, but Jenny met Alice's gaze with bashful pride. "I know," said the child consolingly. "I just wish I'd known her better."

Alice nodded and resumed her seat. "She was a lovely young girl, just like you."

"Thank you," said Jenny, sitting down opposite Alice.

Karen felt her heart fill up with pride at the compassionate, surefooted way in which Jenny dealt with the older woman. She could see Jenny was simply responding from the heart, but still, her guilelessness was almost childlike. The old woman and the girl sat with their knees almost touching. A current of understanding seemed to flow between them. Blood, Karen thought with surprise.

"My father did not kill Linda," Jenny asserted.

Alice looked at her gravely. "No?"

Jenny shook her head.

Alice reached out and squeezed her hand. "You're right to be loyal to him. Your . . . Linda was the same way about her own father. If only he had lived to see her come back. It was a day he dreamed of. And he would have prevented me from doing something I will regret forever. I treated my daughter very shabbily. I did it to please my son, but it was a mistake."

"She told me a little bit," said Jenny. "I don't think she blamed you."

So Jenny knew, Karen realized. She kept her own secrets.

"Linda told you what I did?" Alice asked.

"She told me a little bit. I guess I didn't give her too much of a chance. I was busy showing her pictures and everything. Trying to make up for lost time."

Alice sighed. "You were the only one who welcomed her home. You were the only one who didn't try to punish her."

Jenny looked down, embarrassed. "I'd always dreamed about meeting her."

Alice smiled tremulously. "Maybe I could see those pictures sometime," she said.

Jenny beamed. "Sure. Want me to get them?"

"I don't think she means right now," Karen cautioned her daughter.

Alice smiled. "The eagerness of youth . . ."

"I didn't mean to be pushy."

"Oh, no," said Alice. "I just want to be sure I will see you again."

"Sure," said Jenny.

"It's so strange," Alice murmured. "It's like seeing her all over again—but without the . . . anger. You know mothers and daughters. They can get into a lot of arguments."

Jenny shot Karen a knowing glance. "Yeah. We do too sometimes."

"Well," said Alice, sitting up in her chair, "you know, I was really dreading this. I had to force myself to come."

"Why did you dread it?" Jenny asked.

"Jenny," Karen admonished.

"Well, I guess that's a silly question with all that's happened," said Jenny.

"No, it's a fair question. I guess I was afraid of the unknown."

Jenny nodded.

"Anyway, I should go. For now. But I brought you something." She reached for the shopping bag.

Jenny peered down into it as Alice rummaged around and brought out a pale blue, painted porcelain cat.

"It's a bank," said Alice, shaking it. Coins jingled inside. "It was Linda's. It's probably still got her allowance in it from years ago. She loved cats, and the color blue."

"I do, too," Jenny exclaimed. "This is beautiful."

Alice handed it to her. "Well, she had it when she was your age. Of course, I know girls are a lot more grown-up these days and all. But I wanted to give you something that was hers. That she treasured. I don't have anything from recent years. I've never even seen where she was living. But I had this. . . ."

"I really like it," said Jenny.

"I'm glad," said Alice. She stood up.

"I'm glad you came," said Jenny.

Alice hesitated and then squeezed Jenny in a quick,

sharp embrace. Jenny responded sincerely, clutching the bank.

"And thank you, Mrs. Newhall, for being so understanding."

"Call me Karen. Please, come again."

Alice walked to the door, then looked back thoughtfully at her granddaughter. "How wonderful," she murmured, and Karen had the strange conviction that Alice was speaking across time and space to her Linda.

Chapter Thirty

T here he was, big as life," said Frank Kearny. "I turned to my wife and said, 'You know, he looks mighty familiar to me.' "

After passing Greg Newhall, the Kearnys had eventually made their way to the Bayland Inn, checked in, had their breakfast, and gone on to the wedding of a great-niece in a local church. It was during the reception, when some of the guests started talking about the local murder case, that Theresa Kearny had suddenly realized why she had recognized the face of the man they saw this morning. Although in the version the Kearnys related to the police, the revelation had been her husband's.

Walter Ference, who was hearing the story for the third time, rose from his chair and coughed into his fist. "Mr. Kearny, I want to thank you for taking time out from your family occasion and coming forward with this valuable information. You're going to have to excuse me so we can get moving on this."

Theresa Kearny beamed and started to struggle up from her chair. "Arthritis," her husband muttered, grasping her supportively by the arm.

"Here, let me help you," said Walter, hurrying around the desk.

"Is there a reward for us if you catch this guy?" Frank asked bluntly.

"Frank," his wife exclaimed reprovingly.

"Well, I'm living on Social Security. Every little bit helps. . . ."

"I'm afraid not," said Walter.

"Why not?" Kearny demanded.

At that moment Chief Matthews came rushing up to them, his hand extended. "Are these the Kearnys?" he asked.

Walter nodded. "This is Chief Matthews."

"Chief," Kearny said respectfully, pleased at the attention from the top.

"We can't thank you enough," Dale said, pumping the old man's gnarled hand. "We've had a lot of calls on this that didn't amount to anything. This is a real break for us. It's not every man who would be so civic-minded, to leave the bosom of your family on such an occasion to help the cause of justice. . . ."

"Let's get back to the wedding, Frank," said Theresa. Frank hesitated, as if ready to bring up the subject of rewards again but thought better of it.

"Glad to help out, Chief," he said as his wife urged him away.

Dale turned to Walter. "I've called up everyone we've got—off-duty, vacations, the works. Of course it took the old codger all day to put two and two together, so Newhall could be in Timbuktu by now."

"I doubt he's gotten far," said Walter mildly. "I'm kind of surprised he's still in the area at all. I would have thought he'd headed for Canada or Mexico long ago."

Dale rubbed his hands together. "I've got a good feeling, Walter. We're going to get him now."

"I certainly hope so," said Walter.

"I want everyone to use extreme caution," said the chief. "As far as we know he's not armed, but he's certainly dangerous. And desperate. I have a feeling this guy may have gone around the bend. Now, let's get going. Every minute counts."

Jenny lay on her bed hugging the blue porcelain cat to her chest, thinking about her grandmother. It was a strange concept. A grandmother appearing out of the blue when you were thirteen. No stranger than your biological mother suddenly turning up, she reminded herself. Or finding out that your father was really your father. She wondered what she should call her new grandmother. Everything in her life was strange now. And most of it was scary and awful. All she really wanted was for everything to be the way it was before.

It wasn't that she was sorry that Linda had come—never that. She had wondered all her life, ever since she was little and they told her she was adopted. All these years she had kept in her heart the picture of a girl, young and sad and faceless, cradling a baby Jenny, cry-

ing when she had to give her up. Now, that image had a
face, that empty place was filled. But it seemed like she
had lost everything else just to have her questions answered. Including Linda herself. And maybe her father,
although Jenny refused to think that way. Maybe her
mother was willing to give up, but she wasn't. "You
think he hung the moon," her mother used to say to her
about her dad. Of course, in those days she would smile
when she said it. But it was true. Jenny never denied it.
Still, it was easy to take someone for granted when they
were always there.

Before all this had happened, it seemed to Jenny that
she was usually mad about something, always dissatis-
fied. "Oh, God," she whispered, "if you could make
everything all right, I promise I would never complain
or be crabby again." She prayed it, but in her heart she
didn't really believe that God, or anybody else, could
make life return to the way it was.

Jenny heard the telephone ring, but she didn't stir
from the bed.

"Honey, it's Peggy," Karen called from the bottom of
the stairs.

"Okay," Jenny said, and sighed. She got off the bed
and went down the hall to her parents' room and picked
up the phone.

"Hi, Peg," she said.

"How are you?"

"Okay. What's up?"

"Listen, do you want to go to the movies tonight?
The new Arnold Schwarzenegger picture is playing."

Jenny was tempted. It would be great to sit in the
dark theater and eat popcorn and drink Coke and let the

movie absorb all her attention and forget about everything else for a few hours. And she knew her mother
would let her go. It wasn't that. But she'd need at least
ten bucks to go; everything added up, and she didn't
want to ask her mother for it. She knew how worried
her mother was about money.

"Jenny?" asked Peggy. "You said you wanted to see
it."

"I do," said Jenny. "But I'm tired tonight." She
couldn't tell Peggy the real reason because then Peggy
would offer to pay, and she didn't want that.

"Is anything wrong?" asked Peggy.

"You're kidding, right?"

"Well, I meant anything else."

"Something weird did happen today. I'll tell you
about it when I see you."

"Okay," said Peggy uncertainly. "Well, call me if
you change your mind."

"I will," said Jenny, and hung up the phone. She
started back to her room.

"What did Peggy want?" Karen called up the stairs.

"Nothing," said Jenny, closing the door to her room.
She lay back down on the bed and picked up the cat
again and ran her finger along the design of pink straw-
berries and little white flowers that was painted on it. It
gave her a funny feeling to think of Linda, her mother,
using that same bank to save her allowance so many
years ago. She wondered what kinds of things Linda
saved her money for. They didn't have CDs in those
days. Records, probably. Her parents had a collection
of records from the days when they were young. And
clothes. Girls probably liked to get new clothes back in

the caveman days. Idly Jenny turned the bank over, and the coins clinked inside.

I wonder how much she had saved, Jenny thought, sitting up and looking at the cat with a different kind of interest. She held the bank to her ear and shook it. Besides the clinking, she was sure she could hear a rustling sound. Like dollar bills, maybe. Maybe there was even enough to go to the movies. That would be all right, she thought, if she came up with the money herself. It would sort of be like a little present from Linda to her.

Curious now, Jenny tried to pry the rubber plug out of the bottom of the bank using her fingernails, but the rubber was stiff with age and had been in place a long time. Jenny laid the bank gently on her bed and went over to her bureau drawer to hunt up a nail file.

I probably should save the money, she thought, or give it to Mom. We might need it. But at the same time, she knew her mother would never take it anyway. She found a metal nail file, took it back to the bed, and inserted the tip under the edge of the plug. If it's anything good, I'll offer it to her, Jenny decided. Even if she says no, at least I offered. She began to jimmy the nail file, trying to work it gently so she wouldn't scratch the bank. The dried rubber crumbled around the edges as she worked it. Someday, maybe I'll give this bank to my own daughter, Jenny thought. And I'll tell her about my story.

The plug came loose and Jenny popped it out. She turned over the bank, and a shower of coins bounced onto the bedspread. Then she gave the blue cat a shake and could hear the rustle inside as paper dropped toward the opening. Wiggling her fingers up inside the hollow figurine, she felt paper, but she knew at once, with a sense of letdown, that it was not money. Carefully she worked it around with her fingers and a little help from the nail file and began to extract it from the opening.

What emerged from the hole was a piece of slightly grimy, lilac-colored stationery, folded over again and again, until it was only about two inches square. Jenny started to unfold it and then shook the bank once more for good measure. With a soft rustle, a corner of newsprint emerged from the opening. Carefully Jenny extracted the dry, yellowing clipping, which was also folded repeatedly and threatened to crumble in her fingers. The single-column clipping had been carefully cut out and stapled at the top corner. It was not a long article. The newspaper it came from was the *Des Moines Register,* from Des Moines, Iowa. The dateline on the article was nearly fifty years old. There was a shot of a pale, grim-faced, hollow-eyed man named Randolph Summers at the top of the column. Beneath his photo the headline read CONVICT ES-CAPES AFTER AMBUSHING GUARD. The news story detailed the escape from a state penitentiary of Summers, a prisoner serving a twenty-year to life sentence for armed robbery and assault, and warned the public to be on the lookout for this dangerous criminal.

Jenny read the article over again, wondering why Linda would have saved this particular story—hidden it, in fact, in her bank. There had to be a good reason to hide it with your money stash. It gave Jenny a queasy feeling as she set it aside on the bedspread. Still frowning, she picked up the square of stationery with the tips of her fingers and began to unfold it.

Chapter Thirty-one

The last local train to stop in Bayland left the red clapboard station house at 8:47 P.M. The lighted clock that hung above the platform read 9:00 P.M., and a gentle drizzle had begun by the time Greg reached the Bayland railroad station. The place was as quiet as a cemetery. The station itself was locked, and no passengers would be waiting on this platform tonight.

Greg lurked below the platform, studying the parking lot. He had given this a lot of thought. The fact that no other trains stopped here tonight meant that all the cars still in the parking lot were here until morning, at least. They would not be picked up by their owners until they arrived back the next day. And Greg had need of a car for the night.

He scrutinized the small variety of cars before him,

running a hand over his gaunt, freshly shaven face. The Kingman house had worked out better than he hoped. The Kingmans had obviously taken flight from the construction, and although a security guard patrolled the enclave at intervals, it had been easy enough to get in. There were floor-to-ceiling windows being replaced in the kitchen. All he'd had to do was remove some opaque plastic and squeeze through. He had shaved and showered in a darkened bathroom, then borrowed some chinos and a golf shirt from Mr. Kingman's dressing room. The sight of his dwindling frame in the mirror, even by moonlight, had given him a start, but he didn't have time to worry about it. He threw his own clothes in a hamper, figuring it was the most logical place to hide them. It would be quite a while before anyone did laundry in the house and noticed them. Then, after taking a screwdriver from a toolbox in the construction area, he'd slipped out of the house and made his way to the station.

Now, after perusing the selection of cars, he decided on a black-and-gray Toyota in the second row of parking spaces back from the tracks. He knew a little bit about Toyotas, had fixed a few in his day, and it was an unobtrusive, older car. A station car. It would do. He had to walk authoritatively right to the car, in case a police officer might be cruising by the station. He could not be seen going from one vehicle to another, trying the door handles. He had to make a smooth move, pop the lock, get in, and use the screwdriver to get it started. He'd never much liked his teenage after-school job in a gas station, he thought. But it finally came in handy.

Greg glanced over his shoulder nervously. He had been very much aware of the extra police who seemed to be everywhere in town. That couple had recognized him this morning. He was sure of it. He didn't have the energy to berate himself for his mistake. He had to concentrate on his mission. He crossed the parking lot as casually as possible, the rain misting on his clean hair and his borrowed shirt. He had to get to the Harborview Bar and take his shot. He knew it was a long shot, but what difference did that make? It was better than no shot at all. He would use the car, bring it back, and the passenger who got off tomorrow morning's train would never know the difference.

He walked up to the Toyota and put his hand on the door handle. Just as he did it, a police car drove slowly into the parking lot on the other side of the tracks and stopped. Greg's stomach did a sickening flip. The cop opened his door, and the light went on in his car. Greg watched in terror as the uniformed officer groped in his glove compartment and then got out of the automobile. The officer stretched, and as he did, he spotted Greg standing beside the Toyota in the darkness. He looked curiously across the tracks. Without thinking, Greg gave the man a wave. The officer hesitated, waved back, and then removed a pack of cigarettes from his shirt pocket. He shook one out and, leaning back against his patrol car, cupped his hand around a lighted match to protect it from the drizzle.

In a minute the cop was going to begin to wonder why Greg was standing there beside the Toyota, not getting in. Like a man with a gun held to his head, Greg lifted up the door handle and felt his legs wobble beneath him as the handle clicked and the door opened. It wasn't locked. He couldn't believe it. He closed his eyes and thanked God. It was a sign. An omen. He wasn't much of a believer in that sort of thing, but it had to be. Greg opened the door, slid onto the seat, and, using the screwdriver, turned on the ignition. He was clammy from head to toe, his heart beating wildly in his chest. He switched on the lights, and the cop across the way put up a hand to shield himself from the foggy glare. Quickly Greg turned out of the parking space and, with no license, no keys, and no idea whose car he was driving, headed out into the night.

Walter Ference chewed on his sandwich and stared ruefully at the framed Currier and Ives print that was wedged, at a drunken angle, between the kitchen table and the wall. It had fallen this morning, while he was drinking his coffee, and startled the hell out of him. He was immediately reminded of Sylvia's prediction that it would soon fall, and he was doubly irritated because she was right. He had gotten as far as getting the hammer and nails out of the toolbox to fix it, but so far they remained on the counter where he had set them down. He knew he should rehang the print before Emily got back, but those programs tended to last for a month or more. There was no real hurry about that.

The house was so silent with Emily in the rehab center. It reminded him of his boyhood, coming home from school. He would get home before Sylvia, and his mother would be in her room with the door shut and the drapes drawn. Sylvia often told him that before their father died there were servants in the house, but he could not remember that time. In fact, he had no memory at all of Henry Ference. He just remembered the silence. For a while he would stand at his mother's bedroom door and call out to her, but she never answered him. She was too ill, she said. Often she would not emerge from that room all day, or at least not when the children were home. She told them both Sylvia was in charge. Sylvia was the boss, and Mother did not want to hear any more about it. The door remained closed, no matter how he pleaded.

Abruptly Walter got up from the table and carried his plate to the sink. He looked out the window at the rain and ran his fingers over the wedge-shaped scar in his forehead. It was a mistake to give a pubescent girl that kind of unlimited power. He gazed down at the hammer on the counter, wondering idly if that was the same one she had hit him with. He could not remember what offense had brought on the hammer attack. She was six years older then he, bigger and stronger, and there were many things he did that made her angry.

Emily had always known that he did not like his sister. He'd never told her much about it. Just that Sylvia had a mean streak if he didn't do what she wanted. Emily always said how their mother had placed a terrible burden on Sylvia, and Sylvia probably took it out on him. Walter just agreed with her. There was no use discussing it. Emily was always trying to excuse people's faults. He did not tell her that there were whole days in his childhood when he fantasized about . . . well . . . he never did carry out his plans for Sylvia, and he hardly thought about it anymore. They were old now. He never would.

A knock at the door made him jump, and he looked up at the back door. Through the ruffled curtains at the window, he saw the square, plain-featured face of Phyllis Hodges, distorted by the raindrops on the pane. She gesticulated for him to open the door. The expression in her eyes was eager, almost frantic.

Walter walked to the door and opened it. "Hello, Phyllis," he said.

Phyllis rushed past him like a whirlwind. "Walter," she exclaimed, "I am glad I found you. Where's Mrs. F?"

Walter frowned. "She's not feeling well."

"Oh, sorry." Phyllis dropped her voice to a whisper.

"She's not here," said Walter. "She's in the hospital."

"Hospital?" Phyllis exclaimed. "Is it serious?"

"No," said Walter shortly. "What can I do for you?"

"I tried the station, but they said you went home for supper. The chief wouldn't see me, of course. You know how he loves me."

There was a quality in Phyllis's voice that got on his nerves. It was that strident, bossy tone that was self-pitying at the same time. He hated the sound of it. Phyllis had never been attractive, even as an adolescent. She had never appealed to him.

"So, I couldn't wait. I thought, I'll catch him at home."

"What is it that couldn't wait?"

"I know how to find you an eyewitness to Eddie McHugh's murder."

Walter stared at her. Her face was pink with excitement. His heart did a queer little flip-flop, but his voice sounded impassive. "We're not sure it was a murder," he said.

"Oh, it was," said Phyllis impatiently. "We all know that."

"Phyllis, you're a little out of your depth on this." He leaned back against the corner cabinet and folded his arms over his chest.

Phyllis came closer, hemming him in. "I figured it out. Do you want to hear about it?"

"Sure," said Walter slowly. He fancied he could feel her breath, stale on his face, although that was impossible. The top of her head was barely level with his shoulders.

"Who do you think killed Eddie McHugh?" Phyllis asked. Before Walter could respond, she rattled on. "I say there's two possibilities. First, Newhall came back and killed him. It's possible. After all, Eddie claimed to have seen him beat up Linda Emery. But he might have made that up, thinking it was what the police wanted to hear. The other possibility is, what if he saw somebody else in that room? And that person got nervous when they read my article."

Naturally you would think your article was the crucial factor, Walter thought with disgust. What an arrogant fool. "You can speculate from now till doomsday," he said impatiently. "It's meaningless."

"No, that's just it," Phyllis cried. "I have a plan."

She was too close to him, yapping at him like one of Sylvia's little terriers. He could not stand being cornered any longer. "Excuse me," he said coldly.

Phyllis backed off just enough for him to brush past her. But she persisted without embarrassment. "I remembered reading about this. It just took me a while to remember where, and look it up." She handed him a piece of paper. It had the name and address of a doctor in Philadelphia on it.

"What is this?"

"The engineer," Phyllis exulted.

Walter frowned at her. "What are you talking about?"

"He claims he doesn't remember seeing what happened, right? He just saw Eddie hurtling out in front of him."

"Yes, that's what the man said."

"But he was probably in shock when you questioned him."

"We took that into account, Phyllis. He was questioned again today. He's not in shock now."

"Yes, but he's still traumatized." Phyllis could barely contain her glee. "He can't remember what he saw because he was traumatized by what happened. I mean, he killed a man. Accidentally, but all the same."

"Well, yes, unfortunately."

"So," said Phyllis, her voice rising. "This is a doctor at the University of Pennsylvania, in Philadelphia, who specializes in this sort of case. He hypnotizes people, and under hypnosis they are able to recall what they really saw. I remembered reading about a case exactly like this. A subway driver. And I finally found the article in the library. Anyway, we take our engineer to this guy, and have him hypnotized, and he'll be able to recall the person who pushed Eddie onto the tracks. Maybe he can even describe the perp."

There was something infinitely annoying about the

way Phyllis used police jargon. He knew she felt entitled, because her father had been a cop. And that flushed, triumphant expression on her face was infuriating. He forced himself to think about what she was saying. He could picture the whole thing in his mind. The engineer, deep in a trance, visualizing himself once again at the controls of the train, seeing the twilight, the tracks, the man in his path, the person who pushed him. Opening his eyes and looking straight at Walter, the answer slowly dawning on him. She was right. It was a good idea.

"What do you think?" said Phyllis proudly.

"I think it might work," said Walter.

"That's what I think," Phyllis exulted. "You know, I have a feeling I am going to get a book out of this case. And I'm going to mention you in the acknowledgments. Uncle Walter," she teased, using a sobriquet from childhood days.

"Thank you," said Walter solemnly, slipping the piece of paper with the doctor's name into his jacket pocket.

"Wait a minute," she said, reaching playfully for the paper in his pocket, like a child reaching in her daddy's pocket for candy. "It's my lead. I want to be sure I'm in on this. And that I get the credit."

Walter brushed her hand away like a fly and walked over to where the hammer lay on the counter.

"Now just a minute," said Phyllis in a huffy tone. "I came to you because I need your help on this. But that doesn't give you the right to bypass me."

It was too bad, really, Walter thought. Stan Hodges hadn't been a bad guy. They'd played some poker together, gone to picnics, done the things that cops do. It was a fraternity of sorts. All for one and so on. But

Phyllis had brought this on herself. Even Stan would have to admit that, if he were alive. Besides, he had to silence her. This thing was mushrooming out of control, and if she yapped long enough, and loud enough, people would start to listen to her. He picked up the hammer and turned to face her.

Phyllis, who was in midcomplaint, was abruptly silenced by the look on his face. "What are you doing with that hammer?" she demanded. "If you're trying to threaten me, that is really sick."

Walter did not reply. Behind the glint of his glasses, his eyes were calm and cold. He was staring at her with an intense yet distant look on his face. It was weird. Scary. She had never seen a look quite like it. It made her feel small, like a speck of dirt. His hands worked on the handle of the hammer.

"All right, you can have the stupid paper," she said. But even as she said it, she knew that it was no longer hers to give. She had the sudden, vivid realization that she should never have come here. She was in danger. She did not understand it, but she was not a stupid woman. She knew this was not the time to argue about it or try to figure it out. Just leave, she said to herself. Don't say anything else. Just go. She turned and bolted for the door. In one swift movement Walter stepped in front of her, blocking her way.

"Hey," she protested, but it was empty bravado. Her voice was breathy with fear. Move, she told herself, but she could not budge from the spot. In a moment of terrible understanding, she put up her hands as Walter swiftly lifted the hammer, aimed at her head, and whacked it down.

Chapter Thirty-two

Mom!"
The shriek from upstairs startled her.
Karen cried out and sliced her own finger
with the knife she was using to peel an apple. She fumbled for a paper towel, spattering the roll with blood as she ripped one off raggedly and stanched the oozing blood.

"What is it?" she cried, rushing down the hall, her finger raised, the blood seeping through the paper.

Jenny clattered down the steps, her face white, clutching a creased sheet of stationery and a fluttering, yellowed newspaper clipping. She stopped short when she saw her mother's hand, her eyes drawn to the splash of scarlet. "Are you okay?"

"Yes," Karen said impatiently. "What happened? Why did you yell like that?"

Jenny looked at her mother with wide eyes and held out the clipping. "Look what I found. In Linda's bank."

Karen frowned and reached out.

"No, don't get blood on them," said Jenny. "Let me get a bandage."

"Thanks," said Karen. She went and sat down on the living room sofa. Jenny reappeared with a gauze-padded bandage and, placing her clippings on the coffee table, removed the paper towel with trembling hands and slapped the bandage over the cut and the blood seeping out. Karen sat meekly, feeling like a small child as her daughter repaired her cut finger.

"There," said Jenny, crouching before her.

"Thank you, honey," said Karen.

Jenny looked up in her mother's eyes and rested her hand on one knee. "Mom, I think this is something really important."

Karen smoothed the bandage down and looked curiously at the papers on the table. "What are these?"

"Read them," said Jenny. "I found them in Linda's bank. Read the clipping first. But, be careful. They're old." She wadded up the bloodiest paper towels. "I'll throw these away. You read."

"Okay," said Karen, carefully picking up the clipping and perusing it. Jenny disappeared down the hall.

Karen read the old clipping several times. An escaped convict. Randolph Summers. A forty-year-old news story from the Midwest. It didn't tell her much, although it was surely a strange thing for a teenaged girl to save.

Karen put down the clipping and picked up the creased, faded lilac sheet of stationary. The handwriting on the paper was definitely girlish, unformed. There was no greeting. The words covered the page. There were no margins. No paragraphs. *I don't know what to do,* it began. *There is no one in the world I can tell. I've thought about it over and over, but there's no answer. If I tell what he is doing to me, then he will tell about Daddy, and Daddy will have to go back to prison for his whole life. At first I didn't think it was true, but then he brought me this clipping to prove it. The man in the picture is my father. He's right about that. So, I have to be quiet and let him do what he wants. But I can't bear it much longer. The things he does to me are terrible and so painful, too. And I can't tell. Every day I wake up and wish I was dead. I ask God to help me, but God doesn't listen. I will never be able to get married and have a normal life because he has ruined me and men will just think I am always garbage now. I know it would be a mortal sin to kill myself, but sometimes it seems like the best thing to do.*

Karen read the page over several times. Jenny crept back into the room and sat down beside her, watching her mother's face. Karen shook her head as if to deny the meaning of what she was seeing. "My God," she murmured. "Poor thing. Poor Linda."

Jenny suddenly began to cry and looked at her mother helplessly. Karen kept shaking her head. It was too awful to imagine. She squeezed her hand over Jenny's white knuckles. "Poor thing," Karen repeated, her own eyes welling with tears.

"What does it mean, Mom? Well, I mean, I know what it means, sort of. . . ."

Karen glanced at her daughter, still a child, but,

thanks to movies and television, overly wise to the sordid side of life, at least as far as information was concerned. She clenched Jenny's hand in her own. "Your mother was the victim of a horrible crime. She was being blackmailed with this information about her father."

"Her father was an escaped convict? Do you think my . . . you know, her mother knew?"

Karen shook her head slowly. "No, I don't think so. I think her father kept it a secret. And so did Linda. Just like her tormentor wanted her to do."

"And this person was blackmailing her . . . not for money," said Jenny. It was not a question.

"No," said Karen grimly. "Not for money. That poor girl."

"Wait a minute, Mom," Jenny cried. "You don't think it was Dad?"

Karen looked startled. "Dad! No, no, of course not." She read the papers again, wishing the frightened girl had named her torturer. "No, of course not," she repeated.

Like probing a diseased tooth, Jenny offered, "What about if he blackmailed her into giving me up?"

Karen knew Jenny did not believe this for a minute. She was imagining the questions from the police. Karen felt pity for her, to be so familiar with such matters. She looked up at Jenny, and for a brief, surreal moment, she felt a deep kinship with the murdered woman, an understanding as lucid as if they had shared their innermost thoughts. "There's no way she would ever have let him adopt you."

She looked down at the letter again, thinking of that

long-ago girl, trying to protect her father whom she loved, her family. Paying with everything she had, her dignity and her innocence. "No," said Karen again. "Your mother would never have knowingly given her child to a monster. But, you're right about these papers. They are very important. *This* is her killer. I feel sure of it. Your father is right. This is who she came here seeking."

"What do you mean, Dad is right?"

Karen looked up in confusion. Jenny did not know about their meeting. "I just meant . . . he told me there had to be another explanation. This is it."

Jenny gave a hollow chuckle. "And I thought she came to see me."

"She did," Karen reassured her absently, ruminating on all that these documents implied. "But it wasn't the only reason. . . ."

"But why?" Jenny protested. "Why after all this time? All these years. It doesn't make sense."

"Mmmm . . ." Karen frowned, thinking of the things that Linda had told them. She had come back to meet Jenny. She had come back for Mother's Day. She had come back because she had learned . . . and then suddenly Karen understood why. It all made sense. "Because he's dead now," she said.

"Who?" asked Jenny, confused.

"Her father," said Karen. "She told us her father died a few months ago. That means the blackmailer had nothing over her anymore. Once her father was dead, she was free to come back, to expose him. Her father couldn't be sent back to prison."

Jenny shrieked and jumped to her feet. "You're right! That's right. Mom, you're a genius."

Karen motioned for her to sit down. "Don't get too excited. We still don't know who it is." She looked out the window at the darkness, the rain on the windows, and felt suddenly vulnerable. Someone evil had chosen to entangle them in this, had pinned the blame on Greg. Someone depraved, who knew too much about them. For a minute she allowed herself to wish that Greg were there with them. She hated being alone in the house, just her and Jenny. *No one knows about these papers,* she reminded herself. *No one knows you have them. The killer thinks his secret is safe.*

"Yeah, but the police can find out who it is, now that we have these papers. And Dad can come home."

Karen shook her head. "It's not that simple."

"Why not? Let's call them up and tell them."

"Let me think," said Karen. "We need to do the right thing."

"Come on, Mom. The sooner you tell them, the sooner Dad will be able to come back."

Karen stood up and walked out to the phone in the hall. Jenny followed her, jiggling impatiently from foot to foot.

"Who are you calling?" she asked as Karen dialed and held the receiver to her ear.

"Our lawyer," she said. "Mr. Richardson."

"Don't call him. He can't do anything."

Even as her daughter pestered her, Karen listened with a sinking sensation to the recording on Arnold Richardson's office machine. "Mr. Richardson is away on business. You can contact him at his office on Tuesday morning."

Let down, Karen hung up the phone. "He's away for the weekend," she said.

"Let's go to the police," Jenny cried. She whirled around in a spin and hugged herself. "I've saved him," she crowed. "I've saved my dad."

"Hush," said Karen sharply, staring down at the documents she clutched in her hand. "Hush, I'm thinking."

Chapter Thirty-three

The Harborview Bar was in Dartswich, a fishing town about twenty miles from Bayland. It was a considerably less popular and prosperous town than Bayland, having suffered from the shutdown of a cannery and a much publicized problem with chemical wastes. The bar, like the town, had a dreary, depressed aspect to it. Its decor was a tired, nautical theme, with a fishnet canopy across the ceiling and scarred captain's chairs surrounding the tables. There was a jukebox for music, and hits from the fifties filled the smoky length of the gloomy tavern. Greg found it almost funny that he felt overdressed in his borrowed chinos and golf shirt. Most of the patrons wore T-shirts or rumpled work shirts. A few of the patrons looked up disinterestedly when he came in, then went back to their beers. Greg slid onto a barstool, gave the guy two stools down a forced smile, and then gazed at the female bartender, waiting to catch her eye.

Finally she came down to his end, her hair pulled back in a ponytail, her rather sloppy torso encased in a loose T-shirt that read "Surf's up" on the front. "What'll it be?" she asked.

Greg knew better than to try to get information without ordering a drink, although he was so ill nourished that he was apprehensive about the effect alcohol might have on him. The girl, who had clearly pegged him as the imported bottled-brew type, nodded approvingly when he ordered a draft. She drew it and set it in front of him. Greg placed a five-dollar bill on the bar and waved off the change when she rang it up. It was almost the last money he had, but, he thought wryly, there was nowhere he could spend it anyway. He pretended to sip his beer and waited. As he expected, she drifted back down in his direction when her scattered customers were satisfied.

Greg began a jittery conversation about the weather and segued into the Red Sox. The woman, who answered to Yvonne from the other customers, shook her head as if to separate the greasy bangs that brushed her eyebrows. She lit a cigarette and leaned back against the shelves of liquor. Like any good bartender, she let him lead the conversation. Greg could feel his heart hammering, and his lips were dry as he approached his purpose.

"Look," he said in a low voice, "I'm not just here for a beer."

Yvonne took a drag on her Marlboro, screwed up her lips, and nodded, regarding him coolly.

Greg fished in his pocket and pulled out the picture. "The truth is, I'm looking for some information."

Yvonne shook her head in disgust. "A cop," she said.

"I'm not a cop," Greg protested, placing the picture carefully on the bar. "This is my wife."

"Oh," said Yvonne, ignoring the picture.

"I know she's been running around on me. I found the name of this place in her diary with a notation for a week ago, Monday. No offense, but this is not the kind of place she would ever go to with the girls."

Yvonne smiled ruefully, acknowledging the truth of that.

"I have my suspicions about who the guy is," he said. "But I need to know."

"Why don't you just ask her?" Yvonne suggested, stubbing out her cigarette.

Greg shook his head. He picked up the photo and offered it to her. "Were you working that night?" he asked.

Yvonne thought back. "Last Monday? Yeah."

"Can you just look?"

Yvonne tried to appear disinterested, but curiosity had the best of her. She took the picture and glanced at it. Then she handed it back to Greg. "Yeah," she said.

"Yeah, what?" Greg asked, his heart leaping.

"She was here."

"Just like that?" It was like the car door snapping open. It was his luck changing.

"You want to know or don't you?"

"With . . ."

"A man." Yvonne shrugged.

Playing his role, Greg smacked his hand on the bar. "That bitch. Do you remember what he looked like?"

Yvonne chuckled. "I wouldn't forget those two," she said, enjoying the surprise and curiosity on Greg's face.

"Hey, Yvonne, another round here."

Yvonne gave Greg a Cheshire cat smile. "Customer," she said.

Greg sat back on the stool, amazed. A witness. It was so easy—if you knew where to look. Hope flared inside of him. She could save him. Surely this would save him. It proved that Linda was with someone else that night, someone long after he was home. He would be free. He tried not to think of the problems, the possibilities that awaited him from here. The main thing right now was to be able to rid himself of a murder charge. He looked down the bar at the unlovely Yvonne, and she seemed like a guardian angel.

As she meandered back down the bar, lighting another cigarette, Greg wanted to grab her up in an embrace. Thank you again, Lord. I don't deserve it, but thank you.

Yvonne pointed her cigarette at his glass. "Something wrong with that beer?"

Greg shook his head. "My stomach's in a knot," he said truthfully.

"Beer's good for that."

Greg did not want to waste any time. "I'm surprised you remembered them so easily," he said.

"Oh, they were easy to remember all right," she said flatly. "He's a cop."

Greg stared at her as if she were speaking another language.

"Your wife's boyfriend is a cop."

Greg felt suddenly light-headed and weak. "How do you know he's a cop?"

"How do you think I remembered them?" she asked, pleased with the effect of her revelation. "He came up to the bar, and I noticed he had a piece under his jacket. I thought for sure I was about to get robbed, or worse. But when he went to pay, I saw the shield in his wallet. It gave me a few bad moments, though."

"A cop." Greg slumped on the barstool, hope leaving him like air from a punctured tire.

"Wasn't who you thought, eh?"

Greg shook his head.

"Hey, maybe she's not fooling around. Maybe it's something else. They didn't even look friendly to me, never mind lovey-dovey. Besides, the guy was old enough to be her father."

Greg tried to collect his thoughts. "What did he look like?"

Yvonne thought it over for a minute. "Gray hair, glasses, those wire kind. Oh, and a weird dent in his forehead. Some kind of scar."

Greg recognized the description at once. The detective in charge of Linda's case. Walter Ference. It couldn't be. He did not ever remember Linda mentioning anyone on the police force. Although, he had to admit to himself that there was very little he knew about Linda at the time of their affair. He knew she was troubled, but she was quiet about it. She was secretive, and he had not tried to find out why. But why would Walter Ference . . .? Well, whatever the reason, it explained a lot of things. All along Greg had been thinking that whoever framed him had known about his affair with Linda for years. Walter Ference may only have known about it for hours. After the witness he mentioned came forward with the information, Ference saw a suspect with an ideal motive staring him in the face, and he framed Greg with the room key. He had been in the ideal position to frame Greg. Yes, Greg thought. It made sense. But it also destroyed his hope of exoneration. He tried to visualize himself going to the police and accusing Walter Ference. Hey, guys, I've got a suspect for you. Your boss. He looked back at Yvonne. He had only one hope left, and before he spoke, he had a good idea of what her answer would be. Most people were definitely reluctant to start pointing the finger at the police. But he had to try to convince her.

Greg leaned over the bar. "I need your help," he said urgently.

Yvonne barked out a derisive laugh. "I know what's coming. No way, hon. Forget it."

"Please," he said. "I need someone who can identify him."

Yvonne shook her head. "Rat on a cop? Sure buddy. I've got a death wish."

"You're the only one who can help me," Greg pleaded.

"Look," said Yvonne. "I'm sorry for your problem, but I don't mess with cops. Hire a private dick to follow them and take pictures. Leave me out of it."

Greg felt both light-headed and nauseated. He had only had a few sips of the beer, to placate Yvonne, but combined with the stress, it made him feel sick. "You don't understand," he said helplessly. He realized that he could not explain. He was a fugitive from a murder charge. "Please," he said, feeling muddled, trying not to sound desperate. "I could have a lawyer call you."

Her eyes narrowed at his persistence, his ingratitude. Most of all, she disliked the mention of the lawyer. She wanted to make it perfectly clear that she did not intend to cooperate. Period. "Look," she said in a shrill voice, "get this straight. I never saw you. I never saw them. I don't know anything. That's what I tell anyone who asks me. *Capisce?*"

"But . . ." He tried to reach for her forearm, as if it were a life preserver.

"Are you having problems here, babe?" A burly, red-faced customer approached the stool where Greg was sitting, his glowering eyes on Greg, who averted his face, fearful of being recognized.

"Get out of here," said Yvonne. "Beat it."

Greg slid off the stool. It was useless to try to pressure her. She didn't owe him anything. She wasn't about to change her mind. And it was definitely not a good idea to draw attention to himself this way. He had to think, and he couldn't think here.

"Okay," he mumbled. "Thanks for talking to me. Sorry." He kept his eyes lowered as he hurried toward the door, anxious to get out of range of the suspicious gaze of Yvonne's pot-bellied knight in shining armor.

Chapter Thirty-four

W alter cautiously circled the parking lot of the giant Cape Shore Mall in Phyllis's gray Volvo and finally chose a space in the middle, toward the front. He didn't want an outlying space. Some bored employee might stare at it long enough and realize the car hadn't moved for days. Here, where it was busy, nobody kept track of which cars came and went. It could be weeks before anyone noticed the car. And time was important. He needed time.

The rain was a lucky factor for him. Not even teenagers were idling in the parking lot in this weather. He got out of the car, with his hat pulled down and his collar up, and walked quickly into the main entrance of the mall, just in case anyone had watched him pull in. It would look strange for someone to park a car at a mall and then walk away from the mall. He went up and down two aisles of the indoor maze and then headed back out into the night. He kept his head down and walked quickly to the bus stop. There was a smaller mall within a few miles of his house, one he could have walked home from, but he knew how conspicuous he would look walking along in the rain. He couldn't take the chance that someone might recognize him, might offer him a ride. No, he had chosen the Cape Shore Mall because it was new and huge and out of the way. To bring in the maximum business, the store owners supported a bus service to all the surrounding towns. Walter had plenty of company on the bus on this rainy night. He took a seat near the back. People were trying to keep their distance from one another to avoid wet coats and umbrellas. He looked out into the darkness and saw his own face reflected in the window, raindrops sliding like tears down the glass.

It was a plain, normal face, except for that dent over the eyebrow made by the hammer. There was nothing about his face that suggested he had beaten a woman to death an hour earlier. Walter folded his gloved hands in his lap, and as the bus bumped along, he went over his plans in his mind.

Before he left the house, he had moved Phyllis's body down to the basement. The basement door gave out onto the driveway, and his car was right beside it. Later tonight he would be able to load the body quickly into his trunk and take off. No one in the neighborhood thought anything of his coming and going at all hours. It was part of his job. As far as where he would take the body, he had given that a lot of thought.

He had considered stuffing Phyllis into the trunk of

her own car and leaving her, and her car, at the mall. But, after examining the options, he decided it would be best if it looked as if she had been abducted from the mall. That would make it seem random. He wanted to dump the body where it wouldn't be found for months, so that it could decompose. The less that was left of her, the less evidence there would be. Every cop knew that. He had been lucky with Rachel Dobbs, the girl they all called Amber. Even he thought of her as Amber by now. He had not been so lucky with Linda.

The Dumpster had seemed like a good idea for Linda's body. If only that couple had not been tossing out their trash illegally, Linda would have been hauled off to the nearest landfill without incident. He could not help but feel that things were beginning to turn against him. A frown crossed his face, causing the pale-skinned scar on his forehead to pucker. He had never set out to kill anyone. He was not that sort of person. The thing with Amber had really been an accident. It was really unfair for anyone to blame him for that.

A heavyset woman cleared her throat and glared at Walter. He looked up to see her eyeing his umbrella disapprovingly. He moved it off the seat beside him. The woman made an ostentatious show of wiping off the seat with a shredding tissue, and then she wriggled into it. Walter pressed himself up against the side of the bus.

He found most adult women rather repulsive. For as long as he could remember he had a preference for young teenage girls. His sexual fantasies all involved bondage and discipline, B & D, as the vice cops called it. But they were just fantasies, for years. He'd had a

taste of the real thing in Vietnam, where teenage prosti-
tutes were commonplace. He'd even broken a girl's
nose, but some American dollars had smoothed it over
with the madam of the brothel. When he came home to
the States, he just told himself that he would have to be
satisfied with fantasies. And he probably would have
been. But then fate stepped in.

It started when he was investigating an armed robbery, doing his usual thorough job, and by chance he
came across that information about Randolph
Summers. And he knew he recognized that face. It took
him a while to figure it out. It was ironic—the answer
had actually come to him in church. He was in a pew
behind Jack Emery and his family. He was not paying
attention to the sermon, just sitting beside Emily, staring at the beautiful young girl in front of him, imagining what her budding body looked like under the
flower-printed dress she was wearing. She had a white
lace mantilla resting on her dark, shiny hair, and her father would squeeze her hand now and then and smile at
her. One of those times, it came to him in a flash.
Walter suddenly realized where he had seen Randolph
Summers's face before. It was Jack Emery. If they had
been on the street, he might have collared the man then
and there. But they were in church. He couldn't very
well jump up and rip the rosary out of the man's hand
and haul him in. So he sat quietly, waiting for the mass
to end. And it was while he was sitting there, preparing
to arrest the man, that the idea came to him about Jack
Emery's daughter.

"What street is this?" asked the woman beside him.

Walter started and peered out the window. He had

lost track of time, remembering. "Congress Street," he muttered.

The woman hoisted herself up off the seat and started toward the door. Walter exhaled, glad to be rid of her.

His mind returned to Linda. She had been his to command, for several years. He had acted out every fantasy, enjoyed every release. It had worked out better than he had ever dreamed. And then she ran away. For a long time he had stifled his impulses, made do with pornography, and dreamed of his retirement, when he could return to Asia. He had used all his self-control, knowing he would never come across a situation as perfect as the one with Linda Emery. And then, off duty one day, he had caught Rachel Dobbs in the act of shoplifting a Walkman in a tape and CD store. He'd followed her outside and accosted her. She'd turned out to be a runaway from Seattle. She had no one to vouch for her. She was scared and willing to do anything. And he couldn't resist.

But it had been a mistake. He didn't have the same kind of grip on her that he had on Linda. She started to threaten him, and his temper got the best of him. Something about the way she defied him was infuriating, and that hammer in the toolbox was close at hand. Walter shifted uneasily on his seat. Suddenly the lights in the bus seemed uncomfortably bright.

"Bayland," the bus driver called out.

Walter squinted out at the street signs. He would wait for a few blocks, get off at the main street. It was only a short walk from there. He pulled the cord overhead and waited until the last moment to step up to the back

doors and climb down onto the curb. It was good to be
back in the darkness.

He opened his umbrella, put his head down, and
started the few blocks toward the house. He had gotten
rid of the car. That was one big job out of the way. Now
he had to dispose of the body. Luckily his police train-
ing helped him to avoid costly mistakes, leaving telltale
evidence and so on. He had thought it over carefully
and decided that the best place to put her was a summer
house that would not be in use this year because the
people were going to Europe and had decided not to
rent it out. He knew this for a fact because the police
were supposed to check on the place every week. But
they would not be checking in the two-car garage.
There was no reason to. No one would open those
doors for six months, maybe a year.

Walter glanced up and could see his own house in
the near distance. In the daylight you could see the
peeling paint, the broken shingles, but in the darkness it
still looked imposing. Walter's father, Henry Ference,
had been a famous attorney, and Walter sometimes felt
as if he had inherited his cleverness. He often thought
he could have been just as successful as his father. It
was just that circumstances had gone against him.
There was no money for the Ivy League education by
the time Walter grew up. He had settled for the police
force, but things still seemed to go wrong for him.

Like this business with Phyllis. She had come up
with that hypnosis idea, and she would never let go of
it. She was like a dog with a bone. And Walter knew
that when the engineer remembered the face of the man

who pushed Eddie McHugh, the face would be Walter's.

This whole thing was having a ripple effect. He had never intended to do another killing after Amber. That had terrified him when it happened. But then Linda had come around with her threats. She was going to expose him. Some nonsense about DNA testing, to prove that Jenny Newhall was his child. Only it wasn't nonsense. She could ruin him. He didn't know, at the time, that she'd also told Greg Newhall that he was the child's father. All he knew was that killing her had been necessary—no choice. But once he had put her in the Dumpster, he had to go back to her room, to make sure she had kept nothing that might implicate him. What he didn't realize was that Eddie McHugh had been waiting for her light to go on, ready to peep at her. And he'd seen Walter instead, searching through her things. Eddie let that information drop when Walter was questioning him at the police station. He thought it would get him off of the peeping charge with Phyllis. He'd realized his mistake as soon as the words were out of his mouth. Eddie got a lot more than he bargained for. Walter hated to admit it, even to himself, but pushing Eddie in front of that train had not been that difficult. He had always heard it said, especially by the guys who worked in the prison system, that when a man killed once, it got easier and easier to kill again. He'd always thought of that sort of person as an animal. He was not like that. He was civilized. The only reason he had killed these people was because it was absolutely necessary. It wasn't something he liked doing. But he had to admit that it did get easier.

Walter reached the front steps of his house and bounded up them the normal way. There was no use worrying about it. He was almost in the clear. He just had to concentrate on what needed to be done. He would have a hot cup of tea to take the chill off and then get on with moving the body. He slammed the front door behind him, relocked it, and stared down the gloomy hall. Suddenly a figure appeared in the dark before him.

"Jesus Christ," Walter cried.

"It's me, Walter," said Emily.

"What are you doing here?" he demanded furiously.

Emily looked apologetic. "I couldn't stand it. I checked myself out. I took a cab home. Please don't be mad at me."

Walter just stared at her.

Chapter Thirty-five

"What happened to the picture?" Emily asked timidly, pouring her husband a cup of tea. Walter glanced at the hole in the plaster, the light spot on the wallpaper where the picture had been. He had swept the picture off the table and into a trash bag in his hasty clean-up before he left the house with Phyllis's car. It was automatic. He wanted to rid the room of anything that connoted a struggle, even though the picture had fallen before Phyllis ever arrived. "It fell," he said shortly.

"Did the glass break?"

Walter hesitated. "Yes. I threw it out."

Emily nodded and pressed her lips together. "I'll have to get something to put there," she said.

"Yeah," said Walter, staring out over his teacup. They both knew she never would.

There was silence in the kitchen, except for the loud gulping sound Emily made as she drank a ginger ale. She placed the glass down on the table, then picked it up and wiped the table beneath it carefully with a napkin. "I know you're mad that I came home," she said tentatively.

"No, I'm not mad."

"I just felt so uncomfortable there," she said. "All the personal questions. I didn't mind the withdrawal so much. Honestly. I mean it was bad, but I guess I deserved that. It was more the groups and all the psychologizing. I just hated it. They kept wanting me to talk about . . . you know, the past. They aren't happy unless you're telling them everything. And there's . . . I just . . . I believe some things are between a person and God."

Walter nodded.

"But I really think I'm going to be okay this time. I really do."

"That's good," said Walter, taking another sip from his cup.

Emily sat back and felt the old familiar heaviness settling onto her heart. He wouldn't criticize her. He never did. He never got mad at her or objected to what she did. There was no reason to explain any of it to him. He was the perfect husband, she thought, and she felt that void inside of her again that had temporarily been relieved in the hospital. She knew what other people thought—they thought she should be grateful. Most men would have thrown her out long ago or beat her up or something. Walter never lost his temper with her.

Tears rose to her eyes. She wiped them away. He did not seem to notice.

The ringing of the phone startled them both. Emily looked at her husband fearfully. "That might be Sylvia," she said.

"I don't want to talk to her," said Walter.

"She'll wonder why I'm home," said Emily worriedly.

"It's none of her business," said Walter.

Emily could see that he wasn't going to answer the phone. She wished she was one of those people who could just sit by a phone and let it ring, but it made her feel too guilty. If someone was calling her, it was her duty to answer. Slowly she felt her insides shrivel at the prospect of hearing Sylvia's voice on the other end, critical and shrill. She licked her lips and whispered, "Hello?"

"Mrs. Ference?" asked an unfamiliar voice.

"Yes," Emily agreed uneasily.

"My name is Karen Newhall. I know it's late and I'm sorry to bother you and your husband at home, but I need to speak to Detective Ference."

Emily's heart filled with relief. She knew it wouldn't last. Sylvia would find out before long—but at least for now she was safe. She held out the phone to Walter. "It's for you," she said.

Walter pushed back his chair, walked over, and took the phone. "Yes," he said.

Emily took their cups and saucers and rinsed them in the sink. Then she began to dry them.

"What kind of information?" Walter asked suspiciously, his voice low. He turned his back to his wife.

"Well, you did the right thing to call me," said Walter. "But listen, there's no need for you to come down to the station. I'll come to your house. I'm sure you've seen enough of that place already. . . . Okay. Okay. I'll see you then." Walter hung up the phone.

"I need to go out," he said.

Emily nodded. "That's okay. I'll be fine," she said, although he hadn't asked. "I'll go to bed early." She knew better than to inquire about the call. Walter never liked to discuss such matters at home.

"You might have trouble sleeping," he said. "Maybe you should take something. I have some sleeping pills."

"No," said Emily. "No pills. They're as bad as alcohol. I learned that at the counseling. They call that substituting one dependency for another. No, if I can't sleep, I'll just watch TV or clean out a closet or something," she said, forcing a smile.

Walter sighed and gazed at the cellar door, which was across the kitchen. It was unlikely that she would go down into the cellar. She was afraid of the dark, the cobwebs. It was a chance in a million, but still, there was that chance. And there was no use locking the door. It would only make her curious if she tried it, and besides, it only locked from the outside upstairs anyway. He watched his wife, moving around the kitchen, tidying up, her hands still shaking from the alcohol withdrawal.

No, he thought, there was only one way to guarantee she would be in no condition to go into the cellar, or anywhere else, for a while. He needed to be sure she would be incapacitated tonight. He walked out into the hallway and opened the door to the antique lowboy. He removed a bottle of vodka from where she had hidden it behind the good china in the back. He set the bottle carefully on top between a vase of dried flowers and a framed photograph of his mother. Then he opened the door to the hall closet and called out to Emily.

"Have you seen my other raincoat? It's still raining out there, and this one is wet."

Emily came shuffling innocently out of the kitchen. She had put on her bedroom slippers as soon as she came home. "I'm sure it's in there," she said. "It's probably jammed between two coats."

Walter nodded to the vodka bottle on the lowboy. "By the way, I found that. You'll probably want to pour it down the sink or something."

Emily's gaze rested with fear and longing on the bottle. "Yes, I will," she said.

Walter continued to rummage in the closet and made a display of finding the missing coat. "Oh, you're right," he said. "Here it is." Then he looked down at something on the closet floor as if surprised. "Look at these," he said, reaching back into the closet and holding up a pair of dusty, black tooled cowboy boots. "Now this is the closet to clean if you're in the mood for cleaning tonight," he said. He shook his head and gazed fondly at the boots. "I must have been sixteen when I got these."

"A lot of things need cleaning out," Emily admitted apologetically.

Walter examined the dusty boots and then gave a noisy sigh. "I was saving these for the boys, for Joe and little Ted. I thought they'd wear them someday."

Emily's face turned chalky white, and she could not tear her gaze from the boots in Walter's hands.

Walter shook his head and handed them to her. "They're no use to us now. Here's the first thing you might want to toss out."

"No," said Emily, putting up her hands. "No, don't."

Walter frowned as if perplexed by her reaction. "Well, I don't see any reason to keep them any longer. It's not as if the children are ever coming back."

Emily covered her mouth with her hand and turned her back to him.

He placed the boots on the lowboy, beside the vodka bottle. "Well, you do what you want with them," he said. "I've got to go."

Emily nodded but did not look at him as he left the house. Once he was gone, she walked over to the lowboy and picked up the boots. She stared at them, turning them over in her trembling hands. Then she walked over and replaced them in the closet. She straightened up, but she did not want to turn around. It was as if the bottle on the lowboy was calling to her, in a voice that only she could hear.

Chapter Thirty-six

I'm glad we don't have to go to the police station," said Jenny, pulling back the curtain to see if Detective Ference had arrived in the driveway yet.

"You're going to wear that curtain out," Karen observed. "You'll be able to hear the car when he gets here."

Jenny shrugged and flopped down on the sofa. "I just want to get this thing over with," she said.

"I know," said Karen, looking out at the rain. The rain had actually been the deciding factor. She had debated what to do—whether or not to wait for Arnold Richardson's return or to call the police, as Jenny was urging her to do. It was the rain that had helped her to make up her mind. She kept picturing Greg out there, trying to find shelter from the drizzle. It was a habit of long-standing, to worry about his health, his well-

being. For years, every time he was out on a job and it
started to rain, she automatically worried that he might
get soaked and get a cold. He teased her about it. He
told her she liked to worry. Now she found she couldn't
stop herself from thinking that way. No matter what
he'd done to her, to their marriage, he was an innocent
man, and he was hiding out, God knew where, being
hunted down as a dangerous criminal when he could be
safely back . . .well, maybe not at home, but at least in
some kind of civilized place. It was not fair to deny
him safety, or delay it, even for a couple of days. Jenny
was right. She had to act right away.

Jenny flipped on the TV. The sound of the canned
laugh track on the show she was watching grated on
Karen's nerves. "Honey, would you mind turning that
thing off," she said.

"I'm just trying to pass the time," Jenny said huffily.

"I know, but that noise . . ."

"All right, all right."

Karen looked at the envelope on the coffee table and
wondered, for the umpteenth time, if she had done the
right thing. She had tried to be cautious. Greg had an
office in the finished basement where he did the paperwork for his business. Karen had used the copy machine in that office to make copies of both the clipping
and the letter. Then she had locked the originals in his
office safe. If the police weren't satisfied with the
copies, then they would just have to wait for Arnold
Richardson to get back. At least she would have tried.

"I think it was nice of that Detective Ference to say
he'd come here," said Jenny.

Karen smiled wryly. "Sometimes you remind me so much of your father."

"Why?" Jenny asked.

"Oh, you know how he is when things are going his way. He loves everybody."

"What's wrong with that?" Jenny asked defensively.

"Nothing," said Karen. "Just mentioning."

"Besides, you must have liked Detective Ference, too. That's why you called him, wasn't it?"

"I called him because he is in charge of this investigation. I'm not about to show these papers to whatever desk sergeant is on the night shift."

"But he *has* been decent to us," Jenny persisted. "Compared to some of the others."

Karen sighed. "I suppose so. I'll tell you, though. I won't mind the day when I don't have to see him or any other cop ever again in this house."

"Me neither." Jenny hesitated. "Of course, once Dad gets home there'll probably still be some cops who want to come here and talk to him."

Karen could hardly miss the question behind the awkward statement. "Let's just worry about this for the moment, shall we?"

But Jenny would not be put off. "You are going to let him come home, aren't you?"

Karen looked away from her and did not answer.

"Mom, you have to," Jenny cried.

"I hear a car in the driveway," Karen murmured.

Jenny was torn for a moment, and then she rushed to the window and peered out through the raindrops. "Our watchdog is leaving," she said. "And another car is coming down the drive."

This is it, Karen thought to herself. She got up with a nervous sigh and walked to the front door. She opened it up and looked out as Walter Ference emerged from his car.

"He's here," she said.

Greg crouched, shivering, in the opening of a hedge and stared up at Walter Ference's house. The chills had begun as he was driving back from Dartswich and had intensified after he left off the car at the train station. He had found the detective's address in a phone book outside the station and made his way here. All the way over, he had felt physically worse and worse. At first he thought it might be from the small amount of beer he had in the bar on an empty stomach. But alcohol did not make your bones ache. By now he knew he had a fever.

Greg looked over the big house, recognizing it. He had often driven by it in the past, noticing in a cursory way the myriad signs of neglect on the grand old place. He recalled having wished he could get his hands on it, have a crack at renovating it, thinking it must have been a showpiece in its day.

The drizzle seeped under his collar and accumulated in his already soaked shirt. His throat was scratchy and his joints ached. Even his eyelids hurt to blink. He thought about Karen, always warning him to wear his slicker, worrying when he got caught in the rain. You always said I'd get sick, he thought. Not that it matters much now.

He did not recall much about the drive home from Dartswich. It was partly the fever, partly because his mind was completely preoccupied with what he had learned. He had found out who his enemy was. He just didn't know what to do about it. When he reached the railroad station, he was already trying to think of where he could spend the night—what deserted frame of a house or unlocked utility shed could he cower in—and then suddenly he was struck by a moment of delirious revelation. He was hiding from a man who had framed him for murder. He was hiding, like a rat in a sewer. He could die out there, running from his enemy. And he was an innocent man. With a clarity that had eluded him until that moment, Greg suddenly decided that he was not going to run away anymore, no matter what. It would be better to face his nemesis, man to man, than to die in hiding.

It had been a short move, born of feverish logic, from that revelation to this spot in the hedge, from where Greg now observed his enemy's house. There was no car in the driveway, no lights visible in the place. If ever a house appeared deserted, this one did.

He knew what his intention was. He intended to get into the house. He intended to take Walter Ference by surprise. He wanted to see him jump when he realized who it was who had gained entry to his home. He wanted to confront him with his crimes, show him that he was not going to hide from him any longer. He wanted to threaten him. If Ference was gone, he would wait for him. He would be ready for him, whenever he came back.

Greg scoped out the entrances from his spot in the bushes. The front and back doors were too visible, even in the darkness. The cellar door, which gave out onto

the empty driveway, was probably locked, he thought.
His best hope was a broken windowpane in the founda-
tion window. It was a double-hung window. It could be
lifted, although Greg knew it would not be lifted easily.
The windows were so grimy, they were virtually
opaque. But it was a possibility.

Just as he was about to dart out of the hedge, he
heard the door of the house next door open, and a man
stepped out into a pool of light on the porch. Greg drew
back into the bushes, holding his breath. "Rusty," the
man called out, and waited for an answering bark,
which didn't come. He called back into the house,
"Lillian, did you let Rusty out?" There was an answering murmur from inside. "Where is that damn dog?"
the man muttered, going back inside and slamming the
door.

Quiet returned to the night, and Greg took a good
look around before scurrying out across the narrow side
yard to the wall of the house. He tried the basement
door. As he suspected, it was locked. He crawled down
by the window and pulled the rags out of the broken
pane, examining the stiff lock with the aid of a penlight
he had purloined from the glove compartment of the
Toyota. There were cobwebs growing all around the
lock. This would not be easy, Greg thought. He put his
arm carefully through the window and reached inside,
pressing himself up against the outer wall of the foun-
dation. He did not have a good angle on it, and it was
hard to get a grip on the lock to turn it. He grimaced at
the effort, working it back and forth, hearing the reluctant lock creak with every millimeter it moved.

Greg felt weak and light-headed, but he persisted,

pushing with all that was left of his strength, until finally the wedge shifted, and the lock gave way. Carefully Greg removed his forearm through the broken pane and began to jimmy the window as best he could. He did not think about what he would do when he got inside. He just continued to work the window, rocking it to loosen it. With a groan he pushed with all his might, and the sash lifted. He exhaled a short, triumphant sigh, then froze as he heard panting behind him and felt hot breath on his neck.

He snapped his head around and looked into the dark, inquisitive eyes of a big, shaggy red dog. He looked warily at the animal, but it did not seem hostile to him, merely curious. If this dog belonged to Walter Ference, Greg was going to have to scuttle the mission. He'd never get into the house. Carefully Greg reached out and lifted the dog's tag, looking at it with his penlight. "Rusty," it read. "Lund, 27 Hickory Drive, Bayland, Mass." Greg dropped the tag and gave the furry ruff of the dog a pat. "Good boy, Rusty," he whispered. It felt so good to touch the warmth, the soft fur of the dog, that Greg briefly rested his forehead against the dog's side. Rusty twisted his head around and licked Greg's nose. "Thanks, Rusty," he said. "G'wan now."

The dog did not move but sat, watching curiously, as Greg heaved open the window and stuck his feet, then his legs, inside, oozing under the bottom of the raised sash like a limbo dancer. He fell to the floor of the cellar with a gentle thud. He was in. He slid down the wall, masonry crumbling and pebbles falling into his shirt, and rested there, savoring his victory. He heard

the dog outside get up and pad away, rustling through
the hedge. Greg suddenly felt too weary to move, too
exhausted to do what he intended to do. There were
nonsense images flashing through his mind. He realized, with a kind of detached alarm, that he was close
to passing out.

Greg rubbed his parched lips with the back of his
hand and shook his head as if to shake off the en-
croaching delirium. You have to stay alert, he said to
himself. That seemed to help. He shined his penlight
around the basement, examining the lair of the man
who had destroyed him. Water pooled in patches on the
floor, and the basement ceiling was low. He could tell
that without even standing up. Rusted appliances lay on
their sides, like sleeping polar bears, and pieces of furniture were piled haphazardly about. A series of
shelves holding paints, hardware items, and cardboard
boxes lined the walls. The odor in the basement was
foul and musty.

Greg forced himself to his feet. When he stood up,
the top of his head grazed a rafter. On the opposite wall
to where he had landed, there was a sofa bed that was
open, a tangle of sheets with dark stains piled on top of
it. Using his penlight, he picked a path through the de-
bris, past an old high chair, an overturned cradle, and a
cardboard box full of tax forms. He had to get upstairs,
into the house. He made his way toward the staircase,
his eyes adjusting to the darkness now. He had become
used to living without light. It made him feel like a bat.

He shivered, overcome again by the chills. It was
May, and the outside temperature was not cold, despite
the drizzle. But to Greg it felt arctic. On the wall beside

the back door he saw a bunch of clothes hanging from a pipe that ran across the ceiling. He could see that some were dresses, but there were other, shorter garments, too. A jacket, he thought. It might help. He made his way through the mess to where the clothes were hanging. There were several jackets and some heavy flannel shirts in the bunch. He picked out a flannel shirt, which appeared to have a checkered pattern, and pulled it on. It smelled rank and felt scratchy against his skin, but its warmth was as soothing as a blanket.

He turned back toward the staircase, moved forward, and struck his head against a hanging light fixture. He dropped his penlight but managed not to cry out. The feeble beam shut off as it hit the floor. Above him, the house was silent as a tomb. Swearing to himself, he bent down and began to grope around for the penlight. He would need it upstairs. He did not want to turn on any lights. He fumbled blindly across the floor, seeking the narrow cylinder he had dropped. He reached out, and his probing fingers felt the unmistakable sensation of human flesh beneath his fingertips. Cold flesh. Five fingers. A human hand. He gasped and fell backward, clutching his chest. His eyes made out the dim form of a person sitting, legs outstretched, on the basement floor.

Chapter Thirty-seven

W alter picked up the photocopy of the newspaper article and scanned it.

"That newspaper clipping was really old," Jenny offered. She was seated across from him on the sofa, next to her mother. "It's all yellow and flaky."

Without a word he picked up the other page and read it. For a long time he studied the note, as if he were memorizing it.

Karen watched his impassive expression, holding her breath, waiting for his reaction.

Still staring at the paper, Walter said, "Where did you get these?"

"In Linda's bank," Jenny said. Then she looked up at Karen. "Should I tell him, Mom?"

"Sure," said Karen.

Walter's gaze was inscrutable behind his glasses as he listened to Jenny. Excitedly she recounted how she had come to possess the bank, how she had discovered its contents.

"I see," said Walter when she had finished.

The detective's response was disappointing. Jenny looked at Karen, wondering if her rendering of the tale had been inadequate. Karen leaned forward in her seat and pointed to the papers.

"What do you think? It seems to me this casts doubt on my husband's guilt."

"What makes you say that?" Walter asked.

"Isn't it obvious? Linda Emery was the victim of extortion for sex, as a teenager. She came back to expose her attacker. Now that's a motive for murder."

"Unless the extortionist was your husband," Walter said calmly.

"Oh, come on, Detective," said Karen. "She gave us her baby."

"My mom figured it out," Jenny piped up eagerly. "She had to wait until her father was dead to come back. So he couldn't be put back in prison."

Walter shook his head. "That's quite a theory."

"It's true," Jenny cried.

"It might be," he said. "If these really were her papers."

"They *are* her papers," Jenny insisted.

"Stop it, Jenny," said Karen sharply. She turned to the detective. "I told you, and I am willing to swear to this in court. We found those papers in Linda's bank where she hid them."

"I'm just wondering," he said.

"Wondering what?"

"Wondering if maybe this isn't a rather bold effort on your part to fabricate something to save your husband."

"That's ridiculous," said Karen, her face reddening. It was infuriating to her the way the policeman's suggestion could make her feel guilty, even though she wasn't.

Walter shrugged. "I'm afraid I'm not the only one who's going to think that."

"No," Jenny wailed. Tears sprang to her eyes. "That's not fair. I found these in her bank. Like we told you."

Karen was suddenly overcome by the futility of this meeting. She took a deep breath and stood up. "All right, that's enough. This is just upsetting my daughter. I had hoped that showing these to you might make you realize you were after the wrong man, but I can see I was mistaken. We'll just have to wait until our lawyer gets back."

Karen reached for the papers, but Walter put his hand on them, holding them down. "I'm not saying we're not interested in these, Mrs. Newhall. I mean, if what you say is true . . . well, you're right—this could implicate another person. Even though Linda doesn't mention who that person might be. . . ."

"I understand that," said Karen stiffly.

"But, these aren't even the original documents," said Walter. "These are just copies."

"I have the originals," said Karen.

"May I see them?"

Karen hesitated. Then she said, "I've decided I'm not going to show them to anybody but our lawyer."

"Well, until I can authenticate these, they're really meaningless. We would need to have a document expert in the lab go over the originals, to determine the age of the paper, the ink, and so on. We would first have to prove this is not a hoax."

"Show him, Mom. Give him the real ones," said Jenny.

Karen saw the panic in Jenny's eyes and felt that she had been impossibly naive about this whole thing. Of course the police would want to see the original documents. It was the only thing that made sense.

"Please, Mom," Jenny pleaded. "Please, for me."

Walter Ference looked at her expectantly.

Chapter Thirty-eight

The person did not move. Greg looked again. It's a mannequin, he thought. It has to be. Now that he looked closer he saw that its head lolled to the side. It's got to be some kind of doll, he told himself. They have everything else in the world down here. He felt as if his hands were glued to the woolen fabric of his borrowed shirt. He crouched there, opposite the doll, unable to move. His teeth began to chatter.

Finally he forced himself to breathe. Just turn around, he told himself. Go on. Go up the stairs. But instead he fumbled with the penlight, now recovered, and trained it on the figure against the wall.

The eyes were glassy, staring. Through the blondish bangs on the forehead, something dark made streaks that meandered down the side of the face.

Greg felt his heart leap in his chest. He moved the tiny beam, with trembling fingers, up to the source of the streaks. The top of the blondish head was dark and pulpy. Greg rose to his feet and moved closer, on leaden legs. He bent over and touched the face. The cold flesh made him gasp, as if it burned.

"Jesus Christ," he cried. "Oh, my God."

He leapt back from it, staring. It was a woman. A dead woman. His heart was thundering in his chest. He looked wildly around the dark basement, half expecting her killer to jump out at him. He stumbled away from the body, then turned to look again. Who was she? My God, he thought, what kind of monster is this man? He forced himself to look again at the dead woman. She was unknown to him. A young, square-faced, stocky woman. With her head bashed in.

Run, he thought. Run. Get away from here. But his legs refused to budge. And another, more rational voice was trying to influence him. Here it is, he thought. The proof you need that Ference is a killer. Keep your head. But the panic rose in him again. What do you do? Tell the police what you found in Ference's basement? Sure. It was the same thing all over again. You're the one they're looking for. You're the one they'll blame. How can you explain what you are even doing here?

Greg stood there, wearing Walter Ference's discarded shirt, his eyes riveted to the ruined face of the corpse. After a trancelike minute, he looked around. He had an idea.

Tracing his way back carefully through the cellar, he reached the steps to the first floor. This is it, he told himself. Go carefully. This is it. Gripping the handrail weakly, he climbed the steps. The house was perfectly silent. If anyone was here, they had to be dead asleep. It was a chance he had to take. Before, he almost hadn't cared. He wanted only to meet the devil on his own ground. But, suddenly, he had hope. That poor, dead girl in the basement was his lifeline. Now he had a ghost of a chance, and he had to act quickly. He tried the door at the top of the steps. It opened. He pushed it to slowly and stepped out into the dark room, illuminated by the foggy moon and the dim glow of a streetlight.

He was in a kitchen, neat, empty and old. There was no one around. No sound. He walked over to the kitchen door and closed it. Then he returned to the wall telephone he had spotted when he emerged from the cellar. Greg took a deep breath, picked up the receiver, and dialed. He leaned against the counter for support. The operator came on the line.

"Get me the police department," he said in a hoarse voice he hardly recognized as his own. The sound seemed almost shattering in the silent kitchen. As he waited, he told himself that he should have run from the house and found a phone booth. But what if Ference came back in the meanwhile and somehow got rid of her? Surely he did not mean to leave the body there. Besides, Greg knew that every moment he spent out in the street he was in danger. He could be spotted on his way or in the phone booth. He had to make his move immediately.

A voice in his ear said, "Bayland Police Department."

Here goes, he thought. Greg gripped the phone with

both hands. "My name is . . ." He coughed and groped for the name. "Lund," he said. "I live at Twenty-seven Hickory Drive. I was just out calling my dog and I thought I spotted a prowler outside my neighbor's house. Can you send somebody out to check? I think he went into the basement, and there doesn't seem to be anybody at home there."

"What is that address?" asked the dispatcher.

"Well, I'm not positive. Probably Twenty-five. I'm at Twenty-seven Hickory. It's the home of one of your officers. His name is Ference."

"Detective Ference's house?"

"Yes. You'd better send a patrol car. It could be nothing but—"

"I have a man in the vicinity. I'll send him right over."

"Thanks," said Greg. He did not give the dispatcher a chance to request more information. He hung up quickly. "Don't take my word for it," he said to himself with grim satisfaction. "Come over and see for yourself." He let go of the receiver and turned around.

Emily Ference stood in the kitchen doorway, holding a gun.

Chapter Thirty-nine

Karen shook her head. "I'm sorry. I have to be firm about this one point."

Walter put his hands on his knees and stood up. "Well then, I guess there's nothing more to say."

"No," Jenny cried, clambering to her feet. "Wait a minute. What about my dad?"

Karen hesitated and then held her ground. "So be it, then." She stood up and started for the door. "You may as well leave."

"Mom, you're ruining everything," Jenny cried.

"A day or two more isn't going to matter," said Karen with a conviction she did not feel. "I'd like you to go now."

Walter sighed. "Mrs. Newhall," he said in a reasonable tone, "I'm afraid I can't leave without those papers."

Karen felt herself bristle with indignation. "This is my house, and I'm asking you to go."

"Mom, don't get him mad."

"This is official business," he said. "Those papers are evidence. They don't belong to you. Now you'll have to relinquish them."

Karen felt suddenly shaky. She had blundered ahead when her instincts told her to wait. She should never have called the cops. She had somehow been lulled into thinking that they saw her and Jenny as innocent victims in this whole mess. But she had the sudden realization that in their eyes the whole family was somehow guilty. "Look," she said uncertainly, "don't you need a warrant or a court order or something?"

Walter chuckled as if to belittle the ignorance of her terms. "I don't need a 'warrant,' as you call it, to claim evidence. I don't believe you understand the legal technicalities of the situation."

Karen chewed her lip. It was true. She didn't know much about the law. She'd never had to, for heaven's sake. It had never been a part of her life before this. But this did not seem right to her. "I'll admit that I'm confused by legal jargon, Detective," she said stubbornly. "But what if I give you the papers and they somehow disappear?"

"Aren't you being a little paranoid, Mrs. Newhall?"

"You wouldn't think so if you were me," she said ruefully.

"I'll give you a receipt," he said calmly.

Karen thought it over. Then she shook her head. "No," she said.

"Do you want to end up in jail, too, for withholding evidence?" he demanded.

"You wouldn't even have known about these if it weren't for me," Karen protested.

"Yes, but now we do. And you're obliged to relinquish them."

Karen felt like a butterfly being trapped under a wide net. She'd heard the term *withholding evidence.* Was it like contempt of court? Could he arrest her? Jenny would be left all alone. The situation was impossible. But Karen felt suddenly tired of being pushed around. Tired of being treated like a criminal when all she'd done was try to bring the truth to light, whether the police wanted to believe her or not.

And the same instincts that had warned her to wait for the attorney now nagged her not to give in. She decided to trust herself this time. She did not meet Jenny's beseeching gaze. This was tough enough. She screwed up her nerve and took a deep breath. "You can have the copies," she said. "But until I see my lawyer, you can't have the original papers. The last time I looked, this was not a police state where you could just seize people's property. Now I want you to leave my house."

Detective Ference stepped up to her, raised one hand, and in one dizzying movement smacked her as hard as he could across the face.

Chapter Forty

"**W**hy in the world did you do that?" Emily asked.

Greg stared at her. She had turned the light on with her free hand, and she stood in the doorway, looking like a child holding a toy weapon. She was small and fragile, with large, glassy blue eyes and grayish-blond hair in a Buster Brown sort of haircut.

For a moment he was too startled to understand what she meant. Then he realized that she had overheard his phone call to the police. "I found something terrible in your basement," he said.

"Besides that shirt?" she asked with a wispy smile at her own joke.

There was something eerie about the calm way she was looking at him. She was dressed in a bathrobe and slippers. The gun seemed too heavy for her hand. She did not seem nonplussed to find a strange man in her kitchen. She was not afraid. "Are you ill?" she asked in a solicitous tone.

Greg hesitated. Then he nodded. "Yes."

"Sit down," she said.

He could not figure out if she was crazy or if the delirium of his fever was getting to him. He glanced at the back door. The patrol car was on its way. He couldn't be found here. He remained standing, his body rigid.

"I heard you down there," she said matter-of-factly.

Greg felt the confusion crippling him. "I thought the house was empty."

Emily's smile was painful to behold. "It is," she said. She lowered the gun.

What is she doing? Greg wondered. Why isn't she afraid?

"Why are you here?" she asked.

"Your husband . . . I have a grievance with your husband."

Emily smiled wistfully. "He may be gone for a while. You're welcome to wait."

Greg had a sudden urge to shake her. "Is this some kind of game?" he said.

Emily looked surprised. "No. What do you mean?" The gun dangled, seemingly forgotten, by her side.

"You don't know who I am. I broke into your house. Are you on drugs or something? I could be dangerous to you."

Emily shook her head emphatically. "No drugs," she said. "No drugs, no alcohol. I just got back from a . . ." She pressed her lips together. "I have a problem with alcohol. But I'm sober right at this moment. And as for danger, well, you seem like a decent man. Besides, death doesn't frighten me. I would welcome it. It's living that's so hard."

Greg was suddenly angry. Furious. "There's a woman's body in your basement," he said bluntly. "She's been murdered. And I doubt very much if she welcomed it."

Emily's face turned ghastly pale, and she swayed slightly. Tears welled in her eyes, but she did not protest or cry out. Greg watched her, fascinated. She pulled out a chair from the table and sat down.

"Do you know who it is?" he demanded.

Emily shook her head. Then she looked up at him with worried eyes. "Do you?"

Greg ran a hand through his hair. There was a pounding between his eyes. "Do you understand what I'm saying to you? Someone killed this woman. I think it was your husband."

He expected an argument, an accusation, even a mocking laugh. But Emily just shook her head and stared. "My husband is a policeman, you know."

"Yes, I know," said Greg, "but all the same . . ."

"Policemen are good at keeping their feelings hidden. It's something they learn on the job, you know. They see a lot of ugly things. And they learn not to show it. That's what I always thought about Walter. Even when I met him he was that way, but I just figured still waters run deep. . . ."

There's something wrong with her, Greg thought. This woman is not tracking. Even in his febrile state, he felt sure of that. "I have to get out of here," he said. He turned toward the door. He half expected to hear gunfire, feel the blast between his shoulder blades. Instead he heard the melancholy croon of her voice. "These are my sons," she said.

For some reason her words made the hair stand up on the back of his neck. He turned around. She had removed a well-creased photograph from her bathrobe pocket and laid it on the dull, nicked surface of the table where she had already placed the gun. The boys in the picture were blond-haired toddlers, their gently rounded little bodies bursting with energy and laughter, as if they could spring out of the photograph and clamber all over this frail ghost of a woman.

"I see," said Greg. Family pictures. A murdered woman in the basement. He didn't know whether to laugh or cry.

"I killed them," she said.

Chapter Forty-one

Blood spurted from her nose and Karen stumbled back and fell to her knees beside the sofa. Jenny screamed.

Walter shook a finger at Karen, who was groaning, holding a hand over her nose and mouth. "Don't use that tone with me," he said. "You don't tell me what to do. I tell you. . . ."

Karen stared at him in horrified amazement. She had read about police brutality, of course. But she had an idea that it was something only practiced on out-of-control criminals brandishing weapons or resisting arrest. It was not something that happened to women and children, alone, in their own home, in a quiet little town like Bayland. She stumbled to her feet and wiped her bloody hand on her shirt. Anger and indignation surged through her. A lifetime of obeying the rules, and this was the treatment she got. "How dare you," she said. "How dare you lay a hand on me? I was just trying to cooperate with the police." She looked at the blood on her hand. "I'll see you kicked off the police force for this. I'll make such a commotion you won't know what hit you. There's a cop right out there," she cried, pointing toward the front of the house.

"No, there isn't," said Walter. "I sent him on another assignment."

Something about his tone of voice sent a chill through Karen and stopped her tirade short.

"Now, I have asked you nicely. And I am asking you again. Where are the papers?"

Karen was trembling from head to toe. Her hands felt icy cold. It took her a minute to think of an answer. "They're not in this house," she said.

Walter advanced on her with hate-filled eyes and caught the side of her face with his fist. Karen saw stars as the blow hit her head, and she heard Jenny's wail. She could feel darkness coming over her as she sank down to her hands and knees, but she beat it back. She forced her eyes open. Jenny was on the floor beside her, crying.

"You don't learn," said Walter. "Where are the papers?"

"In the safe downstairs," Jenny sobbed. "Leave her alone."

"All right. That's better," said Walter. "Now, let's go down and get them."

Hate filled Karen's heart as she held herself up on trembling arms. "No," she said.

A dull glint caught her eye as Walter pulled a gun

from inside his coat. He grabbed Jenny by the nape of the neck, like a kitten, and pulled her to her feet. "Are you sure about that?" he said.

"All right," Karen said instantly. "All right. Let go of her."

Walter pressed the barrel of the gun to Jenny's head as he dragged her out to the hall closet. Jenny did not resist. Her terrified eyes locked with Karen's. Karen stumbled to her feet and followed them, tasting blood in her mouth and staring helplessly as the detective forced her child roughly into the closet and locked the door on her. Karen heard the muffled pounding from inside the closet.

"She'll suffocate in there," Karen cried.

"Not if you're quick about this," he said.

"You're a sick son of a bitch," said Karen.

"Get moving," he said.

"All right," said Karen. "All right." She could not swallow or even wince without pain. She forced herself to move, on stiff legs, toward the finished basement. She grasped the doorknob and held on to it. She did not look around at the detective, but her voice was bitter when she spoke. "Do you honestly think you can get away with this? I've lived here all my life. People know me. No matter what you pin on my husband, you won't be able to silence me. I'll see you pay for this," she muttered as he pushed her forward, toward the stairs. "I'll find a way."

"No, you won't," said Walter.

Chapter Forty-two

Greg's head started to reel. He stared at her. Did he have it all backward? Was this the killer? Was Ference trying to protect his wife?

"Oh, not like that," Emily scoffed gently, noting his expression. "It was a car accident. A freak thing. I was driving."

Greg was taken aback. He suddenly saw the frail, distracted woman in a new light. Pity for her welled up in him. "I'm sorry," he said sincerely. The picture was obviously old. It must have happened long ago. Still, there were no words adequate to such a profound loss. No time limit on such sorrow. "How awful for you."

She looked up at him gratefully. Almost hopefully. Then the feeble spark faded from her eyes, and she resumed staring at the picture. "You can't imagine the suffering. All these years." She looked up at Greg.

"Can I tell you something? You are a stranger to me. But you understand, don't you? About children. . . . So you will understand this."

Greg knew he should edge toward the door. But he felt unable to move. She held him with her voice, her faraway eyes, wise with grief. "That's when I first found out, you see. I was in the hospital for a long time, after the accident. And I was weak when I came home. Walter took care of me."

She shifted on her chair and gazed back into the past. "No one could ever know the guilt. The agony." Her words came haltingly, like someone speaking a foreign language.

"No," he murmured, picturing it. "No, I guess not." He could not tear his gaze from her. He had just told her that her husband was a murderer, that his latest victim was here, in her house, and she was rambling on about the past. She must be crazy, he thought. But despite her vague, confused manner, she did not seem crazy to him.

She looked up at him and spoke as if she had read his mind. "I know you think it's strange . . . you say this terrible thing about my husband. And I'm not surprised by it. I want to explain to you. . . . You see, I've known for a long time."

"That your husband was a murderer?" Greg exclaimed.

"Oh, no, not that. No, of course not. But I've known that he was not a normal person. Since the accident. You see, he never mentioned the accident. He took care of me, and he brought me back to this house, and he never said a word about it." She frowned, as if she were trying to assess it again, to piece it together with this new information about her husband. "I told you, I was used to his being . . . reserved. It had been . . . disappointing for a bride, but the children were so full of . . ." Her face lit up, then dimmed. "Well, they were children. But, as I say, after the accident he was kind, and he never, never said a word of reproach. Everybody said it wasn't my fault, and he would always agree. But I figured that beneath it all, he must be so mad at me that he was ready to explode. So, finally, one day, I said to myself, Emily, you have to face him. No matter what. You have to bring it up." Suddenly she looked up at Greg with an expression of embarrassment on her face. "Maybe you don't want to hear all this," she apologized. "I usually keep it to myself. But you seem like someone who would understand. . . ."

"No, go on," said Greg, knowing he should bolt from the house, knowing he couldn't. He had to let her speak.

"I went into the living room, where he was sitting, reading." She pointed across the kitchen as if she could see him there. "And, I said, 'Walter, I have to talk to you. I know how you must hate me . . .'

"And he looked up and said, 'No, I don't hate you.'" Emily looked up at Greg, wonderingly. "Can you imagine how relieved I felt? I could see that he really meant it. There was no anger in his eyes, or his manner. And it was like something was freed in me and I broke down and began to babble and weep. I said, why couldn't I have been the one who died, and about our babies, and how nothing would ever bring them back, and I went on, and then he looked at me and do you know what he said?"

There was an expression on her face of incredulity, almost of wonder, and of horror. Greg shook his head, mesmerized by her face. "What?" he whispered.

"He said, 'It's too bad, isn't it?'" She gazed at him, letting the banality, the indifference, of the words sink in. "Just like that. Like he was talking about some children he had read about in the newspaper. It's too bad."

Greg shuddered. Automatically, without thinking, he tried to explain the man, as a way of comforting her. "Sometimes men have trouble saying . . ." And then he stopped. She was right. Walter Ference was inhuman, a killer. . . .

"No. That was it. Up till then I had always told myself he was a man who kept his feelings hidden. But then I understood. There was nothing hidden. I knew I was alone. Completely alone. I have been alone ever since."

"Yes," said Greg. "You need to get away from him."

Emily shook her head. "You don't understand. It's part of my punishment," she said mildly. "For my sons."

"But you're not to blame. It was an accident."

Emily smiled at him. "How kind you are. You're the Newhall man, aren't you?"

Greg looked at her in surprise. She had known it all along, he thought. "Yes."

"It's strange. Walter went off to your house not long ago."

Greg's heart was gripped with fear. Sweat broke out all over him. "What for?"

"I don't know. Your wife called him. And now, here you are. Are you giving yourself up?" she asked in a small, reedy voice.

"No," said Greg.

A knocking on the door startled them, as if they were waking from the same dream. Emily rose to her feet. Greg gazed at her desperately.

Without a word, Emily turned and walked out of the kitchen. Greg heard her go to the front door and open it.

Larry Tillman stood at the door, another cop on the steps below him. "Emily?" Larry asked. "Are you all right?"

"I'm fine, Larry," she said gently.

"We just got a call from one of your neighbors saying they spotted a prowler outside your house."

"I haven't heard anything."

"Well, Walter wasn't around so we decided to come and check it out for him. This guy, Lund," said Larry, consulting his pad of notes, "thought he saw the guy go into the basement."

Emily nodded, comprehending. She frowned at the floor, and then she looked up. "Well, you'd better go down there and have a look," she said.

She stood back and let in the young cop and his partner. "The cellar door is in the kitchen."

"Thanks," said Larry.

He followed her through the house to the kitchen. The gun was gone from the table. There was no one in the kitchen. Emily led them to the cellar door and opened it.

"Here," she said, flipping a switch at the top of the stairs. "You'll need a little light."

Chapter Forty-three

Karen gripped the railing with both hands and struggled down the stairs on rubbery legs toward Greg's office. Walter prodded her from behind with the gun, so that she stumbled as she went.

"What can you ever hope to gain by this?" Karen mumbled. "You can't get away with this. Sooner or later my husband is going to be exonerated. If not with this evidence, then some other way. . . ."

"Shut up," said Walter. "Open the safe."

Karen looked helplessly from the safe to the detective. Once she gave him the papers she had no more proof. No one would believe her. She and Jenny would just be considered desperate liars. If only she had not called the police. Or if she had just contacted the police chief. Maybe that would have been all right. Or better still, waited for Arnold. This man seemed to have a

personal vendetta against Greg, and he would stop at
nothing to destroy him.

"Why are you doing this?" she asked. "Do you mean
to convict my husband at any cost? Is it because he escaped? Made the police look . . ." She started to say
"foolish" but thought better of it. "Don't you understand? He only did it because he knew he was innocent
and he thought no one would believe him. . . ."

"My reasons are none of your business," said Walter.
"Now open the safe."

Karen felt tears coming to her eyes. In her heart she
said to Greg, I'm sorry, I'm sorry. I had no idea about
the police. She tried again. "Look, you saw the copies.
They don't even identify the man who was assaulting
Linda. . . ."

The pounding started again on the floor of the upstairs closet. "How long do you want to leave her in
there?" said Walter.

Karen looked fearfully at the ceiling.

"Get the papers," he said.

She wanted to threaten him or curse him for his cruelty, but it was too dangerous. He might take his dis-
pleasure out on Jenny. She wouldn't put it past him.
There was no other choice but to appease him. She had
to think of Jenny first. She knew it was what Greg
would want. "Okay," she said. "Okay."

She bent down to the safe, and her hands trembled on
the dial. For a moment she truly could not remember the
numbers. All she could think of was this man standing
over her, willing to brutalize a child to get his way. An
adult was one thing, but how could he be so cruel to a
young girl? Jenny would never forget this. She would

be scarred for life. Karen started to say it. She started to say that only the worst kind of creature would victimize a helpless young girl, and then, all of a sudden, a realization ran through her like an electric shock. She bit back the words, grateful he could not see her face.

"What's taking you so long?" he demanded. He kicked her in the lower back, and Karen gasped at the spasm of pain. She worked the combination with trembling fingers while her mind raced. She tried to do some mental calculations as she rotated the dial. He was the right age. He could have known about Randolph Summers through some kind of police thing. Maybe a Wanted poster or something that crossed his desk. He was certainly in a position to have framed Greg. It couldn't be. But it could. She knew it could. It all made an awful kind of sense now.

She heard the click as the combination caught, and so did he. "Open it," he said.

With stiff fingers she jerked down the handle, and the door to the safe swung free. Taking a deep breath to calm her shaking, Karen reached inside. She put her hands on the papers and pulled them out. This changed everything. Suddenly the most important thing was to satisfy his demand and get him out of the house. Lock the door against him. This was a monster who preyed on young girls. And her Jenny was just upstairs. She had to pretend a defiance she no longer felt. Her stomach was heaving, and a cold sweat broke out all over her. Make it good, she thought.

"You're a disgrace to the police department," she said. "Railroading an innocent man like this."

He kicked her in the side this time, and she doubled

over, gripping the door of the safe for support.
Breathing in caused a shooting pain. Walter snatched
the papers from her hands.

"Get up," he said.

Numbly she rose to her feet. She saw him crumple
Greg's last chance into a ball and stuff it into his
pocket. The newspaper clipping crackled as if it had
been lit by a match. She felt a fleeting sadness, but
there was no time for it. She had to maintain an attitude
of indignation. He must not suspect that she had
guessed his secret.

"Back upstairs," he said.

Limping because of the pain in her side, Karen shuffled to the steps and started up them. "All right," she
said as she reached the top step. "You have what you
want. Now why don't you get out of here and leave us
alone."

"Open the door of the closet," he said.

Karen's heart shriveled with fear. She knew it
showed on her face. She saw his eyes change.

He reached out, grabbed her arm, and threw her
roughly away from the closet door.

"No," she cried.

He unlocked the door and pulled Jenny, who tried to
bite his hand, out of the closet.

Karen scrambled up and grabbed her daughter. He
allowed her to pull Jenny away. Maybe it wasn't too
late, Karen thought desperately. She tried to resume her
posture of defiance. "Get out of my house," she said.
"Take your filthy papers and go."

"I'm afraid not," he said. "I just can't leave you here
with this story. Someone might take you seriously."

The look in his eyes was terrifyingly cold. Karen groped for an answer. "No one in that corrupt police department will listen to a word I say. Even I know that."

Walter gave her a thin, bemused smile. "You won't have a chance to tell them," he said. "Not after your suicide. It's perfectly understandable. A woman pushed to the brink by all the pressures—finding out about her husband being an adulterer, and a killer. Suicide is the most natural thing in the world. And, of course, you would take your child with you. You wouldn't want to leave her behind to face a hostile world all alone. They'll find a gun in your hand."

Jenny began to sob.

Karen realized with a terrified certainty that he was not just toying with her. Not trying to scare her. He was merely informing her of his plans. "That cop outside knew you came here," she cried. "He'll know it was you."

"I thought of that," said Walter calmly. "I told him that you had called me, that you were hysterical when you called, distraught, and that you demanded to see me. The police presence was driving you over the edge. I told him I would handle it. He understood."

"You don't have to do this," Karen pleaded. "I won't say anything. I promise. You're right. No one would believe me anyway. They'll just think I'm an hysterical woman."

"You're too much trouble," Walter said disgustedly. "Besides, you know you wouldn't keep quiet. Women never do."

"All right," said Karen. "Let Jenny go. She's just a

child. She has her whole life ahead of her. I don't care what you do to me, but spare my daughter."

"Oh, I understand," he said. "After all, she could just as well be my daughter. But age is no advantage in this case. Lots of girls her age are just as treacherous as their mothers. Worse, even."

As he spoke he was herding them into the living room. "Now let's try to do this the way it would actually happen," he said half to himself. "Naturally, you would shoot the child first, and then yourself."

"Mom," Jenny sobbed, clinging to Karen, "why is he doing this?"

"So," he said, reaching for Jenny's arm, holding the gun to her head, "let's have you over here."

Karen was paralyzed with fear. If he had chained her to the spot, he could not have more effectively subdued her. The sight of the gun at Jenny's head was the perfect means of controlling her. And she realized that if he killed Jenny, she would no longer care what happened to her. She would not want to live. Suddenly everything was very clear. There was no use in hoping that he was just terrorizing them or that he would hesitate to carry out his threats. This was the man who had killed Linda. There was no telling how many others. He would shoot her child in front of her eyes. If she did not act, there would be no second chance.

Like a lioness, she coiled her muscles tight, then sprang forward, taking him by surprise and knocking Jenny out of his grasp. "Run!" she cried. "Jenny, run!"

Jenny stood where she was pushed, frozen to the spot, staring at Walter's gun.

"You stupid fool," said Walter. "Move." He tried to

shove Karen out of the way to get to Jenny. Instinctively Karen started to shove him back. The gun rose in front of her eyes like a hissing snake. Suddenly, instead of resisting, Karen turned to her daughter, knocked her over and fell on top of her. Jenny cried out in pain as she hit the floor. Karen sprawled on top of Jenny, covering the child's body with her own. She grasped Jenny's wrists beneath her and held her tight. "You're going to have to explain how I shot myself in the back," Karen said.

"Get off of her," Walter growled.

"Go to hell," said Karen. She could fell Jenny's thin little form beneath her, trembling and heaving with sobs. "I'm sorry, honey," she whispered. "Can you breathe?"

Jenny's reply was muffled.

"I said move!" Walter bellowed.

"In your dreams," said Karen.

"All right, bitch," he said. "All right. Have it your way."

Karen did not look up, but she could feel him coming toward them, crouching down beside them. She let go of Jenny's wrists and placed her hands gently over Jenny's ears, as if to muffle the sound of a passing train for a toddler.

Walter crouched down and placed the barrel of the gun at her temple. "All right," he said, balancing on the balls of his feet. "We'll do it this way. You first. Then her. You're not saving her by covering her like that."

Tears came to Karen's eyes as she acknowledged the truth of what he said. "I know it," she said. "I'm doing the only thing I can."

"Too bad," said Walter.

He pressed the gun to her head, and Karen shuddered at the sensation. Jenny was sobbing. "I'm sorry, baby," Karen crooned. "I'm sorry."

Karen closed her eyes, said a prayer, and then heard the thunderous blast of a gunshot.

Walter yelled and fell backward. Karen looked up and saw Greg in the doorway, his stubbly face pale and sweating, his eyes glittering, a smoking gun wavering in his hand.

Walter regained his balance, adjusted his glasses on his head, and sneered at Greg. "You're not a very good shot," he said.

"Move away from my family and I'll do better," said Greg.

Karen scrambled up, and Jenny lifted her head. "Dad!" she screamed.

"You heard me," said Greg. "Drop your gun and move away from them."

Karen and Jenny clung together and held their breath as Walter laid the gun on the floor and stepped back. Then, before Karen could stop her, Jenny jumped up and rushed to her father, throwing her arms around him. "Daddy," she cried, "you're home."

Startled by Jenny's sudden move, Greg, already weak with fever, staggered back and lost his footing for a moment. Walter, seeing his opportunity, lunged at him. Greg pushed Jenny roughly out of the way, and the two men grappled, locked together in a deadly embrace. Karen scrambled for Walter's gun on the floor, but once she had it in her shaking hands, she could not use it. She knew nothing about guns and did not dare shoot at the two men fighting for fear that she would hit Greg instead of the detective. "Call 911," she ordered Jenny as she brandished the weapon helplessly. Jenny turned to do as she was told. Before she could reach the phone, a shot rang out. Greg and Walter stared at one another, and then Greg's grip on Walter loosened. Blood seeped all over the front of his shirt and his eyes rolled back into his head.

"Oh, my God," Karen cried.

For a few seconds Karen could not take it in. Everything seemed to happen in slow motion as Greg's legs crumpled beneath him and he sank to the ground, pulling Walter with him.

"Greg!" she screamed. Before she could think of anything but Greg, broken and bleeding on the floor, Walter turned on her, charged at her, and grabbed at her wrist, wresting the weapon from her hand. She tried to resist him, but it was no use. He was stronger than she was, and it took him only seconds to overpower her and drive her to the ground. She could hear Jenny wailing.

Walter smirked at her. "This is perfect," he said. "I can eliminate the whole lot of you at once. I'll just tell them I walked into a trap."

Karen looked up into his eyes. A weird thought went through her mind. So these are a killer's eyes. This is what a murderer looks like. He had killed Linda, gunned down her husband. He was ready to crush her and Jenny. An eerie calm spread through her. This is the end, she thought. The Twenty-third Psalm popped into her head. The Lord is my shepherd . . .

"Drop the gun, Detective," boomed a shaky voice.

Walter's head jerked up and around. Larry Tillman

was standing in the door, his arm outstretched, holding a gun. There were three other cops behind him.

Walter shook his head. "Larry," he said, "I'm glad to see you. Look who's here." He pointed to Greg's prostrate, bleeding body. "I was ambushed by these people. I'm lucky to be alive."

The redheaded cop kept his gun trained on his mentor. The other officers flanked him, their guns drawn as well. The sound of sirens began to fill the room. Cars were roaring up to the house, and doors were slamming. "We found Phyllis Hodges," said Larry.

Karen pushed herself up from the floor. She did not know what they meant about Phyllis Hodges. All she knew was that Walter had let go of her. She crawled over to where Greg was lying. A pool of blood was spreading out beneath her husband. "Please," she whispered. "Call an ambulance."

Chapter Forty-four

The elevator doors opened and Alice Emery, followed by her son, Bill, stepped out onto the third floor of the North Cape Medical Center. Despite the late hour police were milling about on the floor like rescue workers after a disaster. Alice knew the whole story by now. She'd been up doing needlework, her TV tuned to the all-news network, when she had heard the bulletin about Greg and Detective Ference. She had called the police station right away. A boy she knew from high school was a sergeant, and he had pretty well filled her in. Alice scanned the hospital lounge and then walked up to the nurses' station.

A dark-skinned nurse with a name tag that read Violet Fisher, R.N., looked up at her. "Can I help you?"

"I'm here to inquire about Mr. Newhall," said Alice. "How is he doing?"

"He's still in the OR," said the nurse.

Alice glanced at the clock above the nurse's desk. "Still?" she exclaimed.

"Are you family?" the nurse asked.

Alice hesitated. "No, not really. Well, sort of." She thought of trying to explain but decided against it. "I'd like to see his family."

"They're not seeing anybody right now," said the nurse. "No exceptions." She handed Alice a pad and pencil. "If you want to leave a message, I'll be glad to tell them you stopped by."

"Okay," said Alice distractedly. "I want them to know I was here." She wrote her name down on the pad. "Thank you."

She walked back toward Bill, who was leaning up against the wall. His hair was uncombed, his eyes still bleary. He had been sound asleep when his mother called to say she wanted to go to the hospital. She wanted Bill to drive her because she was afraid to go by herself that late at night. Glenda had rolled over in bed, grumbling that it was ridiculous, but Bill had not argued. He'd pulled on some clothes and gone to her house to pick her up. She had filled him in on the way over, although he was almost too sleepy to take it all in.

"What's the story?" he asked now as Alice rejoined him.

"He's still in the operating room. The family doesn't want to see anyone. They're in seclusion, I guess you might say."

Bill looked at his watch. "God, he's been in there a long time."

Alice nodded.

Bill poised his finger over the elevator button. "I guess we might as well go?" he asked.

"I suppose so."

Bill pressed the elevator button, and they waited in silence. After a few moments there was a *ping,* and the doors opened. They rode down alone and walked out of the hospital toward the parking lot. Bill held an umbrella over his mother. It was still drizzling. "I hope he makes it," Bill said, opening the car door for her.

Alice slid onto the front seat. "Me, too."

Bill walked around to the other side and got in. He shook his head. "I still can't believe it," he said. "When I think what Linda went through . . ." Tears suddenly filled his eyes.

His mother looked at him askance. "Too bad you didn't have more pity when she was alive," she said.

Bill stared through the rain-spattered windshield, squeezing the car keys in his hand. "I was just so angry with her," he said. "I didn't know any of this other stuff, about Dad, and what that bastard Ference was doing to her. All I knew was, I blamed her for ruining my life. And when she came back, that was all I could think of."

Alice felt suddenly out of patience with her son. "There's nothing wrong with your life. You made your own life. If it didn't turn out the way you wanted it, well, that's your own doing. You just want to blame everybody else. Honestly, Bill, I feel ashamed of you when I hear you talk that way."

Bill did not try to defend himself from her criticism. He did not seem to hear her.

"What's so bad about your life, anyway? You have a good job and a fine family," she reproved him.

Bill shook his head and seemed oblivious of the tears that were running down his cheeks. "I guess in the back of my mind I was figuring there was time to make up. You know, one day we'd sit down and talk about it, and that would be it. I just wanted to punish her for a while. But there wasn't time. I never had the chance to tell her . . ."

Alice pressed her lips together angrily as he rested his head on his arms, folded over the steering wheel. She stared out at the raindrops and thought about her husband, who had kept his ugly secret all those years. And the price their daughter had paid for it. The ultimate price. And Alice had never suspected. How could she have been so blind, so gullible? She had accepted Jack's version of the past without question. He was a good husband. It suited me to believe him, she thought. Whenever I wondered, I just made an excuse and went on. The bitter lines of her mouth trembled, and she sighed. She looked over at her son. Then she began to rub his shoulder sympathetically. "Everybody makes mistakes," she said. "We all wish we could go back sometimes."

The hospital had provided a small room where they could wait, out of the range of curious eyes. Even at that late hour reporters wanted to have a crack at them. Even some insomniac patients had come up to their floor, trying to catch a glimpse of them. Karen sat with her eyes closed, but she was wide awake. She clutched her empty teacup in her hands. Jenny moved impatiently from one chair to another, leafing through ancient magazines with no interest.

They had not been allowed to go into the ambulance with Greg. Technically he was still under arrest, although Chief Matthews had come to the Emergency Room and assured them that Detective Ference was being charged, and that part of their anguish was over. Now, they just had to wait.

"Mom," Jenny cried, and Karen's eyes flew open. "One of the doctors."

They both stood up and looked expectantly at the gowned figure who approached them. There was blood speckled all over his scrubs.

"Is it over?" Karen asked.

The doctor shook his head. "We've run into some problems," he said.

Jenny clutched Karen's forearm. "What sort of problems?" Karen asked.

"There was a lot of damage to his organs from that bullet, and there's extensive internal bleeding. This whole thing is complicated by the fact that he had a high fever, probably pneumonia, when he was shot. He's lost a lot of blood, and unfortunately he's type AB negative."

"Why is that unfortunate?" Karen asked, trying to make her voice sound calm and rational for Jenny's sake.

"It's a rare type, and we've about exhausted our supply."

Karen nodded, pretending not to be afraid of the implications.

"We're waiting for some to be sent to us from a

blood bank in Boston," the doctor continued. He looked gravely at Jenny. "The reason I'm telling you all this, is that it would be very helpful if you were able to provide some blood. Being his daughter . . ."

"Maybe I have the same type!" Jenny cried.

"Well, we would like you to be tested. . . ."

"She's adopted," Karen said quickly.

The doctor frowned. "Oh, I see. . . ."

"Mom," Jenny protested, "he's my real father." She turned to the doctor. "Let me be tested."

"No," Karen said sharply. "She's weak. She's been through so much."

The doctor frowned and rubbed his forehead with his forearm. "Is she his biological daughter?"

Karen hesitated. "Well . . . yes."

"I wouldn't ask, but this is a critical situation. Do you know her blood type?"

Karen opened her hands helplessly. "It was never . . . I mean, we never needed to . . ."

"That's not unusual with a healthy child," said the doctor. "Look, time is precious here."

Jenny tossed off the sweater she had draped over her shoulders. "Let's go. I want to be tested."

"Honey, don't feel bad if it . . . you know, proved to be different. I mean, you could have Linda's blood type. That's entirely possible."

"I know, Mom. I take biology."

"Will you give permission?" asked the doctor.

Karen nodded numbly.

"The nurse has forms. Come with me, young lady."

Jenny waved to Karen and squared her shoulders. Karen felt an ache in her heart as she watched her go.

She hadn't wanted to say it aloud, but a repellent possibility kept rising in her mind. It probably started when she read Linda's note, and it remained there, permeating her thoughts like some poisonous cloud. Jenny might not have been Greg's child after all. She might have been fathered by Linda's assailant. After all, Ference had kept Linda in his thrall until she ran away. It was possible that at the same time she had her brief affair with Greg, she was still being used by Walter. God knew, maybe the whole thing with Greg had been a plan, a way for her to get free of Walter Ference. Maybe she was already pregnant when she slept with Greg and she knew it. Maybe, in her desperation, she took advantage of Greg's longing for a child. All the awful possibilities tumbled through Karen's mind as she sat there. No matter what, she would never say these things to Jenny. She didn't want to plant that idea in the child's mind, that she may have been fathered by that monster. But there was no getting around it.

Nurse Fisher leaned into the room and looked at Karen kindly. "How are you holding up?" she asked.

Karen smiled thinly. "I'm okay." She looked at her watch. Jenny had been gone so long.

"Can I get you some more tea?" the nurse asked.

"You're busy. I'll get it."

Violet Fisher laughed. "Are you kidding? This is the graveyard shift."

Gratefully Karen handed over her cup. "That would be great. Thanks."

"Try not to worry," said Violet.

Karen nodded and resumed her seat.

Suddenly Jenny burst into the room, pointing

proudly to the gauze patch on her arm. "Mom," she cried. "Look."

"Sit down, young lady," said the blood bank worker who accompanied her. "You need to take it easy."

Jenny beamed at Karen. "We're the same," she said. "I gave him blood."

Karen's eyes filled with tears and she pulled Jenny to her. Jenny embraced her contentedly. "I think he's going to be okay, Mom."

Karen rested her cheek on the top of Jenny's head and stroked her silky hair. "I'm sure you're right," she agreed, feeling suddenly drained of everything, all feeling. She closed her eyes and thanked God. For the first time since this whole nightmare began, she thanked God that Jenny was Greg's flesh and blood. "You rest now," she murmured. Mother and daughter both drifted into an uneasy sleep.

Some time later, Violet Fisher shook her shoulder and Karen awoke with a start.

Jenny let go of her mother and stood up. "How is he?" she demanded.

"The doctor says you can go in and see him in recovery for a minute, but you can't stay. He's very weak," the nurse said gently.

Jenny was at the door instantly. "Come on, Mom," she said.

Slowly Karen rose to her feet and tucked her shirt into her pants.

"Hurry," said Jenny.

They followed Violet down the hall and stepped past her as she held the door open to the recovery room.

At first Karen didn't recognize him. He was as pale

as the sheets he lay on, and there were tubes attached to him all over. His blond hair seemed to have faded into gray. There was no doubt the stubble of his beard was coming in gray. His muscled arms, under the thin, short-sleeved johnny coat, looked flaccid and useless, outstretched on the sheets. There were gurgling sounds as he breathed, and his eyes were closed.

"Oh, Daddy," Jenny cried, gazing fearfully at the inert figure on the bed.

He opened his eyes and his gaze moved groggily around the bright, sterile room until it came to rest on Jenny. Then his cracked lips curved into a weak smile. "Hi, baby," he whispered.

Jenny rushed to his side and took his hand gently, careful not to disturb the IV tube taped to it, a patch of blood blotched beneath the cloudy, yellow tape. "You're going to be okay," she said bravely. "You just have to rest. Everything is going to be okay now."

His gaze was fastened to her face, as if he were watching her from a great distance. When he swallowed, his Adam's apple moved sluggishly.

"It's all over now," she said, and tears filled her eyes. "They know you didn't do it. So, all you have to do is get well."

"Okay," he whispered. He moved his head with painful slowness on the pillow and looked for Karen, by the door. Their eyes met.

Karen's heart twisted inside of her. She knew the bitterness was still in there, but it was overwhelmed by pity at the sight of the pale stillness of that so familiar, long-loved face. She thought of herself, cowering at Walter Ference's feet, trying to shield Jenny, and then that gunshot, and he had been there. At her worst moment, when she opened her eyes, he had been there, ill and weak and trying to save them. Being the man she knew.

Jenny reached over and stroked his hair. "You just get well and come home, okay?" she pleaded, and her voice was thick with tears.

His eyes seemed to grow cloudy and he dropped his gaze.

Jenny turned to Karen. "Right, Mom?" she cried. "That's what we want, isn't it?"

Karen hesitated for a moment. The thought of revenge crossed her mind. She couldn't deny it. She could turn and walk away from him here and now, and it would hurt him as much as he had ever hurt her. More, even. In his weakened state, it might kill him. The complete revenge.

And then who would suffer the most? she thought. She knew the answer. She knew herself well enough to know. Truth time, she thought. She walked to his bedside, and he looked up at her. He tried to gaze at her steadily, but his illness was betraying him. She saw him flinch and she felt ashamed.

"That's right," she whispered fiercely. "I need you." Then she did what she wanted to do. She leaned over, held his face gently, and kissed him.

Don't Miss Any of
Regan Reilly's Adventures
from Bestselling Author
CAROL HIGGINS CLARK

☐ **DECKED**
(A36-470, $4.99 USA) ($5.99 CAN.)

☐ **SNAGGED**
(A60-076, $5.50 USA) ($6.99 CAN.)